WHEN
INVISIBLE
CHILDREN
SING

When
Invisible
Children
Sing

DR. CHI HUANG

with IRWIN TANG

TYNDALE
MOMENTUM

An Imprint of
Tyndale House Publishers, Inc.

Visit Tyndale online at www.tyndale.com.

Visit Tyndale Momentum online at www.tyndalemomentum.com.

TYNDALE is a registered trademark of Tyndale House Publishers, Inc. *Tyndale Momentum* and the Tyndale Momentum logo are trademarks of Tyndale House Publishers, Inc. Tyndale Momentum is an imprint of Tyndale House Publisers, Inc.

Visit the Kaya Children International website at www.kayachildren.org.

When Invisible Children Sing

Designed by Beth Sparkman

Library of Congress Cataloging-in-Publication Data

Huang, Chi-Cheng.
  When invisible children sing / Chi-Cheng Huang with Irwin Tang.
    p. cm.
  ISBN 978-1-4143-0616-2 (hc)
  1. Missions, Medical—Bolivia. 2. Missionaries, Medical—Bolivia. 3. Orphanages—Bolivia. I. Tang, Irwin A. II. Title.
  R722.H83 2006
  610.73'70984—dc22   2006010371

ISBN 978-1-4143-5311-1 (sc)

Printed in the United States of America

18 17 16 15 14 13 12
8   7   6   5   4   3   2

DEDICATION

This book is dedicated to
George and Deb Veth
for allowing me
to continue my dreams
of caring for our children
during difficult times,
to my sister
(Mingfang Huang),
and to the millions
of street children worldwide.

CONTENTS

FOREWORD

This is an extraordinary effort by a sensitive and knowing physician deeply interested in young people and their manner of living. I've read of his work with enormous interest and with great respect—a doctor transcends barriers of geography, nationality, and class. In so doing, Dr. Chi Huang gives us much to consider: how young people, no matter the odds against them, affirm their humanity even as they struggle day by day to stay alive and consider and understand the world around them.

If only more of us in the United States would get to know the people of Bolivia through the words in this book—words that tell of others we very much need to meet and come to know! Yes, we who now try to ascertain what is happening in that far-off nation can learn of it mightily, knowingly, through a doctor's carefully chosen observations—reflections which one hopes and prays will be attended by many of us in the United States and elsewhere.

Finally, here is a doctor who lives up to so many ideals. Some of us in medicine have unfortunately lost sight of these ideals. As I read this book, my mind went back to the work of Dr. Albert Schweitzer many, many decades ago in Africa; and indeed, Chi Huang, the physician who does this valuable and instructive work in Latin America, very much belongs to the tradition of honorable and valuable medical work that Dr. Schweitzer pursued in the early decades of the twentieth century.

Dr. Robert Coles
James Agee professor of social ethics at
Harvard University, professor of psychiatry
and medical humanities at Harvard Medical
School, and author of *The Moral Life of Children*
and *The Spiritual Life of Children*

INTRODUCTION

Angry. Not a great word to describe a future physician or someone hoping to care for street children. But angry accurately describes what I felt as a kid. When my naive eyes saw the black and white of the world, I was angry and confused about injustices such as poverty and famine. I was also angry about getting beat at basketball. I was angry about those three points wrongly deducted from my English grammar test. I was angry about my little sister getting more and better gifts than I got. My father, in his charity, called this anger my "temper." When my mother witnessed this temper, she would roll her eyes, shake her head from side to side, and tilt her head back, laughing.

Christmas Day 1987. The day my life changed. The day I began to question all that I knew. Why was I alive when so many others die from cancer, HIV, TB, war, and famine? Why was I born in South Carolina and not in a developing country, earning less than a dollar a day? Why did I have two caring parents rather than abusive parents who beat me every night? Why was education stressed in my life and not just getting by? Was it luck? fate?

The meaning of life. As an agnostic, I was officially clueless, questioning everything and searching. At Texas A&M University, I learned about existentialism—we're like ants scurrying around doing everything and maybe nothing. It made some sense, in a world that seemed to make no sense.

Having grown up in South Carolina and East Texas, I had heard the word *Jesus* many times, both in prayers and curses. Slightly coerced and slightly out of guilt, I had occasionally attended church with a Christian friend, although I sometimes avoided going to church with him. Most of the church stuff was a sack of lies, in my opinion. I saw how some of those Christians lived very differently Monday through Saturday.

Nevertheless, one day I opened the Bible, desperately hoping to find an answer to the chaos and senselessness around me. Upon comparing the prophecies of the Old Testament with the events of the New Testament, I faced the same questions that Josh McDowell had asked years ago: Who was this Jesus? Was Jesus a liar with a knack for miracle making? Was Jesus a lunatic who convinced himself, and others, that he was the Son of God? Or is Jesus the Messiah, the Son of God, as prophesied in the Old Testament?

After three years of careful study and much resistance, there came a time when the research and studying did not lead me any closer to believing in God—Jesus. I had walked to the edge of the cliff, and intellectually I had accepted the evidence as proving the existence of God and Christ, but my heart was light-years away. I peered over the cliff and made that proverbial leap of faith, hoping to land on the other side. Years later, I landed. I became a Christian. While I reserved the right to ask God many questions once I made it to heaven, my faith did make some meaning of a maddening world. My faith allowed me to bring some structure to a chaotic humanity. Eventually, some of that anger transformed into a passion.

I wanted to become a politician. As a college student, I joined a Quaker peace mission struggling to stop the Serbian-Croatian War. When I was in Belgrade, a refugee girl named Nadia looked up at me with big hazel eyes: "Where is my father?" Maybe he was dead. Maybe he was killing others. "I don't know," I said. "I don't know."

"Why do you murder the Croats?" I asked an eighteen-year-old Serb soldier named Tomas. "Chi, if I do not shoot forward in the tank, there is a gun right behind my head ready to shoot me. It is not hard to kill. What is hard to accept is that my best friend, a Croat, is on the other side, trying to kill me." In some respect, I gave up politics that day. The politicians might as well have been negotiating in an orbiting space shuttle. I was too impatient, too passionate, too ready to spit angry, honest words to be a politician.

I applied to Harvard Medical School. When the acceptance letter arrived, I stared at it in shock. I packed my bags and moved north of the Mason-Dixon Line with excitement and fear.

In medical school, I struggled to keep up with my classmates. They studied two days for a test, and I studied a week. I learned from wonderful teachers and toiled in superb hospitals. After four years of medical school, I needed only a couple of additional classes to graduate and begin my career as a physician. I reread my medical school application essay. Did I really write that? My face burned with embarrassment as I whispered to myself, "Save the world? Cure for cancer?" Did I sincerely believe in what I wrote? Hypocrite.

Call it youthful arrogance, if you may be so kind, but I wanted to change the world. And after four years of medical school, with passion intact and hundreds of hours of hard work logged, I had not changed the world one iota. I feared, in fact, that the world had changed me, softened me, bought me out. I decided to put off graduation. I asked Harvard for a yearlong sabbatical, and it was granted. My father worried that I had quit medical school strapped with a one-hundred-thousand-dollar debt in order to join the Jesuits. When I told my mother, well, my mother just rolled her eyes, shook her head from side to side, and tilted her head back, laughing.

During the first six months of the sabbatical, I studied the Old and New Testaments one page at a time. It was difficult and challenging. I was not a sitter or a thinker. I was a doer, and I was getting antsy. I was ready to serve. I did not really know what it meant to serve, to help, to assist—I just knew that I wanted to do it. I knew one other thing, something I had known since I was a little boy: I wanted to work with the poorest and most marginalized children. I wanted to treat severely malnourished children

living in the jungle and suffering from kwashiorkor. I wanted
to care for children with AIDS. I wanted to treat street children
who, well, lived on the street. I stuffed a hundred letters into the
mailbox.

Dear Organization X:
   I am a fourth-year medical student from Harvard Medical
   School looking to spend up to six months in some service
   capacity. . . . I would be greatly appreciative if there are any
   volunteer opportunities available.

   Sincerely yours,

   Chi Huang

A handful of organizations responded, and one of them fit the bill
perfectly. Scott Womack, the pastor of Iglesia de la Comunidad, was
willing to let me work with street children in a poor Latin American
nation called Bolivia. Just as I had applied to Harvard not knowing
it was in Boston, all I knew about Bolivia was that it was south of
Boston.

   I knew nothing about street children. I knew that they were
children and that they lived on the street. I had read *Oliver Twist*
by Charles Dickens, or maybe I had only seen the movie. Wasn't
Oliver Twist a street child? There was very little written about
street children in 1997, and I did not hunt it down. I was a doctor,
almost, and they were children; my knowledge and my stethoscope
were all I needed. As I got closer and closer to leaving for La Paz,
Bolivia, I became terrified of working with street children. Do these
children carry knives? Do they snort cocaine? Will they accept me,
or will they kill me? How will I introduce myself to them? Do they
have a booth on the street that says, "Come and meet the street children, five cents please"?

   What difference could I make in their lives? I was not a social worker, psychologist, teacher, or reverend. I wasn't even a doctor. I was a twentysomething, privileged, idealistic medical student unsure of who he was or what he was doing with a plane ticket to La Paz.

Oftentimes in book introductions, writers give statistics and histories concerning the people in their book. I will offer here only the same knowledge that I had walking off the plane in La Paz: nothing. Your introduction to the street children and their world comes with no numbers, no contextual spin.

I will tell you this one thing. At the end of my first year in Bolivia, I sat on the cold cement blocks of downtown La Paz, wondering what difference I had made in the lives of the street children on all sides of me. I asked a girl prostitute, "What do you want from me?" She did not want money or drugs or anything immediate. She said she wanted me to be present in her life. She asked me to build a home for the street children. She asked me to tell others about her life and the lives of other children of the street.

This book honors the last of those three promises, even if it is ten years later. I have attempted to portray five street children— Mercedes, Gabriel, Daniela, Vicki, and Rosa—as objectively as possible. They are real children growing up in a raw environment, and their language is often raw as well. I have used their own words whenever possible, in an attempt to depict an accurate snapshot of their lives. It is with great reservation that I write about myself. By nature, I am an introvert and private about my personal life. I have tried to describe my life and my transformation, to the possible dismay of my parents, with warts and all, so that you can understand these children through my eyes. Over the past decade, the street children and I have changed one another. In the end, I want this story to be about them and not about me. I have only lent you my glasses so you can see the children.

We've Been Waiting for You

Noon, August 1, 1997;
Plaza San Francisco, Downtown La Paz, Bolivia

A child.

His hands all too visible, cupped as if holding water, but holding nothing. His eyes adhering to my every twitch. His eyes glazed over from sleeplessness, from 3 a.m. flights into the sewage system, from wincing too hard trying to forget, from seeing everything, even the eyes of all those who see straight through him. He is invisible.

I reach into my pocket for a small metal disk that will make him more visible. These disks are almost magical, the way they work. The child is watching and waiting. He speaks poor Spanish. He is Aymaran—of blood indigenous to the Andes mountains. I fumble the metal disk. It falls to the pavement.

The street. This is his workplace, his bed, his table, his plate, his fine crystal. This is his home, Mother Street. I pick up the metal disk and place it in his cupped hands. Now they are not so empty. Now he is not so invisible.

Money. The metal disk is known here as a *boliviano*. It is the currency of Bolivia, worth about twenty American cents.

Everyone loves children, as long they belong to someone. When they belong to the street, few love them. And the children know it. Those cupped hands never ask for love. They ask for money.

I crouch down to ask him his name. He looks at my face. He knows I am new to La Paz. He knows it is my first day to walk the street. He knows he might get easy money from me. But he is not sure what I want now. Most people drop the coin in his hands and walk away, returning to their own sweet oblivion.

The child looks into my eyes, and he walks away.

The hill is steep and covered by cobblestones. The stones warp my feet as I lean forward, walking fast, as I usually do, marching double time to the girls' orphanage at the top of the hill.

By the time I reach the door of Yassela Home for Street Girls, I'm grabbing my sides and ready to vomit. A young girl runs by, giggling at me. Mountain climbers wear oxygen masks at ten thousand feet. *Paceños*—the people of La Paz—live their entire lives at more than twelve thousand feet.

I look around me at the snow-covered, craggy peaks of the Andes mountains. Each year, tons of silt roll down from these mountains, enriching the soil of the altiplano, the five-hundred-mile depression from which La Paz springs. The mountains only partially shield the 2 million Paceños who live there from ice-winds that blast through the altiplano. I'm told the wind is cruelly cold at night.

Panting for air, I bend over to catch my breath in front of the orphanage door. A little eyeball peers through a low peephole and examines my face. The peephole slams shut, and feet pitter-patter away as a little girl's voice shrieks, "Strange Chinese man! It's a strange Chinese man!" The door swings open to reveal a middle-aged mestiza woman, her hands clasped before her food-stained apron. "Dr. Chi," she says. "You're here already. My name is Señora Lola."

Señora Lola leads me silently down the stairs into the cozy main activity room where girls from three to sixteen sit quietly in groups of three or four. They knit. I take my position in the center of the room. "Hello, my name is Chi. I am going to be the orphanage medical doctor here for the next seven months." The girls glance up at me, return to their knitting.

A little girl peers up at me with her twinkling, starry eyes. Her rich chocolate skin is accentuated by her simple pink dress, with which she obscures her face. She lets down her dress slowly, slowly, and ever so carefully she reaches out to me. "Do you want to see my room?"

I put my fingers in her hand. "Sure. What's your name?"

"Sara."

"My name is Chi," I say.

"*Chinito*," she says. Chinaman.

"Actually," I say, "it's simply Chi. Chi Huang."

Señora Lola and I follow Sara to her room. The air is stale with mold. Posters of teenage singing sensations spice up the pastel pink walls. Sara hops onto her bed. From under her covers, she brings forth a ragged doll, its head secured by thin cloth. The doll has one black plastic eye and one imprint of an eye long gone. "Her name is Isabel," Sara introduces.

I kneel down so I'm eye to eye with the doll. "Isabel, how long have you been here?"

"Long time," Sara says.

"Do you like it here, Isabel?"

"Sometimes."

"Sometimes?"

"I miss my mommy."

"Where's Mommy?"

"In El Alto."

"Where's El Alto?"

"It's high above, in the mountains. It's far, far away. And it's very, very poor."

"Why are you here, Isabel?"

"Because Mommy does not have any money for us to live with her."

"Do you get to see your mommy?"

"Yes. She visits every week."

Sara's shoulders slump, and her eyes look far away.

"Will you show me the rest of your house?" I ask her. Sara's face lights up again. She jumps off her bed and scurries out of the room. We walk into the concrete courtyard, where a nurse grabs my arm. Nurse Olivia is a large woman, a strong woman. With her rouge thick and her silver hair pinned tightly into a bun, she looks like a big-limbed Tammy Faye Bakker. "Chi," she says, "I know it is your first day, but I need you to see this girl's arm." She raises her eyebrows and peers into my eyes. "Her name is Mercedes."

The bedroom hosts six sets of bunk beds. Mercedes, about fifteen, sits on her bed, which is a lower one and neatly made. Her hair is a bird's nest beneath which her face is safely sequestered. Her clothes hang loosely over her slender frame, her faded pink sweatshirt having seen the scrub brush one too many times. Her skin is a dark olive; her brown eyes are encircled by black rings of makeup. She looks down and away, deep into a bedpost.

"My name is Chi," I say, as I sit down on a parallel bed. "I am the new orphanage doctor. What's your name?" I ask. She studies the bedpost inside and out. A lightbulb hanging from the ceiling yellows everything. "Señora Olivia wants me to take a look at your arm."

No response.

"Can I look at it?" I ask gently.

"No," she says.

"Why don't you tell me what it looks like since you're not going to show it to me? Is it red? Is there blood coming out of it?"

"No."

"What happened?"

"I have a cut."

"When did it happen?"

"Last night."

"How did your arm get cut?"

"I cut it," she says.

"With what?"

"With Gillette," she says. With a razor blade.

I try to slow my breath. "How come?"

"Because I wanted to."

"Were you mad at yourself? Were you sad?"

"No, I just felt like doing it." She looks as far away from me as she can. "It feels good. I enjoy cutting myself," she says.

I feel my stomach turning. "It doesn't hurt?"

"It hurts later," she says. There is no pride in her confession, but no shame either. I am sickened, perplexed, and my throat tightens out of anger. Knowing the tremendous odds against her survival, why does she make her life even harder? "Is there any pus coming out of your wound?"

"Yes," she says.

"I need to treat it."

"It doesn't need to be treated," she tells me.

"If you don't treat it, the wound will become necrotic," I say. "You'll not only get the skin infected, you'll get your muscles and bones infected."

She stares at nothing. "If you get your muscle and bone infected, I will have to cut your hand off."

She looks at me, and for the first time I see a young girl in her eyes. She is wondering who I am, why I am here, and if she can trust me. She looks away for a long spell. "Okay," she says.

We walk to the orphanage examination room, a small room stocked with only bandages and hydrogen peroxide. Mercedes sits down on the wooden examination table.

"It is 2 p.m. now. What time did you cut yourself?" I ask her.

"Midnight."

"Fourteen hours. I can't sew up your wound. I'd be closing a wound filled with germs, keeping them in your arm. So we'll have to disinfect your wound and bandage it. Please uncover your arm."

She uncovers her right arm. I disguise my gasp as a deep breath. Over twenty razor blade scars run up the palm side of her arm, tracing ragged lines from wrist to elbow. By their color and texture, I discern that the scars vary widely in age. Has she been cutting herself since the age of twelve? Ten?

"Uncover your other arm," I say.

Dozens of parallel scars line her other arm.

"Do you have razor blade marks elsewhere?"

"No," she states with a twitch of the eye.

She's lying to me. But do I have the right to insist on seeing the other cuts? If not the right, at least I have the obligation. But if I insist, will I squander what little trust I've earned?

"Do you have any razor blade marks on your legs?" I ask Mercedes.

"No."

"This is my first meeting with you, Mercedes, I know. But I need to make a full examination. Are you lying to me?"

Nurse Olivia shouts at her, "How you can do such things to your body, and before the eyes of God, is a mystery to me! You don't love yourself and you don't love the Lord!" Only the vitriol hurled at this child can distract from the horror unfolding before my eyes. Five razor blade marks of six centimeters line each of her thighs. Longer scars cover her stomach, stretching from one side of her rib cage to the other. Is this real? I feel like I am a minor character ("DOCTOR") in a tragic play. With scars closing up over other scars, she has probably cut herself at least two hundred times. If she continues, by the time she is an adult, her entire body, save her face, will be covered by this street map of razor scars.

"Did you do all this yourself?" I ask Mercedes.

"Yes," she utters robotically. As soon as Nurse Olivia went into her tirade, Mercedes tuned out of reality.

"She is a cutter," states Nurse Olivia.

I clean her arm wound and bandage it up. A putrid odor has been emanating from her lower body and getting worse. I don't want to offend young Mercedes by gagging, so I open the window and the door for air. The odor recalls for me the time I relieved a man who had been constipated for two weeks. She's fifteen! She should be clean and happy. I take a deep breath and reach for a speculum, and then I remember where we are. I have essentially no medical equipment here. I manually examine the labia. As I examine her for herpetic sores, green pus flows steadily out of her.

I sit there dazed. I didn't expect anything like this. I had hoped for docile children who just needed some antibiotics and a break in life. Whatever I envisioned, now that I'm here, I wonder what I can possibly offer these children.

"You probably have a venereal disease," I inform Mercedes.

She looks at me oddly.

"You should never have sex again, Mercedes!" shouts Nurse Olivia. "God has punished you!"

"Please," I implore Nurse Olivia, "let me take over here." Taking a calming breath, I look into Mercedes's eyes. "You have a sexual infection," I tell her, the words altering neither her face nor her breathing.

"Please take these samples, Señora," I tell Nurse Olivia. "I'll be right back." I walk to a neighborhood pharmacy and return with enough antibiotics to cover most venereal diseases. After explaining to Mercedes her schedule of medication, I ask Nurse Olivia to send the blood and cervical samples to the nearest laboratory in order to identify Mercedes's disease. And then I walk to the boys' orphanage.

Bururu. This is what the street children say when they are cold. You can hear them saying it at night when the cold wind blows.

"Welcome to Bururu Home for Street Boys." Señora Lydia opens the door to Bururu and then points eastward. "As you can see, we are located in the downtown area, not far from the old cathedral of San Francisco and the grand city square known as Plaza San Francisco, where the *campesina* women set up shop and the street children sell drinks and shine shoes."

Walking past Señora Lydia, I extend my toe past Bururu's threshold. *Whuff!* A quartet of boys tackles me, staggering me but not felling me. They each grab hold of a limb and try to pull me down, giggling the whole time. I finally catch my breath, and I play-fully punch a chubby boy in the chest, swing a skinny boy around by the arms, drag a boy in a *fútbol* (soccer) jersey across the room, and try unsuccessfully to shake the fourth boy off my leg. My back grows weaker with each giggle, and they pull me to the brown Spanish tiles.

Then one of the boys speaks to me. He stops to see if I under-stand him, which I don't, before he continues. I'm not even sure if he is speaking Aymara—which is spoken by 1.6 million people around Lake Titicaca—or Quechua, the official language of the Inca Empire, spoken by 13 million people along the Andes mountains. A second boy tries to explain what the first boy said. He is speaking a different but similarly incomprehensible language. Slowly, though, words such as *la* and *el* stand out. They mean "the" in Spanish, a language I do speak, shakily.

"My name is Chi," I tell them. "I am your doctor."

The boy with the soccer jersey tells me, "I am Marcos. I am

a fútbol player. When I grow up, you won't see me playing in the street leagues anymore. You'll see me only in the stadium. Do you play fútbol?"

Before I can answer, the boys all say, "Upstairs. Let's go upstairs!"

"What's upstairs?" I ask.

"The bedrooms," Marcos tells me.

Room 1 stinks like feet unwashed for a fortnight. A dozen blankets laid side by side on the floor mark the boys' sleeping territories. I walk over to a beautiful, brightly colored blanket and pick it up. The indigenous women, or *cholitas*, weave these blankets, and every boy seems to own at least one.

"*Ahuayo*," says Jesús.

"Ahuayo," I repeat.

The children burst into laughter at my pronunciation.

"Ahuayo," I say.

More laughter. I grow popular through incompetence. I study their giggling faces. We look alike, the boys and me. We are all brown. They are short kids, and I am five-six. Their hair is straight, coarse, and black. Mine is so straight that it stands punk-rockishly vertical after a shower. Broad strong cheeks. My fleshy face-flanks make deep dimples when I smile. Eyes like fat or skinny almonds. My eyes are pretty round, but I retain the almond flavor. Yes, this twenty-five-year-old Taiwanese American medical student can pass for their indigenous older brother.

"It is time for the meeting." Señora Lydia stands in the doorway to Room 1. She is of pale Spanish skin, her white, oval face shining through a shower of dark curls. Dressed "Euro," like an Upper West Side art dealer, she escorts me through the carpentry room. Aged five through seventeen and of both *indio* and mestizo blood, the boys hammer together bookshelves and footlockers. *Bang! Bang! Bang!* They are dressed in cotton shirts and blue jeans or beige slacks.

"Many of these children came from off the streets," Señora Lydia tells me. "The others were dropped off by parents who could not afford to care for them."

We enter the meeting room, and four women sitting in a semi-circle stand up and give me solemn smiles. "Some of you have already met him," says Señora Lydia. "Let me introduce him formally. This is Chi Huang."

Nurse Olivia shakes my hand. "God bless you for coming here," she says.

"I am the social worker at the Yassela Home," says Señora Lola, who seems to possess a knowing peace. "I handle fights and hurt feelings, and I keep order."

"Hello." A woman in blue jeans and a collared shirt waves. "My name is Jessica. I do whatever needs to be done. I pick up the loose ends."

A psychologist named Eva tells me, "The boys need more men around here."

"The girls will like him too!" exclaims Nurse Olivia. "He is a godsend! A blessing!" She opens her arms to the heavens.

Señora Lydia clears her throat. Although she is now the head administrator of three orphanages, in earlier years Señora Lydia Morales spent many nights on the streets of La Paz coaxing street children to leave the street and join her orphanage. On the streets where women get beaten, raped, and murdered, Señora Lydia earned the trust and respect of the children by practically living in alleys and nooks. That is why some tiny fraction of the La Paz street children population is willing to leave the familiarity of the street to live in her orphanages.

"Dr. Huang," declares Señora Lydia, "we have been waiting for you."

"Waiting for so long," says Jessica.

"Is it true that you are from Harvard Medical School?" asks Señora Lola.

"Yes."

Harvard. They nod their heads as if the word itself were a panacea, even here, thousands of miles from the seat of global superpower, deep in the southern hemisphere among the crevices and crags of the Andes mountains. One 60-watt lightbulb hangs from the ceiling, flickering furiously to light the three-hundred-square-foot room. Boys galloping across the orphanage interrupt the uneasy silence. These women think that I am some kind of godsend. What's going to happen when I ineptly sew a boy's hand to his chest? I doubt I even qualify as an effective charlatan.

"So, Dr. Chi," says Señora Lydia.

"Um, Señora Lydia," I say in halting Spanish, "I'm not a doctor yet. I still have a few more classes before I graduate from medical school. I'm still learning."

"For the next seven months, you will be the staff *doctor*," says Señora Lydia. "Do you understand my Spanish? You will be a doctor for fifty boys and twenty girls living at two orphanages: Bururu for boys and Yassela for girls. They are orphanages for street children, Dr. Huang. Street children learning to live an ordered and meaningful life, learning to bake bread in our bakery, cook in our kitchens, and build things with their hands in our carpentry rooms. All this so that when these children leave the orphanage at age eighteen, they will survive and, if not prosper, at least sleep under a roof and within four walls. Dr. Huang, are you familiar with street children?"

File image: cold concrete; naked, protuberant bodies; rain. "Yes," I say. "I am."

Señora Lydia takes a deep breath, relieved.

Then I open my big mouth. "Park Street Church is my church in Boston," I announce, "and they sent me here to work at these two orphanages. But I must also treat the children still living on the street." My voice trails off. "Treat the children on the streets," I repeat weakly.

The staff members stare gravely into the floor. "For you to pay a visit to the streets is wonderful," says Señora Lydia. "When do you plan on going?"

"At night. I plan to work most every night on the street, and I want to go as soon as possible."

Señora Lydia tilts her head and frowns. "Do you know how dangerous the streets are at night? Especially for a foreigner?"

"Nighttime is the only time when the children are not working the streets for food and money. And they usually sleep in the same place. By visiting at night, I can establish a consistent relationship with them, as a doctor." I know she knows this; now she knows I know it.

"Dr. Huang," says Señora Lydia, "exactly how familiar are you with street children?"

"One hundred million children live on the world's streets. They are our silent canaries in the mine shaft, shouting to the world the state of the poor."

"Eloquent. How familiar are you with street children?"

As I look around the room for a good answer, my own trite words echo in my ears. Nativity scenes the children made out of paper and clay sit on the shelves behind the staff members. Their creativity warms my heart. My silence answers her question.

"Yes," says Señora Lydia, "and the streets will teach you."

I walk southward. I am living in a partially constructed church in the southern district of Obrajes. Partially constructed means a few bricks here and there along with running water, albeit cold. I stop on the sidewalk, trying to recall how to get there, and I notice a campesina woman looking at me. She is selling bags of Brazil nuts and Coca-Cola, which she pours into plastic bags for the customers. Bolivia cannot afford to throw away its glass bottles, and she saves them to be recycled. She is a typical campesina mother. She wears

a dark bowler or derby hat, the color and shape denoting the area
of Bolivia from which she originates. Her loose, full red skirt only
accentuates her pear-shaped body. And on her back hangs a multi-
colored shawl, in which she holds extra food, recent purchases, and
her young child.

Several street children come up to me with their dirty faces and
ask for a peso. Somehow these children lost their parents or had
to let go of that colorful shawl. I give them some pesos. I walk on.
Street girls sell fruit drinks for one boliviano. Masked, homeless
shoe-shine boys, looking like banditos, offer to shine my sneakers.
I want to buy all the drinks from all the girls; I want to offer Imelda
Marcos's entire collection of footwear to the shoe-shine boys. But
I cannot. My pockets are already empty. I walk on, past grandiose,
all-knowing colonial edifices. Past modern utilitarian architecture.
Past more and more and more street children.

Why does God sentence these children to life on the streets?
Why does God let Mercedes cut herself? I could quote Saint
Augustine, who asked similar questions. I could devise logical syl-
logisms about an omnipotent, inviolable, immutable God who allows
such suffering. But it brings me no closer to the answers I have
sought since my first days as a Christian. Since that Christmas Day
almost ten years ago.

Theologically, my brain knows that God is in control; my heart
has miles to go. I scramble forth like an ant whose mound is being
kicked away. A lifetime could be spent helping the children living
within these four blocks. Can hope sustain me? Can injustice invigo-
rate me? Can I make a difference within one square block?

Yes, I can. "I can," I insist. And yet, as I walk, I cry. And no matter how many times I tell myself that crying is weak and useless,
I cannot stop the tears.

2

Slash, Slash

August 1997, Yassela Home for Street Girls

In mid-August, it is the dead of winter in Bolivia. The morning air
stirs little as I meet Nurse Olivia at the entrance of Yassela Home
for Street Girls. "Buenos días," I say to her, and she returns the
salutation.

"How often do you see girls like Mercedes?" I ask her.

"Girls like what?" she asks.

"Girls who cut themselves."

"They are everywhere, Chi. Nearly all the girls cut. But they
don't all cut as much as Mercedes."

"Why?"

The nurse looks at me as if the answer is self-evident. "What do
you mean, why?"

"Why do these girls cut themselves?"

"Because they enjoy it," she tells me.

I close my eyes. Slash. Slash. Two red lines gush along a thin brown wrist. Mercedes inhales deeply. I shake the image out of my head. "Did we get the results of the cervical culture? Is it gonorrhea? Chlamydia? Is it herpes?"

"I don't know," replies Nurse Olivia.

"What do you mean you don't know?"

"I never got the results."

"Why not?"

"I don't know."

"Did you take the sample to the laboratory?"

"I don't remember."

Anger seeps to my temple as I realize that Nurse Olivia never intended to send the sample. Was she angry at me? Does she want to take care of the children herself? Luckily, I gave Mercedes a battery of antibiotics that would treat most major sexually transmitted diseases. Not HIV. I can't test for it; I can't treat it. Not in Bolivia.

"Anyway, Chi"—she shoos me along—"enough talk. We need to get to work. Work, work, work. You have to complete physicals for nearly fifty boys at Bururu and twenty girls at Yassela."

"Yes, I know. I will start in half an hour."

"Start immediately. At Bururu. You will finish in three days."

"I'll meet you there in thirty minutes."

"Thirty minutes, no later. Be careful with Mercedes. Her bites hurt."

I look at Señora Olivia. I still misunderstand jokes. "What?" I ask.

"You will find out soon enough," she replies. "Soon enough, you will know."

I find Mercedes sitting alone in a corner of the activity room. I sit down beside her. I try to look her in the eyes, but her clumpy hair blocks my view. "Mercedes," I say. She doesn't respond. "Have you taken your medication?"

"Leave me alone," she grumbles.

"How is your wound?"

"Fine."

"Can I see the cut? I need to check up on it."

"No," she says numbly to nobody.

"Remember what I said about necrotic wounds? You could lose your whole arm." She doesn't seem to care about her arm. "What's going on, Mercedes? Don't you want to get well?"

"What will you give me if I let you look at my cut?"

"Nothing," I say.

"Let me listen to your Walkman," she tells me.

"What?" I ask.

She doesn't deign to repeat herself for me.

"You want to listen to my Walkman?"

"Give me your Walkman," she says.

"Can I ask you a question, Mercedes?" I want to know her. I want to figure her out, as if a human being can be deduced like a scientific fact.

"No," she says.

"Did you want to kill yourself when you cut your arm?"

"No!" She shoots an indignant and quizzical look at me. At least she is looking at me now. "What do you mean?"

Not knowing exactly what I mean, I rephrase, "Did you want to die when you cut yourself?"

"No." She laughs at me. "Are you crazy?"

To her I am the strange one because I think that slicing open one's wrists is suicidal. "So," I ask, "why do you do it then?"

"Because I like it." She looks at her sleeved arms, as if dozens of badges of honor were laced across them.

"You have a new cut, don't you? How often do you cut yourself?"

"Every day," she says.

"How many cuts do you have?"

"A few," she states.

"Why do you cut yourself?"

"Because I need to do it."

"What happens when you do not cut yourself every day?"

"I feel bad."

"Where do you feel bad?"

"On the inside."

"How do you feel bad inside?"

"Tension," she says. "Tension inside." She holds her fists to her chest. Her brows furl up, meeting to form a summit. She looks at me with such force built up in her body that I believe she might burst forth and break my nose.

"So," I say, "what happens when you cut yourself?"

"I feel good." She takes a quivering breath. "Tension goes away. Far away."

"Far away?"

"So far away. I am not here anymore. All the tensions in my body are released. I am free, so free. I feel wonderful. You will never know unless you try it. Do you have a razor blade?"

I use my razor blade to shave. "So, it doesn't hurt?"

"Of course not, silly." She looks into my eyes. "You should try it," she implores. She really, really wants me to try it.

"No thanks," I say, trying to steady my voice. "It never hurts?"

"It hurts later." She silently recalls the pain. "It always hurts later."

"Why do you have tension inside?"

"I do not know. I always have felt bad inside."

"Always? Since you were little?"

"Yes, quit asking so many questions."

"Okay. But why did you leave your home?"

"Because it was boring," she snaps.

"What do you mean it was boring?"

"There was nothing to do at home except chores."

What child would leave the secure boredom of home for the danger of the streets? "And the streets? What are they like?"

"The streets are fun."

"What do you think about your mother?"

"I hate her. She always yelled at me to do my chores."

"Your father?"

"I hate him."

"Why? Did they mistreat you?"

"Shut up, Chi! I just hate them. I hate you. Leave me alone." Mercedes turns her back to me. What do I want from her? Answers? And when I get the answers, what then? Ask more?

She walks away.

"Mercedes." I reach toward her. She whirls around, her hands again at her chest, this time clasped together. "Chi!" she says. "Take me dancing! Take me dancing this weekend!"

"Dancing?" I step back.

"Yes, dancing. Don't you dance?"

"Yes. I dance. But . . ." I say. "Who do you dance with? Your girlfriends?"

"No. Guys."

"Boys from the orphanage?"

"No, silly." She chuckles. "Guys. At the club. Some are business-men. They are older men. They pay my cover; they buy me drinks. They buy me whatever I want. They show me a good time."

"You're only fifteen, Mercedes."

"So?"

"So. Don't you think you are too young to do these things?"

"No."

"Why do they dance with you?"

"I give them what they want."

"And what's that?"

She giggles. "You should know. You are the doctor."

"Don't we have a curfew at 8 p.m.?"

"Yes. They are so strict here. I hate it."

"Maybe the counselors are trying to protect you from getting into trouble."

"What trouble is that?"

"These men in the clubs can be dangerous."

"They aren't dangerous, silly. I know them."

"Do they care about you?"

Mercedes rolls her eyes. "Who cares about anybody in this world?"

"Would they take you dancing if you refused to give them what they want?"

She cackles. "Dr. Chi, everything comes with a price. Nothing is free. You have a lot to learn."

"Hmmm. Everything comes with a price, huh? Are you paying rent here at Yassela? Or buying your own food?"

"No." She scowls at me. "My payment is that I have to follow these stupid rules and curfews."

"Tell me the truth, Mercedes. Do the men ever hurt you?"

Mercedes is quiet.

"Do they ever beat you?"

Mercedes is silent.

"After you are with these men, do you cut yourself?"

Mercedes turns her back on me again.

"Mercedes," I say. She walks away, up the stairs. I follow her to the rooftop. A gust of wind throws her matted hair up into the air, and I notice many colors in it—dark red, black, brown, auburn; she's colored it over and over, never finding the perfect shade. She ducks beneath the clothesline, under a line of little girls' dresses and pants dancing on the breeze. She stands at the edge of the building and looks down onto the street a few stories below.

Perhaps she is sad because she thinks that I have figured her out. That I've taken her personality, divided it by her secrets, multiplied that by every one of the two hundred scars on her body, and come up with the answer. The answer of exactly what she is. Maybe she is sad because that formula—what makes her tick, what makes her cut—seems so simple, maybe even to her. Perhaps she doesn't realize that I need her to be simple. I need her to be easily explained. I need the answers. But I know she is not simple. Knowing all her secrets, all her life history, will never explain her, never simplify her. But I ask her for answers anyway, believing in my gut that knowing those answers will help her.

Another gust of wind nearly blows Mercedes over the edge of the building. "Mercedes." I stand beside her. "Have you ever danced with anyone else? Anyone besides the guys at the clubs?"

"No," she says.

"Anybody in your family?"

"My uncle sometimes."

"So you went dancing with your uncle?"

"Yes."

"Was that odd for you?"

Mercedes twists a tangle of hair in her fingers, shielding her eyes from me. "No. It was fun in the beginning."

"Then what happened?"

"It was not as fun as it was before."

"What do you mean, Mercedes?" I try to angle my way into her sight. "You didn't like dancing with him?"

"I didn't like dancing with him."

"Did he ever do anything with you besides dancing?"

"He used to hurt me afterward."

"What do you mean, 'hurt you'?"

"He made me his lover."

I am quiet. I am silent. Behind me, the little girls' dresses do flips. Below us, a car holds a long note on its horn. Eventually, someone will move on and the car will stop singing. Before me, the slender ribs of Mercedes cut through the wind as she turns slightly.

"Yes. His lover," she says, twisting that curl in her fingers, razor scars crawling up her wrist.

"When was the last time you saw your uncle?" I ask her.

"I haven't seen him since I left home."

"Does he or your parents know where you are?"

"No one knows."

Mercedes turns to face me. "Chi, take me dancing." She tries to smile. She sees that I see her trying too hard. "Take me dancing, or I'll cut myself."

American Dream

Winter 1971

A petite Taiwanese woman in her early thirties, her hands holding her protuberant abdomen, waddles to the end of a queue of women, each carrying her own bulging belly. The line to the shower moves slowly. There is always a line, and it is always slow. The Taiwanese woman looks back at the room. Twenty beds arranged perfectly parallel to each other, side by side and without dividers. The room reminds her of army barracks.

At night, it's hard to sleep. With twenty pregnant women, some going into labor at all hours, she wakes up and wonders if she, too, will scream and groan like her sisters. "Ahhh!" they scream. "Make the pain go away!" She's not used to hearing so many expletives.

Taiwan was better. She gave birth to her first child—a girl—in her home in the southern city of Tainan. Her mother was the midwife. They were together, smiling and sweating, welcoming the baby girl to the world. Her mother had gentle hands and encouraging words.

This time she will give birth in Richland Memorial Hospital in a city called Columbia in a province known as South Carolina.

A woman asks her a question. She does not understand. People in America speak too fast. The lady seems friendly enough, so she smiles back and says yes. She thinks about Taiwan again. Her family. Her friends. Her language. Her job as a schoolteacher; her life as a ballet dancer. She left everything she knew to live the American dream.

A sharp kick in her uterus rouses her from her thoughts. Her baby. Her son, she hopes. A son to bring honor to the family. A son to be cherished. Her son will make her proud. Her son will be a doctor. He will support the family. She feels her water breaking.

At three in the morning, at nine pounds and seven ounces, her son is born. Her son. Chi-Cheng Huang. Huang means "yellow." Chi-Cheng stands for "your passionate heart will bring about great success." Her baby boy.

Spring 1973, Columbia, South Carolina

Mrs. Huang arrives early at Stone Manufacturing Company, maker of undergarments. She does not want to be late. Polite and deferential, she wants no trouble. She needs the money to feed her daughter and newborn son. No English, no problem. Just sew. Always faster. Her job today is to sew the bra straps to the bras. She sews until she loses track of time and place.

The buzzer shakes the metallic walls of the warehouse. All the sewing machines stop suddenly. A sigh of relief permeates the air. It's five o'clock. Mrs. Huang blows on her red, painful fingers and notices a drop of blood seeping out of her cracked right index finger. The supervisor announces how many bras and pairs of underwear each assembly line sewed together today and then encourages the women by saying, "Good work today. Let's have a better day tomorrow."

Errrkkkkk! The bus screeches to a halt. Mrs. Huang now stands before Henley Homes housing development: small two-story, red brick buildings lined up side by side; identical in size, shape, and construction. Just like the hospital beds.

And now for the happiest moment of Mrs. Huang's day: she walks toward Wilma's apartment. Mrs. Huang found Wilma through a tedious process. She went door to door, saying to each resident, "Hello. Take care of my children. Pay money." Astonished, her daughter often pleaded, "Mommy, you don't even know her."

Knock, knock.

"Hello, Wilma," says Mrs. Huang.

"Hello, Mary," says Wilma.

Mrs. Huang's four-year-old daughter runs to her with open arms. Mrs. Huang carries her up the stairs to find baby Chi-Cheng. He is in the crib, his diaper wet. Again. She won't say anything. Mrs. Huang will find a better babysitter when she sews the bra straps faster. Right now, she can afford to pay only five dollars per day. Her husband is a graduate student in mathematics at the University of South Carolina, and his teaching assistant salary barely covers tuition and books. She hardly ever sees her husband, except at dinner.

Mrs. Huang thanks Wilma and quietly leaves. Mrs. Huang walks behind her apartment to the grassy backyard where her family's clothes hang on a clothesline. They did it again. Someone has stolen her husband's underwear. Four pairs are missing, and strangely, four remain.

It is quiet now. Nighttime. The South. Crickets chirp their midnight songs in search of a mate, interrupted only by the humming of passing cars. Mrs. Huang feeds her son.

Boom! Boom! Boom! Boom! She looks out the window. The four windows of a car have been shattered. Two men jump into the car and look for valuables. They run away without any goods. She looks at her son. Feeding comfortably. Her husband is snoring loudly on the bed. Tears trickle down her cheeks. The car belonged to her husband. They had saved for years to buy it. A blue four-door Plymouth. It is too dangerous to look at the damage tonight.

She does not sleep. She stares through the window. In the morning she will drop off her children at Wilma's and take the Route 41 bus to Stone Manufacturing Company to sew bras together. She will come home to cook and wash. She will sleep tomorrow night.

1976, Columbia, South Carolina

I am Chi-Cheng Huang. I am almost five years old. My older sister is Chiufang. She is nine. She's on the front page of the *Columbia Record.* That's the city newspaper. She's famous. She's the first Asian student at A. C. Moore Elementary School.

I'm at home watching Bugs Bunny. Sometimes I go out and ride in my plastic car and deliver mail to all the neighbors. I am going to be a mailman when I grow up. I used to want to be the garbageman. He gets to ride on the back of the truck and throw trash into the truck mouth and talk to everyone.

A blonde lady comes on the television. I think her name is Sally Struthers. She's walking through a village of poor people. There are tons of kids around her. They're not playing. They're starving. They don't get fed by their moms and dads because there isn't enough food to go around. They don't even have clothes. They walk around naked, asking Sally Struthers to give them food.

Whenever I watch this, I can feel my heart. It's like a bowling ball in my chest. I don't like having a bowling ball in my chest, so I say,

"Mommy!" And my mom runs into the living room as if there's something wrong.

"What?" she says.

"Mommy!"

"What is it?"

"Mommy, why are their homes made out of boxes?"

"They are poor."

"Why don't they live here with us? In Henley Homes?"

"It is too hard to fly to the United States."

"And why don't they have clothes?"

"Because they are poor."

"Why is the little boy on television during cartoon times, Mommy?"

"The lady is asking for help."

"Can we help them?"

"Chi, we can't help right now. Not for a while."

"Why?"

"Stop asking questions."

Why can't they just feed the hungry people? It's simple. Go to the grocery store, put food on a plane, and fly it over there. Everybody always says to share. We have plenty of food. Why not mail it to them? Why is everyone so stupid? Why doesn't anyone listen to me?

I have a secret plan to change everything. Everybody laughs at me right now because I'm a kid, but when I grow up, they'll be asking, "What happened to all the Sally Struthers commercials? What happened to all the naked kids?" Because there won't be any.

1980, College Station, Texas

Fifth grade. I am a timid kid. Especially around my father. He tells me what to do, and I don't say anything. I just do it.

But at school I am very competitive. I don't like to lose. I hate losing. Even when we play the Quiet Game. I study really hard so I can be the best student in the school. And when no one can beat me, I try to beat myself. It's not easy because I compete against a lot of professors' kids. Now we live in College Station, Texas, also known as Aggieland, the home of Texas A&M University, where my dad is studying.

Right now I'm running my thirty-third lap around the black asphalt playground. I run every day during recess for forty minutes straight. Everyone thinks I'm crazy. I'm training for the presidential medal for physical fitness, which is given to the best 10 percent of kids who do sit-ups and chin-ups and run the mile. I started out unfit. But I've been training like Rocky for six months, and soon I'll be as good as Lance Stratton. His father won the Olympic gold medal in discus. I've got Lance beat on sit-ups. I can do 120 sit-ups in a minute. I can do ten chin-ups; I'm going to get that up to fifteen. I'm way behind Lance on the mile run. I have to shave off at least a minute and a half.

Ringgggg! Recess is over and we run to stand in line for class. My clothes are drenched in sweat. Thirty-three laps in forty minutes. A new record!

"Hey, look. Chi doesn't have any underwear on!" The girl giggles.

My white shorts are drenched with sweat, and my buttocks are bare through the cloth. I stand in line with my legs close together. Why aren't we moving?

The bully of our class looks down between my legs. "Look! It's a tee-tee!" All the children start to laugh hysterically. "Hey, why don't you have underwear on? Your mommy thinks you'll wet your pants?" One girl is on the ground laughing so hard she's crying.

Underwear? What's underwear? My father just wears his boxer shorts around the house. He wears his boxers to water the lawn. So I just wear my boxer shorts when I run and put my jeans on afterward. Who needs underwear?

"Yep. A tee-tee!" the bully exclaims.

I feel my chest caving inward. My mouth starts to quiver. My eyes get watery. Don't cry, you weakling!

Today is my first day in college. I'm ten years old. One hundred
Texas A&M summer school students focus their eyes on me as
I walk into class. They burn holes in my head. Hopefully, they
won't beat me up for being different. I stare at the floor tiles and
sit down in the back row. I am wearing my favorite white shorts
and my Mickey Mouse T-shirt. I pull out my Mead notebook and
the mechanical pencil that my daddy purchased for me. *Click. Click.*
Pentel 0.5 HB lead.

I sit in the orange plastic chair, and my feet don't even touch
the ground. I rest my chin on the desk. I can't see the board—
"Jim Bob," sitting right in front of me, has a big cowboy hat on
his head.

Why can't I just go to summer camp like other kids? I get up at
7 a.m. At 7:30 we leave the house. At 8:00 I take swimming lessons.
From 9:00 to 10:30 I take beginners' tennis lessons. At 11:00 my
mother takes me to Tinsley's Chicken and we eat a little box of chick-
en. Then my mom drops me off at the Texas A&M library and gives
me a bunch of homework I have to do. It's mathematics my father
has assigned me, along with homework for my university class.
Every few days I also have to finish reading a book, such as *Ramona
the Brave* or *Charlotte's Web*. In the afternoons, my mother gives me a
quarter and lets me go to the Texas A&M video arcade in the basement of the student center. Sometimes I play a video game such as
Galaga, but it's hard to get the hang of it when you get one quarter
a day. So most of the time I end up spending the quarter on a pinball
machine. Other kids think I'm weird because I don't know who Luke
Skywalker is, but it's normal to me. I don't like to watch TV or waste
time anyway. I'll have time to play after medical school.

The syllabus is coming around. Jim Bob turns around. "Do you
want a handout, kid?"

Of course I want one! "Yes, thank you," I tell him.

"Are you some sort of savant, kid?"

What's a savant? Leave me alone. Are you some sort of cowboy, sir? "No," I reply. "I just like math, and I'm auditing this course."

The professor begins his lecture.

"Hey, kid, do you understand everything?" asks Jim Bob.

I shrug my shoulders.

"Hey, kid, have you always been this smart?"

I look down again. I'm not naturally smart. I just get a lot of practice. In fact, I completed all the odd-numbered questions in the book already. Why I am taking this class is still a puzzle to me. The only time I get out of doing math is when I pretend to be asleep. You see, my dad's weakness is that he will never bother me if I am sleeping or sick. I wish Jim Bob would turn around. I can feel my eyes watering. Don't be a big baby.

"Hey, genius, I bet you a hot dog that I'll beat you on the next exam."

"Ummhh. Okay. I bet you a hot dog that *I* can beat *you*." I stick out my hand to shake on the deal. Three exams and one final equals four hot dogs or four dollars or sixteen pinball games. Thanks, Jim Bob.

Jim Bob never made another bet with me.

1982, College Station, Texas

It's 7:10 a.m. I sit where I always sit in the mornings—on the low cement wall next to the junior high school bike racks.

"Hello, Colin."

"Hello, punk."

Colin is the seventh grade bully; he's a grade above me. He steps up close to me. I feel precarious on my perch.

"What's up with the pants, punk?"

"What do you mean?"

"You're a dork. Look at your pants. You have four folded rings at the bottom of your blue jeans. You look like a tree ring. Does your mommy unfold your pants every year?"

I look down at my blue jeans. There are four successive rings. Whenever I grow a little bit, my mother unfolds the legs. I never thought it looked odd.

"Your mom can't afford Levi's, punk."

I don't answer. My head is hot. I am so angry. I want to make him shut up, but I can't. I am a dork. A nerd. I'll probably cry before I have enough courage to hit him. A wimp. A dork and a coward!

"See you later, punk." *Whack!* He kicks me in the stomach. I fall off of the wall and keel over in a fetal position. Everything turns black for a split second. *Phhhh!* I can't breathe. I can't breathe. I look up and the sky is gray with ominous clouds. Oh good, I am still alive. I don't think I can stand up. Maybe I have internal bleeding or something.

1987, College Station, Texas

I want to be a tennis superstar. I am fifteen, and tennis is my life. For the past four years, no one in my age group in College Station could beat me in tennis. Not even Lance Stratton—he can't hit a tennis ball.

For the last four years, I have been able to name the top fifty tennis players in the world by name and rank. They change every week, and I can tell you why the rankings changed, and who beat whom.

Right now, I am playing in the finals of a citywide tournament at Royal Oaks Racquet Club—a country club. I'm already up a set. I'm about to win the tourney. I've already won first place at the Brentwood Country Club. I wear underwear these days. And I wear the one pair of Adidas shorts my mother bought for me.

I like it when my mom can watch me play tennis. I want to make her proud of me. We don't belong here at the country club, though. I wish we did, but we don't. People here are rich. And yes, I am jealous. But winning all the tournaments takes the pain away.

I serve an ace. I win. Again. My mother stands up and walks into the country club store and looks for cheap shorts. I'll meet her there later.

I love winning. I'll do anything to win. My father and my older sister are just like me. We all have to win. The only one who is different is my younger sister, Mingfang. But she's unusual in our family. The rest of us, we've got to win.

4

Be Careful

August 15, 1997; La Paz, Bolivia

I have been here. In La Paz. For only two weeks. *Slash, slash.* It's been one week. *Drip, drip.* Since my conversation with her on the rooftop.

She has not changed. She will not change. She finds a man to take her into a nightclub. She drinks. Sometimes she has sex. She cuts herself with a Gillette razor blade. She flashes the wound at me, pretending I won't notice. She will not let me treat her wounds unless I let her listen to my Walkman. She asks me to take her dancing. I say no. She finds someone else who will.

Mercedes.

I have been moping around for the last couple of days. I don't want to think anymore. I don't want to think about the street children; I don't want to think about her. Today, after working at the orphanage, I came here, to Scott's home, located among the cluster of buildings that make up La Iglesia de Dios.

Scott is an atypical missionary. He sees Bolivia as his home and

Bolivians as his brothers and sisters. He lives here with his wife and three children. His children go to Bolivian schools and have Bolivian friends.

On my second day in Bolivia, Scott took me to a "welcoming" party in the altiplano. It was a convention for area pastors. When we arrived, no one else was present, so we walked around the small village and each had a soft drink. Eventually, a bus came and thirty men and women poured out of it. Everyone was warm and friendly, but I felt awkward and out of place. They were speaking Aymara. Most indigenous Bolivians speak Aymara or Quechua. A portion of the Bolivians also speak the national language, Spanish.

Lunch was served as we sat on wooden benches. Scott sauntered by and whispered in my ear, "I guess you are the guest of honor." I didn't pay him any mind. I looked down into my soup and saw the toenail of some beast floating just below the surface of multiple grease globules. I grabbed my fork and poked at the toenail ever so carefully. The toenail dived into the deep abyss of the steaming soup. A three-digit claw floated upward. I waited for the claw to burst up and grab my face. I placed my fork on the table. Across the long table, everyone looked at me with a serious face. They were waiting for the "guest" to take the first bite. I looked across the room. Scott was leaning against the wall laughing hysterically, tears falling from his cheeks. Two thoughts repeated themselves: *The Claw. Cultural sensitivity. The Claw. Cultural sensitivity.* I took my fork and stabbed my enemy. Two bites. One swallow.

Scott is gone now. He is on furlough in the United States for the next four months. I am in his living room alone, watching Monday Night Football by satellite. Watching U.S. television lets me tune in to America's superpowered cleanliness and prosperity. It makes me forget about Mercedes and every other street child. It's a brief jaunt back into the blissful oblivion from whence I came.

Troy Aikman throws a pass to Michael Irvin. Yes. Touchdown. So this is what it's come to. For fifteen or twenty years now, I have

wanted to help the poorest of the poor children. I decided a year or
two ago that the best way to help the poorest children was as a physician. Although the word *missionary* conjures up images of insensi-
tive right-wing fundamentalists to my friends, and despite all my
personal failings, I desire to live my life in a godly manner. I have
taken a year of leave from Harvard Medical School. Upon learning
of my desire to work as a medical missionary in Bolivia, my Sunday
night congregation at Boston's Park Street Church flew into action
and paid for my entire trip and expenses.

All so I could come to Bolivia and prove my whole life a sham. Is
this where I stop being me? The me that I thought I was? I don't
want to get off of this couch and be me. Perhaps I ease into another
identity—one that takes things easy. One that does not fixate
unhealthily on the suffering of children. Who is the real me? The
one that thinks, reads, and writes about the poor but is not ready to
relinquish the finer things in life? Perhaps I will manage to "adjust."
Is there a special therapy for sellouts?

Slash. Drip. Drip. Drip. Blood polka-dots the floor. Mercedes wipes
the razor blade on her pants. I press my fingers into my eyes. Stop
thinking about it, Chi, or you'll be paralyzed forever. Think about
how happy the children are, living in their tiny, smelly rooms. Their
lives are full. Think about the carpentry classes you join them in,
about how each table and cabinet is like a personal work of art, a
very real triumph for each of them. Things get better each day.
More tables, more cabinets. The blood clots into gelatinous globs
along four parallel segments on her wrist. It is done.

In Yassela's open-air patio, a circle of girls make bracelets. Little
Sara strings together a complex pattern of plastic beads, her brow
furrowed in adorable concentration.

"Pretty, isn't it, Chi?"

"Yes. I like how you choose the bright colors."

"Um-hmm," she replies. "I will make you one later."

"Thank you."

As the other girls in the circle work earnestly, Mercedes sits out-side of the circle, making herself a necklace. "Why isn't Mercedes sitting with you, Sara?"

"She is in a bad mood. She is always in a bad mood. She is no fun to play with."

I walk over to Mercedes and sit a couple of feet away from her. "Hello, Mercedes."

"What do you want?"

"Nothing." I take a deep breath. "How's your wrist?"

"Fine."

"Why aren't you with the other girls?" I ask in a nice, high-pitched voice.

"Because they are stupid," she pronounces carefully.

"I don't think they are stupid," I say. "What's bothering you, Mercedes?"

"I just got grounded."

"Grounded. Why did you get grounded?"

"I was playing a game last night."

"What game?"

"Nothing."

"What game, Mercedes?"

Silence. She fears my reaction. Yet she wants me to know this, to know this part of her. "What game?" I repeat.

"My game."

"What game is that, Mercedes?"

"The cutting game."

"The cutting game?" My voice cracks.

Mercedes presses an invisible razor blade against her wrist. "We cut ourselves"—she drags the invisible razor up her forearm into the crook of her elbow—"and see who has the longest cut."

"What?" I whisper harshly. "Who did you play with?"

"Sara and—"

I run over to Sara. "Sara," I say, bending down to face her. "Show me your wrist."

A fresh two-centimeter slash crosses her right wrist.

"Who did this?" I ask her.

"I did," she says innocently.

"Have you ever done this before?" My voice rises.

"No."

"Why did you do this?"

"It is a game that Mercedes taught us?" she says, almost as a question, sensing my disapproval.

"Where did you do this?" My heart pounds.

"In our bedroom late at night."

"Where was the counselor?" My face is red.

"Asleep."

"Sara, how old are you?"

Sara looks at my face, unable to speak and about to burst into tears. She spreads her fingers, signifying five.

"Sara. Listen to me. This is not a game. Do you understand me?"

Tears trickle down from her brown, almond eyes. She looks down. "Yes, Chi. We were just playing. I'm sorry."

"You will promise me that you will never do this again. Okay?"

"Okay." She sniffles.

I am on the verge of screaming. I feel betrayed, though Mercedes never promised me anything. I put my trust in her youth. Maybe she does not know any better. She has long ago betrayed her own youth. I am the young one here, betrayed by my own naïveté. I take a deep breath. Tugging Sara by the arm, I take her to Mercedes. "Mercedes. Where did you find the razor blade?"

She grins.

"Answer me!" My temper flares. "Where did you find the razor blade?"

"I have my own collection." She smiles.

"Where is it?"

Silence.

"Tell me." I soften my tone.

"The counselor took it away from me last night."

"If you ever teach these girls to cut again, you will be kicked out of the house. Do I make myself clear?"

Mercedes looks me in the eyes. "I hate you!"

"Let's go, Sara." I treat Sara's wound as she cries and screams, but I redeem myself by placing a Mickey Mouse Band-Aid on her cut. Sara runs down the stairs and finishes her bracelet.

10:30 a.m., Bururu Home for Street Boys

Badly tardy, I walk into the carpentry room at Bururu to see Señora Olivia running up to me. "Where have you been? I have been waiting for you!" She leads me to a storage room. "This is your examination room."

Lining the back wall are ten-gallon bags of carrots, potatoes, and *chuña*—miniature potatoes freeze-dried in the icy ground of the Andean peaks. Hundreds of species of potato are used to make chuña. Fifteen mattresses are stacked neatly beside the potatoes. A 1950 Singer sewing machine sits lonely in the corner. Before me is a four-by-two-foot table covered with sawdust.

"Let's get started." Señora Olivia walks out of the storage room, shrieking, "Jorge! Jorge!" I clear my mind for the task before me; work is good for clearing the mind of disturbing, repetitive images. I lay my stethoscope, ophthalmoscope, otoscope, and blood pressure cuff neatly in a row next to my two medical texts. A small, semi-disheveled boy enters and stands on the other side of the table. He looks up at me sheepishly. "Chi, can you take care of my feet for me?"

His hair is jet black and his cheekbones wide. Pure indigenous. He cannot be older than nine years old. He looks up at me with his mop-styled haircut. I look down at his feet. They stick out of a pair of filthy, tattered Converse sneakers.

"Are you Jorge?" I ask him.

"No!" he announces. "My name is Fernando."

I kneel down and untie Fernando's shoes. I am bombarded by waves of putrid odors. I open the door to let some air out and return to his feet. Sheets of white skin exfoliate themselves from his pruned and damp feet, which are jungles of fungus. I look up at him. He gives me an innocent grin, and I force a smile back at him. I am going to have to clean his feet. Maybe I can put on gloves. No. That would hurt his feelings too much.

"What's wrong?" he asks me. "I don't smell anything."

"What do you mean, you don't smell anything? When was the last time you washed your feet?!"

"I don't wash my feet," Fernando says indignantly.

"What about when you take a shower?"

"I go swimming in the river. That's my shower. That's how I take a bath."

My instinct nudges me to tell him I cannot help him. I look up at him once again. His dark brown eyes sear into my heart. I take a deep breath through my mouth and begin pulling sticky sheets of skin from his feet.

"You go swimming?" I ask him.

"Yeah. That counts as a shower, doesn't it?"

"How about I get you some socks?"

"I don't want socks." Fernando tilts his head. "Did I ask you for socks?"

"You need to wear socks, Fernando."

"What for? I'm fine. They just itch."

"Okay. How many times do you think you should take a shower each week?"

"Once."

"How about three times?"

Fernando pauses to consider. "Well, I'll think about it. But that's a lot, you know. What's wrong with my feet?"

"You have a fungal infection."

"What's a fungal infection?"

"A fungus is an organism that lives on your skin, especially if you don't wash your skin and keep it clean."

I wash his feet with a towel. More sheets of white skin peel off. He giggles. "That tickles!"

"So, Fernando. How often should you take a shower?"

"Three times a week. Monday, Tuesday, and Wednesday."

"Okay. But how about spacing them out?"

"I'd rather get them done quick."

I rub antifungal cream on his feet. I squeeze out the entire tube.

"When you take a shower, Fernando, what do you use to clean yourself?"

"Water."

"I suggest soap."

"No," he tells me.

I wrap Fernando's feet in gauze. "You need to use soap," I tell him. In future examinations, I would discover that all the Bururu boys feel the same way about soap. I continue with the physical examination.

Temperature:	98.4
Heart Rate:	80
Respiratory Rate:	21
Blood Pressure:	100/60
Weight:	35 kg
Height:	4 feet 2 inches

Fernando's ears are filled with wax. He has cavities in his right lower molars. But otherwise he seems to be in good shape. During the examination, I explain to Fernando that I am conducting a survey of street children to learn how they got on the street and how they live and survive. "So, Fernando. Why are you here?"

"What do you mean, why am I here?"

"Where is your mother?"

"She's dead," he says uneasily.

Silence. "How did she die?"

"Bus wreck."

"When did this happen?"

"Two months ago."

"I'm sorry, Fernando." I pause out of respect and then ask him, "So it's just you and your father."

"I never knew my father."

He must hate me for asking all these stupid questions. "Why did you never know your father?" I continue.

"He left when I was a baby."

"So what did you do when your mother died?"

"I went to my aunt's house."

"What happened there?"

"She did not want me there. I was just another mouth to feed. She always shouted at me, made me work all day, and called me bad names . . . so I left."

"Where did you go?"

"I slept on the streets. And then some of the children told me about Bururu. So I came here."

"What do you think about this place?"

"It's beautiful."

"Why?"

"Because I don't have to be out there anymore." He points at the open doorway.

"What's so bad about being out there?"

"Are you crazy?" His brows wrinkle together toward the bridge of his nose. "It's dangerous out there. Drugs. Knives. Fights. The adults."

"The adults?"

"You're crazy! If you talk back at them, they will give you a good beating and call you trash. Knives are everywhere. You never know when one will suddenly appear in your back. We stuck together as a pack watching each other's back. Thinner kept me warm at night. It messes up your brain and makes you crazy. Just like you."

"You're right. I am crazy. How are your feet?"

He peers down toward his toes. They wiggle in a synchronous manner as if they have a life of their own.

"You should wear these socks." I hand him a pair of tricolor cotton-polyester socks still in their shiny wrapper. Fernando holds the socks in his nubby little hands. "I'll think about it." He skips away with his bandaged feet sticking out of his Converse shoes.

Alejandro is a lanky boy with a perennial smile on his face. Seventeen years old. He is tall for a Bolivian. Five feet eight inches. There is a small scar across his left cheek. His age and the amount of time he has spent at the orphanage place him as the biggest brother among the band of boys. He stops fights and encourages the children to do their homework. I have worked here only a week, but I have grown to like Alejandro for his heart and his kindness.

"Hello, Alejandro. How are you?"

"Good, Chi."

"Alejandro, I am going to perform a physical examination and ask you a few questions." I press my stethoscope against his chest. "How long have you been at Bururu?"

"Six years."

"Where are your parents?"

"They are dead. My mother died when I was two years old. I don't really remember her. My father left me when I was five. He just left me and went down south. I heard he died recently of old age or something."

"Are you sad that your father is dead?"

"No. He didn't do anything for me. He left me like a piece of trash."

"And your mother. How do you feel about your mother?"

"I never knew my mother, so I don't have feelings."

"What did you do when your father left you?"

"I stayed with my uncle and cousin, but that was not a good situation. My uncle had many different women around all the time. He would beat me and shout at me. At times, he didn't feed me. I suffered this for three years, and then I left when I was eight years old."

"Where did you go?"

"The streets, of course."

"Which streets?"

"Everywhere. All the streets. I did not know where to go. I ate and slept on the streets. That was how I spent my days for three years. I shined shoes. I begged. I asked for odd jobs. I slept in warm corners of the city. I watched my back. I survived."

"And then you found Bururu."

"Bururu is my home. My family. I am very happy here because Bururu has provided me with a trade. I am a cook. I have studied cooking for three years. Each month it costs about sixty bolivianos. My school is at the University of Sanchez Lima. The people at Bururu helped me to take the next step in life, to someday live on my own."

"Why do you like cooking?"

"Because cooking is very beautiful. And in the kitchen I can eat whatever I like. Ha ha ha!"

"Aren't you doing an internship in cooking?"

"Yes, at the Hotel Presidente."

"Hotel Presidente? Isn't that one of the premier hotels in La Paz? A five-star hotel, no?"

"Yes, but I have not started yet. I've had trouble obtaining my certificate of citizenship."

"But you've lived in Bolivia your whole life."

"But I do not have any idea who my mother and father are. As a result I do not have anything. They have looked through all the records. Record after record. I am not there. I do not exist. I have been trying to obtain my citizenship for the last three and a half years."

I shake my head. A young man who has pulled himself up by the bootstraps despite not owning any boots is being denied the opportunity to work because he is not considered a citizen in his native land. His Aymaran ancestors have been in Bolivia for several thousand years, but since the Spanish conquered this land, being an indigenous Aymara or Quechua has held no advantage. "Well," I say to him, "I am glad that you're here. You help out a great deal and the younger boys look up to you." Reading from my survey, I ask Alejandro, "Did you use drugs when you were on the streets?"

Alejandro shakes his head vigorously. "I never did those things. I believed in myself—in life. I did not learn those evils of the streets." Alejandro thinks for a moment; he wants to tell me something, perhaps something about his past? Alejandro stands up. "You must have patience, Chi. You need to make them understand. Little by little. Give them food once a week. Once a month, check their wounds in order to make sure that they are healing properly. Talk to them. Teach them. Tell them about God. Show them love. Show them which actions will give them a good life. Show them which actions will inflict pain in their lives and lead them to death."

I remain silent. I feel intimidated but inspired. I pump up the blood pressure gauge. "I will try," I tell him. "I will try."

He walks in wearing red jeans seven sizes too large. Folds of denim hide his feet. His shirt is buttoned up to the top. His hair is wet and neatly combed. Wood chips litter the ground, and perhaps this explains his cautious shuffle. The wood saw in the adjacent room roars and shakes the windowpanes. I imagine the windows exploding and scarring this distinctly dysmorphic little boy. His

brow juts forth from his large, wide head. Does he have an underlying chromosomal or hormonal abnormality? I have no book
to refer to. Even if he has a defect, I can't do anything about it. I
barely have enough money to care for the common cold. He sits
calmly on the end of a chair with his feet hanging, unable to touch
the ground. He looks around the room, his gaze settling on the
potatoes.

"I think we are going to have potatoes for dinner tonight," I say.

"Good. I like potatoes."

"What's your name?"

"Jorge Limachi."

"How long have you been in Bururu?"

He counts on his fingers with great precision. "Four years."

"Four years! Four years is a long time, Jorge."

"Yes."

"Do you like it here?"

"Yes."

"Why?"

"It is nice here, and Señora Lydia buys me clothes and shoes."

"What else do you like about Bururu?"

"We get to go to school. We learn everything. We do our chores
and homework. We also get to sleep and wash ourselves."

"Before you were here, did you live on the streets?"

"I didn't live on the streets."

"How's that?"

"One day I arrived at the square, and two young ladies and
a young fellow found me."

"Why did you leave your house?"

"Because I did not like my father."

"Why?"

"My father used to make me work all day on the farm and then
he would beat me."

"Why did your father beat you?"

"I don't know."

"Did you misbehave?"

"No. My stepmother would tell him to beat me."

"So what did he do?"

"My father would tie my hands like this." He places his wrists one on top of another. "Then he would whip me with wires or large sticks until they broke. Sometimes he would use rubber hoses and hang me from my neck."

I stare at Jorge in disbelief.

"Um," intones Jorge, "one day my father got very, very angry. He placed me in an iron barrel. I remember it was very early in the morning. He filled up the barrel with water. He kept me in the barrel for two hours, and I almost drowned."

"So how did you leave?"

"My father left me at my aunt's house."

"Do you like your aunt?"

"No! She was a perverted woman."

"What do you mean, 'perverted'?"

"She would often get angry and bathe me in cold water. One day she told me, 'Tonight you will take a bath with cold water.' I said, 'Okay.' After the bath, I slept on the floor, covered only with a plastic foil. The very next morning she told me, 'We're going to sell some food.' I said, 'Okay.' As she was cooking that morning, I took about five bolivianos. Then I told her, 'Auntie, I am going to pee outside, okay?' She replied 'Go, but come back quickly!' Once I got outside, I ran and ran until I could not run anymore. I walked down a dirt road. A nice man with a truck gave me a ride into the city. He drove me all the way to the downtown area. He did not ask me why I was all alone at night. If he did, I would have lied to him. When I arrived at Plaza San Francisco, I walked and walked, trying to figure out what was the next thing to do. Then two cholitas who were selling trinkets asked me why I was not at home at such a late hour. I did not answer them. They eventually let me sleep with them at night under the tarp covering of their market stand. They were very kind to me and helped me with many things."

"So how long did you stay with them?"

"One and a half months. They asked me if I knew about Bururu. I said no. So they took me here."

"So, Jorge, what happened to your mother?"

"She died in a fire when I was very young." Jorge thinks for a second. "I have a picture of my mother." Jorge pauses again to consider this fact. "Do you want to see the picture?"

"I would love to see a picture of your mother."

"Follow me," he says. Señora Olivia and I tail him as he runs out of the storage room, up the stairs, and into his bedroom. He unbuttons the top button of his shirt and retrieves a key tied precariously to a tattered piece of yarn around his neck. His entire worldly possessions are kept in a two-by-two-foot wooden box in the second-floor hallway of Bururu Home for Street Boys. He opens his wooden locker, the hinges of which are only halfway screwed in. He rips open his Velcro wallet and carefully pulls out a discolored one-by-two-inch photograph. His mother is a young woman with a pearlike body wearing a brown bowler hat. She must be from the southeastern region of Bolivia. The cholitas identify their origins by the color of their hats. Jorge's mother is a cholita without a smile.

"She is very pretty, Jorge."

"I know." He carefully places his most prized possession in his wallet and places the wallet back into the locker.

"You miss your mother, don't you?"

"Yes." He looks down at the floor. "Yes, but she is safe now. She is in heaven. I say a silent prayer every night, for her and for the people who help me."

It is 5 p.m. and I have done six physicals today. Most of the orphanage children are surprisingly healthy. Besides the occasional skin infection, the children need a dentist more than a doctor. Nearly all the children have severe cavities requiring extraction. I walk out of Bururu and down tiny cobblestone roads. The old women who sell llama wool sweaters watch me.

"Who is that Chinese man?" asks one to the other. "He is here every day."

The sky is a brilliant light blue. I walk down to Plaza San Francisco. Five street children are sprawled out supine on a grassy area. They are asleep, perhaps drugged up. Another street child carefully sifts through their pockets in search of a few bolivianos. The homeless stealing from the homeless. I should do something. Do something! What? Perhaps I should rearrange the deck chairs on a sinking *Titanic*. Now that I am here, among so many in need, I am incapacitated by sadness, overwhelmed by the work before me. I walk to Burger Center, a restaurant that caters to first worlders, and I order a cheeseburger with fries and a large Coke. I remember *Titanic* really is playing tonight at the cinema. I hate romantic movies. I might go see it.

I find Mercedes on the roof of the Yassela building. She lies on her left side in a fetal position, the morning sun splitting her evenly between light and shadow. She wears a dark peach knitted sweater and black sweatpants. She rests her head along her extended arm, but she is completely aware that I have come to re-dress her wound. Two days ago, she showed me a new gaping wound on her left wrist, but she needed me to play her silly game, and I didn't play long enough to win the prize: the privilege of treating her wounds.

I crouch down beside Mercedes and whisper gently, "Mercedes . . . Mercedes . . . Mercedes, it's 9:30. Time to wake up."

She does not respond.

"Wake up, Mercedes."

"Leave me alone."

"I need to treat your wound. We made a deal. I let you use my radio, and you allow me to wash and re-dress your cuts."

"I hate you. Leave me alone."

"I love you too. Now get up," I say rather harshly.

"I hate you!"

She doesn't really hate me, I tell myself. She just wants me to get out of her face. "You can hate me all you want," I tell her, "but you still need to get up. You are living in Yassela, so you need to listen to what the staff asks you to do. Besides, this is for your own good."

"I hate you!"

"Would you rather have your wrist infected and eventually become necrotic?"

"Yes. I hate you."

"Let's go to the examination room, Mercedes. Let's walk down the stairs and get your wounds cleaned and bandaged. It won't take but five minutes."

"Give me your radio, and I'll do it."

"I'll let you listen to my Walkman if you want."

"No. Give it to me."

Blood rushes to my face. "No! Do you think Yassela is a palace for you?"

"I hate you."

Something needs to change. She'll never get anywhere in this world if she continues hating everyone who tries to help her. Eventually, her wounds will become infected. Her arms, her legs, her body, even her soul, will become necrotic. I grab her good arm, the one without the fresh cut. The arm is limp, as if it were already dead. I pull Mercedes. I try to pull her up, to lift her up, to help her help herself up, to use the loaded language. She doesn't budge. I pull harder, more laterally. I will drag her to the examination room. Her back scrapes along the rooftop floor like that of a nonviolent protester being removed from the premises.

I drag her several feet toward the stairs and she shrieks, "Leave me alone! I hate you!"

Nurse Olivia appears in the stairway. She motions to me calmly, and I walk over to her. "Chi," she says, "if she does not want your help, don't give it to her. We have so much work here that we cannot waste our time. Look at all these little girls here. If that isn't enough, look at all the little children on the streets."

I look at Mercedes lying motionless on the tile floor. "Mercedes, do you want to have your cuts treated or not?"

"Leave me alone. I hate you."

"I have seen girls like Mercedes," Nurse Olivia tells me. "Unrecoverable. Incorrigible. If she wants to die, then let her die."

I take a deep breath. I crouch down next to Mercedes, and I speak to her as gently as I can. "Mercedes, all I want to do is help you. To keep you healthy. I am not here to make you feel bad. Do you want me to treat you?"

"I hate you."

"Well," I say, "I hope your arm becomes necrotic." I immediately feel terrible. How could I say such a thing to a child? I walk away with my head bowed.

The next morning, I hear that Mercedes has left the Yassela orphanage. I stare into the bustling downtown streets as if asking them to take pity on her. I have truly failed. I have helped to send a girl back out there. Of course the truth is more complicated. Mercedes was preparing to leave Yassela anyway. She was about to be kicked out by the Yassela staff. In some ways, it is better that she is gone, so that little girls like Sara do not learn to cut themselves and exchange sex for clothes and drugs.

And that was at the crux of our short relationship. She expected me to be another sugar daddy. Instead I treated her like a big brother treats his sister. In the end, I lost control, and she got what she wanted: the feeling of rejection, of being only an object, not worthy of simple brotherly care. She loves pain. She savors the razor slash, the puncture of her skin, the sharp agony running up and down her limbs like lasers bouncing between two mirrors and gaining strength, until she finally feels something other than heartache and emptiness. I have failed. Failed tremendously. I could not draw the girl out of Mercedes; I could not make her feel loved.

Perhaps the toughest maneuver of the streets is to accept love. Should I take up the responsibility of teasing out the youthfulness of broken children? If I don't, who will?

5

Introduction to the Street

August 29, 1997

It is 10:40 p.m., and I pace in my room in the half-constructed church, counting the minutes until midnight. My thin twin mattress rests snugly in the pine bed frame. Atop it lies my heavy-duty sleeping bag. Next to that, a small space heater blows warm air into the spacious room; the buzzing noise comforts me. On a metal table next to the window sit my most prized possessions: my Bible and my Macintosh laptop. The window rattles; the wind wants in. My walls are decorated only with pocks of plaster undone. Even for my minimalist taste, it's a sad-looking room.

In exactly one hour and twenty minutes—at midnight—I will meet David at Kennedy Plaza in El Alto. A counselor at Bururu, David talks to street children in El Alto every Tuesday and Thursday night. He befriends the children and eventually gains their trust so that they might join the orphanage. I have been trying to get on the streets ever since I arrived in La Paz, but most people politely tell me "okay" and then don't show up on the night of our planned outing. I have a feeling that whether David shows up or not, I will introduce myself to the street tonight.

"Ayweirea! Wnkiknnaa! Eireiis!" So chants, in her high and eerie voice, my neighbor Ximena. Sometimes I wonder if her family is committing a ritual sacrifice with all their chanting. They are squatters from a rural area. They don't speak Spanish, but every week or so Ximena mimes a request for water. I drag my water hose over to their buckets and give them a week's worth of water. Her family has no plumbing, indoor or out. But somehow they "borrow" enough electricity to keep their rooms lit. Unlike Ximena, I have my own bathroom, supplied with cold water. I take showers at noon, when it's warmer—the sun, not the water.

Eleven-thirty. I'm tired of waiting. I slip on my hiking boots. I tie them hard. Double knot. I stuff one hundred bolivianos into my right boot. "Lord, help me and protect me from the dangers that lie ahead. I pray that what I am about to do is not foolish. Amen."

I gently close my front door. I look up. It's a full moon. Past the rocks and the scrap wood on the half-built church's grassless front yard, I come across a small cat. It looks at me, meows hungrily, then dashes away.

"Good evening. I need to go to El Alto." The taxi driver and I look at each other in the rearview mirror. He doesn't believe me. "It costs eighty bolivianos to go there," he says.

"That's funny. It cost forty the last five times I've gone there. Did the price of gas double today?"

"Forty it is." He shifts gears and begins our forty-minute trip. "Are you meeting someone at the airport?" he asks me. The local airport is in El Alto because landing in La Paz would be a steep and deep dive. As it is, landing in El Alto is a winding descent between frozen Andean peaks. An airline jet once crashed into the side of one of the mountains, killing all the passengers upon impact. At twenty thousand feet, I don't know if the recovery effort was ever fully successful. Dead bodies may still be up there.

"No," I tell him. "I want to meet a friend of mine who works with street children."

"Have you ever been in El Alto at night?"

"No."

"You know, I don't work in that area because it is not worth the risk. There are gangs and knifings. It is where the sex trade is prospering. A woman was raped and then killed just last week. Left strangled and naked."

"Uh-huh." I remind myself that the kids on the street are more like Mercedes than Sara—older, tougher, maybe less trusting, maybe more violent. Those who live in the orphanages have chosen to subject themselves to the rules of the orphanage. They trust that this orphanage world ruled by adults will not be worse than the street. Those who still live on the street prefer the rules of the street. The streets are dangerous. The streets are cruel. But on the streets, at least in part, they write the rules. I want to go to the street. I must walk into their world, abide by their rules to some degree, and try to help them. It is there that they need help the most.

"You know where your friend is?" asks the taxi driver.

"In the Kennedy. Do you know about it?"

"Kennedy. Yes, there are dozens of street children there. But they are gangs. Are you sure you want me to take you there? I can take you back home."

I rub the black plastic covering of my Swiss army knife over and over again. Its greatest deed thus far is cutting hard German cheese. "Yes," I tell the taxi driver. "I am sure I want to go."

I fall into a trance, hypnotized by the blinking night lights of La Paz as they recede slowly into the deep hull of the valley. The engine of the taxi hums loudly as it crawls up the northern mountain, up to El Alto. As we penetrate the mountainside outskirts of El Alto, I cannot tell if I am entering a gigantic construction site or a bombed-out war zone. The taxi weaves between potholes that could easily engulf it whole. A lot of people stand around on the streets, seeming to do nothing, just looking at us. There is dust everywhere. It no longer forms clouds but is simply the final layer of atmosphere here.

Along the roads are the homes. It's hard to tell if they are going up or coming down. I look closer and I can tell. They are tiny, half-built houses made of oven-baked red bricks stacked together haphazardly. As a family comes into more money, they add more bricks. When a family suffers a crisis, the house begins to rot amid the elements. Survival races decomposition.

El Alto is a shantytown suburb of the capital city of the most impoverished nation of the contiguous countries of the Americas. El Alto is the burning fringe of the periphery of the periphery of the global economy. Its population, more than 750,000, grows up to 10 percent each year. More people live in this shantytown suburb than in many U.S. state capitals—and El Alto has no sewage system.

El Alto is a holding cell for rural indigenous people wanting to trade in thousands of years of indigenous culture for a modern urban job. The lucky make their way down to work in La Paz; others die in El Alto. Meanwhile, the children of these migrating families trip their way into the streets. Poverty begets homelessness, and El Alto is a font of street children.

The cars before us slow to a halt. It is around midnight, and on this four-lane road, the nonstop honking, revving, and human barking make my head rumble. I look out at a dozen teenage boys playing fútbol in a park the size of a street intersection. "This is the Kennedy," says the driver.

"Can you wait for me to come back?" He pulls over to the curb, reclines his seat, and begins his nap.

Along every side of the raised hexagonal park, cholitas dressed in blue and white checkered aprons grill meat. They'll be here until 5 a.m., serving the drunks, prostitutes, and late-night streetwalkers. I walk around and around the park looking for David, to no avail.

Why do I need to be introduced to the street children? I can introduce myself. My legs carry me between stumbling middle-aged drunken men. In my ears I hear the trickling of liquid. I stop. A drunk urinates at my feet. He looks at me. I look at him. I walk on. Inebriated men dressed in 1960s-era polyester shirts stumble out of bars with women at their sides. One woman lies on the sidewalk getting her face pounded in by an angry, drooling man. Scantily dressed females switch their hips as they search for tricks. I step into a puddle of urine; thank God for Gore-Tex. I turn at the next corner and find more bars and more neon signs advertising hourly rates. But no street children.

I turn in to a dark alleyway. If I feel uncomfortable, I'll just turn around. I walk several steps down the alley. I make a turn down another alleyway, and then another alley; this seems like the kind of area a street child might hide out in. This is where the poorest of the poor are forced into the solitude of cold pavement. This is where I belong, serving the children. I see movement. A group of young men approaches. At first I suspect that they are drunk, but I can tell by their purposeful gait that they are not. They see me, but they don't say anything. I turn around. My heart races. I look back, and they are still there. Jogging toward me. *Boom. Boom. Boom.* I begin to jog lightly. Now they are running. I run. I make a turn. Another turn. Another dark alley. I cannot see the men. Nor can I see anyone else. Where am I? I run. I try to think. How do I get back to the Kennedy? How? Think! Dark alley after dark alley. Turn after turn. Adrenaline courses through my arteries. I expect to see the gang at my very next turn. Where are they? Did they even notice me?

I stand motionless in an alleyway. The Andean wind claws at my face. Did I think there would be children huddled in these back alleys, innocent and shivering, saying "Burururu," waiting for me to rescue them? A sympathetic rat looks up at me, sniffs, and then abandons me to my fate. I hear voices. Voices of young men. They are yelling. What was I thinking, coming here? Did I actually think that a foreigner could show up at midnight and all the street children would come? What an act of idiocy. I can't do this alone; I need help. Especially right now. The voices get louder as I walk farther down the alleyway. They are screaming, laughing, yelling. Louder, louder, louder.

They are the voices of teenagers playing fútbol. I am near the Kennedy. My entire body relaxes. I walk out of the alleyway into the green lights. I take a breath of joy when I see the prostitutes, the men in suits, and the drunks and their puddles of urine. I wipe the sweat of fear from my eyes and rap my knuckles on the taxi window. The taxi driver wakes up, half startled. "Any luck?" he asks.

"No."

"You didn't find the kids."

"Not exactly."

"Good thing you didn't get into any trouble."

Several Days Later

Plaza San Francisco is a blurry tangle of human activity. The campesina women break down their outdoor shops and prepare their makeshift tents for the night. Couples hug each other, necking like American teenyboppers. Trash hovering an inch above the pavement scoots along, drawing unusual polygons. Puddles of vomit and urine give the area its pungent smell and add color to the gray rock floor. I stand in the middle of this activity watching a young woman eat a cow's heart—a common Bolivian delicacy often sold on the streets.

Rodrigo walks up to me and shakes my hand. "Hungry?" he asks me. He is a Bolivian medical student who attends La Iglesia de Dios. Next to him stands Elizabeth, a Danish college student who has been volunteering at Bururu. Both of them want to see what the streets are like; they want to help the street kids.

The cold Andean wind whips my face. I zip up my jacket and stuff my hands in my pockets. A drunk wearing a shirt and tie walks up to Elizabeth. "You have the most beautiful eyes," he says and stumbles toward her, hoping to get a free rub. She gives him a look of disgust. I slip between the two of them. "Back off," I tell him.

We take a circuitous route from Plaza San Francisco to Bururu in order to avoid the dark alleys. A scantily dressed, toothless woman approaches Rodrigo. We march ahead without missing a beat.

"Wow, Chi, that was a huge woman!"

"Uh, Rodrigo, 'she' was a 'he,' not to mention a prostitute."

"That was a man?"

"Rodrigo, her arms were bigger than my thighs, and she had a five o'clock shadow."

We get to Bururu, tiptoe up the stairs, and sneak into Room 4, the most "senior" room that the orphans aspire to. I shake the leg of Alejandro, who is sleeping in his street clothes. "Alejandro," I whisper, "do you still want to introduce us to the streets tonight?"

We double-check our gear—the medicines, the guitar, the soccer ball, and so forth. We bow our heads and say a prayer.

My body courses with electricity. Tonight is the first night. The veil will finally be lifted. I will know the children. We walk. We get to a concrete, fenced-in park that I've passed half a dozen times. We go inside. The clock strikes twelve. The white fluorescent lights in the park produce an eerie feeling as the damp, cold air wisps by my face. "You know about this place," says Alejandro. "Don't you?"

"No, not really."

"This place is Alonzo de Mendoza. Over against the back portion of this park is where all the drug dealings occur. Along the edges, the street children sit and talk on the benches. Up the street is where the prostitutes sell their bodies every night. It is also where all the bars are located. It's Friday. Singles night."

"Singles night?"

"Yes, singles night. It is the night when men, married or unmarried, become single. They go into town, drink, and have sex. On Saturday, they return to their wives or girlfriends as if nothing happened."

"Oh."

We walk up to four kids sitting on a bench—three boys and a girl. They range from five to twenty-five. Each one of them holds a fist to his nose. None of them are looking up. When they do, I see an impenetrable glaze on their eyes. A teenage boy's eyeballs roll back into his skull. I take a step back. "Are they high on cocaine?" I ask Alejandro.

"No, Don Chi," Alejandro says, using the highly respectful term usually reserved for older people. I can't ask him to stop using it without hurting his feelings. "No," Alejandro says, "they're using paint thinner."

"What's paint thinner?" I ask.

"What they inhale."

"Why?"

Alejandro shrugs his shoulders. "It keeps you warm in the cold. It makes your hunger pains go away. It gives you an unbreakable armor. No one can hurt you when you are high."

"Why don't they use alcohol?" I ask.

"Because it's too expensive and does not last as long."

"What do you mean it's too expensive?"

"The street children can buy a whole gallon of paint thinner for one American dollar," Alejandro explains, pantomiming each step. "They buy it from the store, and they give it to all their friends in small bottles. The street kids soak strands of yarn in these bottles, then they hold it in their fists and breathe in the thinner. When the police come by, they throw the yarn away."

In the past, the Aymara and Quechua Indians often kept coca leaves in their mouths all day. It also kept them warm and warded off hunger. I guess thinner is the new coca leaf, only cheaper, more toxic, and mass manufactured by industrial companies.

Alejandro announces to the four kids on the bench, "This is Chi. He is a doctor from America. He can sew up your wounds. He's here to help you."

The four kids lift their faces from their fists and then lower them back onto their fists. Some of them don't even look at me before they sniff again.

I turn to Rodrigo. "Should we play one of the songs?" I open up my backpack and pass out the lyrics to one of the songs. Rodrigo begins strumming. We sing. It is a duet; none of the kids join in. They hold the song sheet in one hand and their thinner in the other. Some of them hold the song sheet upside down. Every once in a while one of them looks up at Rodrigo or me, when we miss a note. We get to the end of the song, and I take back my song sheets. I open up my backpack again. I have printed up some verses from the Bible and cut them into individual strips. I hand each of the four children a strip of paper upon which is neatly typed a Bible verse.

"Okay." I kneel down on the ground. "Can someone read this verse for me?"

Alejandro taps me on the shoulder. "I think they might have a problem reading."

"What do you mean? Because they're high?"

"No. A problem reading."

"Can anyone read?"

A boy, high as a kite, says, "I-I-I can reeead."

"Okay," I say.

"Gawwwwwddd . . ." he says.

"Yes?" I say.

"Gawwwwwddd . . ." He nods off into his paint thinner.

This is not working. My heart sinks. Then a young boy walks up from behind. "Is that a Bible verse?" he asks.

"Yes," I say. "Ephesians 2:8."

"Oh," says the boy. "I know that one already."

"You know that verse already?"

"Yeah," says the boy. "I say it every day on the bus. Ephesians 2:8: 'For by grace you have been saved through faith, and that not of yourselves; it is the gift of God.' Then all the old ladies give me money. I could use some new verses. You got any?"

I'm walking around and treating a few minor ailments when a skinny boy of about thirteen years walks up to me with a bloody wound on his hand. I open my tackle box full of medicine, and the kids stare wide eyed into it. "Look at all the drugs he has," the wounded boy says. "He's pretty cool." A dozen more kids gather around. "Look at all these drugs! Whoa!"

"Sit down," I say. "These are antibiotics, not narcotics."

"I don't care," says the wounded boy. "Can I have some?"

I look at the wounded boy. "No," I say, and I treat his hand.

Later, a ten-year-old boy limps up to me. His foot has a big red gash across the top of it. I need to clean out the wound, debride it. It's going to hurt intensely. He's going to need lidocaine, so out of the fishing box comes the syringe.

"Serious drugs!" says a kid. "He's got an IV!"

"I'm not shooting up," I say.

"Hey, mister, did you know that's bad for you?"

"No, it's an anesthetic."

"You mean you're going to go to sleep?"

"I'm not injecting it in myself. I'm injecting it in his foot." The kid with the foot wound looks at me with concern.

"You mean you're going to put him to sleep? Wow! That's even better!"

Later a teenage boy with a huge bloody gash in his right leg staggers up to me. Acne has taken over his face. He is five foot four and stocky. He looks mean as a rabid dog. He looks at me without saying anything. He just looks at me.

"What'd you do?" I say.

"I stabbed another kid."

"What do you mean, you stabbed another kid?"

"I tried to kill him."

I think about this for a moment. "Do you have a knife on you?"

"Of course I have a knife."

The other kids chime in. "If you treat him, he won't stab you." All the children laugh.

I take out the syringe. "Is this going to hurt?" he asks.

I say to him, "You just stabbed someone. I bet that hurt!"

The other kids laugh hysterically. "I don't want to do this," says the boy.

I give him a serious look. "If that wound gets worse, it'll get necrotic, and we'll have to cut your leg off. You have two choices: Either we stick you with the needle or we cut your leg off."

"Cut his leg off! Cut his leg off!" chant the kids. "Cut his leg off. What does he need it for?"

"Shut up!" says the boy. "You better shut up!"

"Close your eyes," I tell the boy. "I need to inject you three times. Each time I inject you, I'll count to three."

"One, two, three. . . ." Down goes the lidocaine. "One, two, three. . . ." Down goes another dose. As I fill the syringe with lidocaine a third time, two men walk up and stand behind me. I only know they're behind me by their shadows. I've heard bad stories about what happens on the streets, where bodies end up. I'm on my knees trying to aim the syringe into the right spot on the boy's leg. By the looks of their shadows, the two men are tense, ready to strike. I can hear them mumbling to each other. Sweat pours out of my head. I can't concentrate. "One . . ." I say. My patient looks worried for me. Then he looks at the syringe shaking in my hand and he starts worrying about himself. "Two . . ." I say. I'm just waiting for the blow to come down and crack open my head. I'm not going to turn around. I'm just going to wait. When I see movement, I'm going to dodge and run like a madman. "Three . . ."

The boy spits out, "Be careful with that, buddy."

My hand is shaking so badly I don't dare inject him. I'll probably hit a bone or something. Finally, Alejandro whispers in my ear,
"Calm down, Chi. They won't bother you." Alejandro tells the men
behind me that I am a doctor here to treat the street children. That's
all I'm here for. I take a few deep breaths and inject my patient a
third time. I clean out his wound, give him some antibiotics, and
send him on his way. The men leave, the show having ended.

"Does anyone else need any help?" I ask.

"No," says a boy walking by.

I take the soccer ball out of my backpack. "Does anyone want to
play soccer?"

They inhale their thinner.

I sit around, twiddling my thumbs for a while. "Okay," I say to no
one in particular, maybe myself, "I'll be back tomorrow."

As Rodrigo, Elizabeth, and I walk back to the orphanage with
Alejandro, I say to him, "That was a total waste of time."

Alejandro does not seem to miss a beat, as if he knew I would say
that. "Chi," he says, "you have to be patient with these kids. You have
to be there for the kids, that's all. They'll come around. Many people
want to change these kids too quickly. That includes the orphanage.
They're all wrong. These kids aren't going to change overnight.
You have to do it step by step. A little less thinner. A little less violence. A little at a time."

We walk past a row of child prostitutes. "The kids won't listen to
you this month. They might listen to you in seven months. They don't
want your charity—actually, they don't mind taking your money. But
they want you to be part of their lives. They won't listen to you until
they know you care for them. They won't assume that you're there out
of the goodness of your heart; they think you're out to get something.
Everything comes with a price. You have to prove it's free, always free,
that you will always be there for them, even if for no reason."

6

Miguel and Pilar

October 1997, Plaza San Francisco

The mantra repeats itself in my head: "Get them off the streets. Get them off the streets." The words never seem tiresome or repetitive.

I am drawn to abandoned street children. They are the poorest of poor children, the forgotten of the forgotten. Even the orphanage workers have abandoned them. Though La Paz is dotted with dozens of orphanages, the social workers don't walk the streets. They are too busy in the orphanages, taking care of the children they already have, many of whom have never slept on the streets; these children are dropped off by poor parents who cannot afford to care for them. Where does that leave the street child living alone on the street? On the blind side of averted eyes.

I want to help them. Most of the time, they don't want my help. I stitch wounds. I treat diseases. Upon closing my medicine box, I ask my patient if she wants to live under a roof. A leery look washes across her face. Adults are enemies; men beat them, berate them, and sexually abuse them. Being alone with the wrong man will get you killed. "No." The answer is always "no," or rather, "next time," since in Bolivia refusing an invitation is impolite.

"Stay however long you want," I eventually learn to say. "A night, a day, an hour, a minute." Just an hour under a roof will convince them, my theory goes, that life is better in a home—even an orphanage.

"No." Still no. Always no.

But I don't give up. I tap the testimonies of former Bururu kids, as the kids trust each other more than they trust me. "Is Bururu a good home?" I ask those who once slept on pavement. "Yes," they say. "Are kids abused there?" The kids tell the truth: "No."

And then I turn to the child. "Do you want to go to Bururu?"

The truth. Always the truth: "No."

Tonight is breezy. I am leading some street children in a prayer song, but the song rings hollow. Singing of hope, joy, and God feels patronizing when there is little hope and joy here. When enough street children have gathered around our singing, I unlock my backpack and take out the soccer ball. I ask more than twenty children if they want to play soccer. They shout a resounding "Yes!" It's a "yes" to a return visit to childhood, however brief. And they don't even have to sleep in a scary orphanage employing unfamiliar adults. We walk down Calle America, passing unconscious drunks.

A gargantuan statue of a head casts an irregular shadow in the empty plaza. I don't know if he has a name. He is the Statue of Heroes. People pay their respect to him by urinating on him every day. During the day, Plaza San Francisco bustles with food vendors, street evangelists, and shouting shamans selling crocodile oil; at night the plaza belongs to the street children. Two boys scurry about, pick up two rocks each, and place them on the cool concrete. Here are the boundaries for the goals. Two boys take turns pointing their fingers at the other children. Here are our teams. The ball is dropped, and here in the plaza a heated battle commences. These street kids, malnourished and mistreated, play fútbol as well as any kids in the world. The melee rages on.

Down the dozen stairs leading to the plaza steps a little girl. She sets both feet on each step before taking on the next one. She wears solid blue knitted pants and a red sweater. She sits down on a step and digs into her paper bag of potato chips. Her fingers and cheeks, covered in potato chip grease, glisten under the streetlights. She lets out a periodic giggle as she watches the soccer game.

She notices me and shouts, *"Chino! Chino! Venga aquí!"* She waves her greasy fingers and winks. I walk toward her and take a seat beside her on the cold stairs.

"Why are you here at 2 a.m.?" I ask her.

"I need to earn money."

"How do you earn money?"

"I sell stuff."

"What stuff?"

"Just stuff. Chino. Give me five bolivianos." She pleads with her brows.

"I'm sorry, but I can't give you money."

"Please. How about one dollar?" She scrunches up her eyes and sets her thumb and index finger a centimeter apart.

"I'm sorry, but I can't give you money. . . . Where do you live?"

She stretches her left arm behind her back, "Far, far away. Do you see that boy with the soccer ball? He's my brother."

"Oh, really? What's his name?"

"Miguel."

"How old is he?"

"Eight."

"What's your name?"

"Pilar."

"And how old are you?"

She shows me four of her fingers.

"So, Pilar, where are you going to sleep tonight?"

"Here." She points down at the cement sidewalk.

The soccer players stop in their tracks. The ball rolls off the field.

"Give me my money!" a three-hundred-pound drunken man barks.

A fifteen-year-old street boy crouches against the wall, protecting his head with both arms.

"I don't have your money!" shouts the boy.

"I told you I was going to come back tonight! Where is it?" The man slams a large stick against the boy's back, and the boy's scream echoes across the square. The boy jumps up and flees along the wall. The soccer players run to the side of the street boy, ready to take blows in his defense.

"I don't owe you anything!" shouts the street boy.

As one, the human wall of boys and girls puffs up its collective chest and braces itself to be struck. The drunken man holds his stick high.

"He doesn't have any money," says one of the older children. The stick comes down, slowly. The drunken man walks down the street, and the tension subsides.

The boy runs down El Prado. The rest of the children resume their soccer game. Shouts and grunts pepper the air along with the periodic "Gooooallll!"

I stand and shout, "Last game!" They grumble. They plead. They play harder for the final defining point. And when it is scored, the mighty roar of "GOOOOOALLL!" can be heard by every street child and every police officer in town.

"We will return tomorrow night." I pick up the ball.

"Promise, Dr. Chi."

"Yes. Promise."

As the children disperse, I seek out Miguel and introduce myself. He reciprocates politely. I ask him why he's on the street.

"My mother dropped us off," he says, "and she's going to pick us up in the morning."

"Do you want to come with me to the orphanage?"

"No, I'd rather stay on the street."

"You would rather be on the street," I say, "and you're going to have your sister stay on the street with you."

"Yeah."

"Your sister is only four years old, and when you were playing soccer, she was left all alone. You're the big brother. You need to take care of your sister. How can you allow your sister to sleep on the street? It's one thing to have you sleep on the street because you're a bigger boy, but it's another thing to have your four-year-old sister sleep on the streets." I say that he can stay at Bururu for how-ever long he wants. I ask other street children if Bururu is a good place, and they say yes.

Miguel thinks about my words. He says, "No."

Alejandro signals for me to give the child a little bit of breathing space. I walk across the empty plaza. I glance at my watch, and it says 2:34 a.m. A sudden feeling of exhaustion sweeps over my body as I realize that I will have to wake up in less than six hours for church. As I walk away, I realize that Alejandro and Luis (another boy from Bururu) are discussing matters with Pilar and Miguel. I grow impatient waiting for them and decide to expedite the situa-tion. As I walk closer to the children, I notice that Miguel is nod-ding his head, but I can see in his eyes a glassy fear. He knows that some of the orphanages are notorious for violence and robbery. But Alejandro and Luis do not relent. At times, the silences persist, but after fifteen more minutes, Miguel says, "Bueno."

We walk past fetid trash and fresh urine. Pilar walks alongside my left leg, attempting to match my long strides. Her dark black eyes peer up at me, and she reaches up her hand to hold mine. We walk a couple of strides together, and I realize that I am nearly dragging her along the sidewalk.

"What if I carry you?"

She giggles and holds her tiny, chubby arms out.

As we walk back to the Bururu house, Pilar and I see stumbling drunks and men in business suits looking for sex. Pilar mumbles something into my ear. It saddens my heart as I realize the harshness of the lives of these children. The desire to adopt every single child on the street grows with each step. As we turn the corner, we see a gang walking toward us. I tell everyone to cross the street and walk slowly without any appearance of fear. As we jaywalk away from the young gangsters, taxis honk and zip around us. The women street vendors are still grilling greasy beef at three in the morning. I walk past them to the front door of Bururu orphanage.

I dig deep into my pockets to retrieve my keys. I turn to let the orange streetlight illuminate the keyhole. I almost tip over as I turn the key four times counterclockwise while holding Pilar in my arms. As the misaligned door drags along the kitchen floor, the unoiled hinge creaks a high pitch. I flip on the lights. Miguel stands on the threshold staring at the big ovens, sink, and stove.

"We have a huge kitchen along with a bakery. Every day we make lots of rolls, hot and fresh. All the children eat three times a day. It's all free. All you have to do is do your chores, follow the rules, and go to school."

I crouch before the boy. "Miguel, listen to me. You have to look after your little sister. You may be tough and able survive the streets, but you have to think about your sister also." Miguel nods in agreement; his sister has fallen asleep in my arms.

"Which place is warmer? Bururu or the streets?"

"Bururu."

"Where can you eat three times a day? Bururu or the streets?"

"Bururu."

"Where is it safe? Where are there no violent men, prostitutes, knives, and drugs?"

"Bururu."

"You have to think about your sister."

We walk down the hall and turn on the lights.

"This is the medical office. We have nearly every medicine you may need. I am here Monday through Friday."

We walk up the stairs and flip on the hall lights. I open Room 1 and present to Miguel the dozen or so boys sleeping there on the floor, beneath their ahuayos. "This is Room 1, where the newest boys sleep. After you sleep here for a month or so, doing your chores every day, you can move up to Room 2, where the beds are better, and so are the boys. Room 4 is the best room." Choco, the Bururu dog, wakes up and barks fervently at Miguel. Pilar stirs in my arms. One of the boys tells the dog to quiet down; he looks up at Miguel and says, "Grab a blanket. There's plenty of room."

Alejandro carries in a mattress from another room, and I retrieve a blanket. I search Miguel for drugs and knives and tell him, "Miguel, there is no fighting, no stealing, and no drugs in the home. We have breakfast at 8 a.m. and then you will have a chore to do. This will be your bed with your little sister. She can stay with you tonight. But since this is an orphanage for boys, Pilar needs to be with you at all times. Do you have any questions?"

"I don't think so." Miguel and Pilar lie down on the mattress. As I back out of the room, little Pilar waves her arm. I walk back toward her, between the bare soles of the sleeping children. She cups her hands against my ear. "You will come back. Won't you?"

"Yes."

"Promise."

"Promise. I will be back tomorrow."

She takes off her tiny, worn-out tennis shoes and gets under the cover. She snuggles up to her brother and quickly falls asleep.

I return from church the next morning to find Miguel and Pilar gone. Alejandro tells me they left around ten that morning. They did not say where they were going. Back to their mother, I hope. Hope is all I can do. Anxiety eats at me as I realize they may have returned to the streets. When I don't see them on the streets over the following days, I want to believe they have gone home. Of course, they could simply be sleeping on the streets in a different area of La Paz, or they could be hiding in trees like some children, or they might have moved to a different city altogether. "Get them off the streets." The mantra. Get them off the streets. "Promise"— her one word to me echoes. Promise. I never see Miguel and Pilar again.

7

Gabriel

32°F, Midnight, Alonzo de Mendoza (the Red-Light District of La Paz)

Bam! Bam! Boom! Plack! Feet scrape concrete. Chests bump chests. A child's body smacks the ground.

Another night in Plaza San Francisco watching the children play soccer. An evening of fútbol is a cool oasis in the hell that is every other minute of life. To most children in the developed world, playing is an assumed part of childhood. To girl prostitutes and street boys, kicking a leather soccer ball between two stones and into a puddle of urine is a gift from heaven. Every time I hear the children shout "Gooooalllllllll!" it is music to my ears.

Bop! Bam! The ball careens off of a young boy's head into the aforementioned pool of urine. One team raises their hands in triumph. The other team looks to me. "Chi, come and play with us," pleads a girl. "We need help. The boys are being rough, and we are losing."

I jump into the arena and play fútbol with my two left feet. The air is still thin for my lungs. A heavy pant beats a quick rhythm for my fatigued body. Sweat pours down my face, which is cooled only by a whizzing ball. "Goooallllll!" The opposing team scores again, and the children celebrate by running to the steps and whipping out their tiny plastic bottles of paint thinner. They inhale and enter into their other world.

One boy's head stands out, high above the younger ones around him. A red, tattered cap covers his brow but cannot hide the black hair that falls to his shoulders. A knifing scar crawls across his left mandible. Pimples dot his face like cities on a map. I can't see his eyes. He's a big kid, maybe fifteen, but already five foot three. The average Bolivian man stands about five foot four. From his baggy jeans he brings forth a half-liter bottle of clear fluid. Girls and boys, young and old, crowd like vultures around a fresh kill.

"Give me some!" they plead in asynchronous voices.

"Wait. Everyone will get his share," the taller boy announces with calm authority. I often see him breaking up fights and leading a pack of younger boys through the streets. A couple of his "followers"—José and a black boy named Mario—keep the crowd back as he pours paint thinner into two-ounce plastic bottles. Street kids always share their thinner; they never keep a surplus. The kids snatch up the bottles as soon as they are filled.

A chill courses through my body. I watch from a distance the surreal tragedy occurring four feet in front of me. Little boys not older than eight years old clamor for more inhalant. Little girls who should be jumping rope shove others aside to get more of this brain-damaging fix. The drug is more precious than food itself. My mind zips from one scenario to another. Confiscating the drug would only deter the children from it temporarily. Asking or telling them to stop would be futile. And so I watch as the children inhale the amnesia-inducing poison, the antidote to memory, the thinner that thins out brain cells.

The euphoria goes on for several minutes. They return to earth. They disperse.

Another night on the streets. For a couple of weeks now, I have been watching the confident boy who shares his euphoria, noting his mannerisms, actions, and reactions. I know his name.

"Hello."

"Hello," he replies. Same drug. Same clothes. Same cap. His hood hides his eyes; I see them only as sparks intercepted by the light as he turns his head away from me. Our eyes bore holes into the concrete at our feet.

"Your name is Gabriel, isn't it?"

"Yes. And your name is Dr. Cheeeeee! Even though I sniff"—he inhales deeply—"I am still as smart as a cat." He's been watching me, these nights, longer than I've been watching him.

I offer my hand. He takes it. I shake his hand with as strong a grip as I can muster. "You've been on the street for quite a long time."

"Yuuuuuppppp!"

"Where do you live?"

"Oh, you know, here and there."

"In the sewers, right?"

"How do you know?" He's surprised.

"I've seen you walk down into the sewers."

"I live way far down. Deep. It is very dark. No one can see me. It is my hiding place."

"Do you like the sewers?"

"It is better than the streets. Life is horrible on the streets and in the sewers. But I feel safe down there. Not even the violent men are willing to walk into the sewers. I have ten furious mutts and a few drunks sleeping with me!" He speaks with pride. "The rule on the streets is survival. You either live or die by your actions. I choose to live."

He respects me, I can tell, as I respect him. I take a deep breath, relax, ready myself to ask the big question, the silly question for a tough kid like Gabriel. But I must: "Would you be interested in living in the home?"

Gabriel looks at me with an eye of suspicion.

"Why would I want to live in a home when I can be outside and free?"

"We have a bed with blankets, food three times a day, school, and arts and crafts for you to learn." An uneasy silence. "Plus, in a home, no one can beat you."

He walks away. I guess that means no.

The fútbol game is even fiercer tonight. Older boys have joined the nightly game. With his yarn pressed against his panting mouth, Gabriel dribbles the ball past one defender and shoots. The goalie leans and deflects the ball with her right hand. Gabriel's teammate kicks the ball to him, and for once he takes the thinner from his face, to head the ball. Although his cap is soaked with sweat, Gabriel is not tired; his body has adapted so well to the inhalant that it doesn't slow him down.

My mind flutters from one thought to another. Sleeping five hours a day over the past week has taken a huge toll. It is only half past midnight, but I will call it a night and go home. Gabriel approaches me. I stick my hand out to shake. "Have a good night," I tell him. "I will see you tomorrow."

"I want to go."

I squint at him. "You want to go where?"

He looks me in the eye for the first time ever; he stares hard, as if trying to catch a glimpse of my soul. "To the home."

"Are you sure?"

"Yes."

"It will be tough, you know."

"I want to go."

"There will be rules and everything."

"I know."

"No drugs. No knives. No fighting."

Gabriel does not avert his eyes from mine. Here is a proud kid, a kid who understands dignity and its absence. A kid who stays warm at night by hugging a sewage canal but who hasn't a toilet to use in the day. A kid who speaks of survival as a religion unto itself but who must steal the very essence of life—water—from other human beings. A kid who knows where he stands in the eyes of mainstream Bolivia and yet wears his street stains with the armor of thinner and the pride of a lion. "I want to go."

"David! David!"

Boom! Boom! Boom! I slam my fist harder against the door. I hear the clinking sounds of David's belt buckle as he attempts to hastily dress in the dark.

"Hermano David. Please wake up."

The door opens and a short, pear-shaped man steps into the light.

"I am so sorry to wake you at this hour."

"No problem." He smiles at me.

"Gabriel wants to live at the house."

David's smile disappears. He leans over to the side to catch a glimpse of the boy hiding behind me.

"Step to the side, Gabriel," I tell him. "Come on."

He drags his feet and enters into view.

"What's your name, kid?"

Gabriel's cap is nearly covering his eyes. His head angles downward.

"Gabriel, David asked you a question. He is the counselor, the boss of the house."

"Gabriel Garcia." Metamorphosis. Gabriel transforms from a confident, gangsterlike street teenager into a timid boy uncomfortable with himself.

"Go ahead. Tell David why you want to live here."

"Because"—he points toward a dirty window overlooking the city lights—"I am tired of being out there."

"He knows the rules of the house," I tell David. I turn to Gabriel. "Give me your drugs." He hands me his ball of yarn and the plastic container. I turn his pockets inside out and search his body for knives. David fiddles with his motley array of copper keys and walks slowly to the first room on the left.

The door opens to darkness. Two large yellow eyes stare into the light. A low rumbling growl emanates from their direction. Room 1: You sleep with the dog. Two young boys lift up their heads and squint their eyes at me. "Hermano Chi, what are you doing here?" asks the shorter one, Carlos.

"Gabriel's going to live with us."

The two boys look at Gabriel. They begin shaking the other boys awake with vicious trepidation. Startled, one child jumps out of bed, confused and puzzled. He looks at me. He looks at Gabriel. "We don't want him."

"He is dangerous, Chi." Carlos wags his finger at me. "Don't let him stay here. He'll ruin everything." Gabriel can't even catch a break from other street kids; do they not understand that living on the street is what made Gabriel dangerous, that now that he has been removed from that environment, he will behave differently? But I have no time to explain all this. I tell Carlos, "It's not really your choice, is it now?"

"Chi," says Carlos, "do you know on the street sometimes a kid with a bad reputation sits down on a bench, and all the younger kids get up and walk away because they fear him?" Carlos glances at Gabriel, as if I might not know of whom he speaks.

Without a word, Gabriel trudges to the far left corner where none

of the children are sleeping. He lifts a blanket over himself and goes
to bed. Not even the street boys want him. No one wants him except
for some scraggly mutts and a few cirrhotic homeless men. And a
small gang of street boys for whom he supplies thinner. And me.

"Take off your shoes, Gabriel."

Gabriel reluctantly sits up and unties the tattered shoestrings of
his almost sole-less shoes. I know he can be rehabilitated. I know it
like I know the sum of two twos. "I'll see you in the morning," I say.
Gabriel nods his head and pulls the llama blanket, with its colors of
the sky, mountains, forests, earth, and blood, over his face.

It is 7 a.m. I did not sleep well this morning. My chest feels tight.
Did he leave the home? Did he hurt anyone? Did he break anything? Is he feeling unloved? Has he returned to Mother Street?

I walk to Bururu and stand at the back door, petrified of what
I might find. He will be gone. I walk into the Bururu dining room.
Gabriel stands before a small, shaky wooden table. With his stubby
fingers, he meticulously shapes a lump of clay into a Mary-like
figurine. Entranced by his work and seemingly swimming within
his element, he does not even notice me until he comes to a stopping point. He looks up at me, and a smile transforms his face. His
face! I can see his face! His cap, his hood, and even his long hair are
gone. And his smile—he is like a person who for years suffered from
Parkinson's disease and is now taking medication for the first time,
awakening and stretching long-atrophied muscles.

"Chi!" he exclaims.

"How is it going?" I ask him.

"Good," he replies with glee.

"Have they treated you well?"

"Yes." He signals with a wink and an okay sign.

"Do you like it here?"

"Yes, I like it a lot here."

"What do you like about it?"

"I get to work with my hands." He shapes the face of his clay figurine. "I want to be a mechanic."

"Do you need anything?"

He looks at me as if to ask why he would need anything when he has everything. I am proud of him.

"Do you need anything?" I ask again.

"No, not really."

"How about some shoes?"

We both look down at his tattered shoes with toes sticking out of the front. I want to reward him with new shoes, to show my pride in him.

"I guess so," he says.

"Great. I will come back this afternoon."

"Okay, Chi."

"You did a good job, Gabriel. You did good. What happened to your hair?"

He makes a scissors sign. The barber must have visited the orphanage today.

"It looks good, Gabriel. You looked like a girl before." He acknowledges my joke with a smirk and an ambivalent nod.

We walk up the steep, cobblestone street to Mercado Negro, the black market. Hundreds of wooden stands sell thousands of imitation goods. Tourists are rarely seen among these crowded alleyways. Bolivians zip in and out of stands looking for underwear, socks, soap, and in our case, tennis shoes.

"How do you like the other kids at the home?"

"They are okay," says Gabriel. "Can I have these shoes, Chi?" Gabriel hands me a pair of fake Converse canvas shoes. The white rubber sole is loosely stitched to the red cloth. The interiors have little sole support.

"How about these Aadidases?" I hand him a sturdier pair of counterfeits; the soles are double-stitched to the leather. He turns them around in his hands and rubs his fingers over the double a's in Aadidas.

"Sure."

"How much do they cost?" I ask the campesina woman.

"One hundred."

Anger swells up through my neck and into my head. My scalp feels hot.

"Are you crazy? Quit ripping us off! Let's go!"

The woman runs after us.

"I am sorry, *joven*. I thought that you were a foreigner. I will sell it to you for eighty bolivianos."

Gabriel looks at me. Is this a test? "Seventy," I say.

"Okay," she says.

I hand her the seventy bolivianos, equivalent to fourteen American dollars. The shoes are quite expensive by Bolivian standards, but I know if I buy Gabriel cheap shoes, they will be torn up in the first week of street fútbol.

"Thank you, joven."

"Thank you," I reply.

Gabriel looks at me. "You did good," he tells me.

"I am going to mark your shoes with your name on the side so that nobody will steal them at the orphanage. Is that all right with you?"

"Sure."

I know Gabriel won't return to the streets. I know he won't. But he might try to sell his shoes to someone on the street; that's why I write his name on the shoes. I still don't trust Gabriel with all my heart.

8

Stabbing

Sunday Morning, November 5, 1997;
Obrajes District (an Affluent Southern Area of La Paz)

I listen to Scott's sermon with only one ear, as I turn every fifteen seconds to look at the door. There's only half an hour left of the Iglesia de Dios service, and none of the street boys have shown up. David leads them in the hour-long walk from Bururu, and they usually arrive before the service begins.

My leg bounces up and down anxiously. It's been one month since Gabriel joined the orphanage. Gabriel has transformed himself, with the encouragement of the Bururu counselors, into a model Bururu boy. Every day he takes a shower, cleans his room, and makes his bed. He has purged himself of all the traits of the street animal he was, showing his core innocence, proving that the hide he wore on the street was simply his original skin callused over by the beatings of his environment.

I nearly spring out of my seat when I see Daniel, a Bururu boy, standing on the threshold of the church entrance with his hands behind his back. His horizontally striped shirt is soaked with sweat. He signals to Jessica (a Bururu staff member), and she escorts him outside. Could it be Gabriel? Could he have stolen some thinner? Did he bully another child?

Ten minutes and a gallon of sweat later, I walk out of the service to find Jessica and Daniel outside in the sun and the breeze. "Tómas has been hit by a car," she tells me.

"Is he okay?" I ask.

"He might have broken his leg. They have X-rays."

"Good. I'll take a look. How'd it happen?"

"The boys ran across Avenida Hernando Siles at the same time. Tómas was the last boy of the group. A taxi hit him on the leg. I've told the boys so many times to use the crosswalk. They never listen."

"Did the taxi driver stop?"

"He stopped. We got his name and driver's license. The police are talking to him right now." He's probably already in jail. In Bolivia, drivers who hit people are immediately thrown in prison, regardless of culpability.

"Thanks, Jessica," I say. "I'll go to the hospital after church." I take a deep breath. Am I relieved because Tómas lives or because Gabriel hasn't screwed up? Does it matter? All's well. I turn to walk away.

"Chi, something else happened."

"What?"

"There was a stabbing."

"Who got stabbed?"

"A boy in the park got stabbed."

"One of our boys?"

"No."

"Um, so what happened?"

"It was Gabriel. He stabbed another boy in the back. The boy is in surgery right now at Methodist Hospital, three blocks down the street."

I walk toward the hospital. I know Gabriel has done some things in the past, but he's reformed now. There must have been some confusion about what happened. I trust Gabriel. I know him.

I stand at the hospital entrance. A fat, elderly man is rolled out of the hospital on a stretcher, his family scooting along around him like cytoplasm. The man is so deathly pale he blends in with his sheets. And yet there is neither an intravenous line attached to him nor any medical personnel around him. I look inside the "ambulance." It is an empty van. No people, no medications, no defibrillators. Into this shell the man is inserted and driven away.

I spot Daniel in the hospital parking lot, talking to a national police officer. After the policeman finishes his interview, I ask Daniel if Tómas is all right.

"Yes," Daniel says, "but the boy Gabriel stabbed is real bad."

"How bad?"

Daniel shakes his head and his eyes glaze over as he remembers the scene. "There was blood everywhere. We were in the park playing before church. Gabriel was sitting next to a tree just relaxing. Then one of the boys in the park gave one of us—Coco—a dirty look. Suddenly, Coco and this other boy started punching each other. A mob fight broke out between our boys and the other boy and his friends. Coco was taking these kids down. It was amazing for someone who never says anything. I didn't think Coco had it in him. Then Gabriel took his eight-inch knife and stabbed the boy who started the fight in the back. The boy fell to the ground, yelling. Screeching and everything. Blood just pouring out, gushing, and his stomach getting bigger and bigger. It was scary. David took him to this hospital. He's in surgery."

"Where's Gabriel?"

"He's long gone. Probably in another city by now."

I walk into the hospital and climb its green marble stairs. Floor three. As I walk toward the end of the hall, I look into each room and see nothing. No doctors, no patients, just beds. No one walks the dimly lit hall. When I get to the end of the hall, I am looking into the eyes of four teary- and weary-eyed campesinas. A fiftysomething-year-old cholita wears the traditional clothing of a countrywoman.

"Is your son inside?" I ask her.

"Yes, do you know him?" she asks, wringing her hands.

"I heard about him. I work with Bururu Home for Street Boys."

The woman puts her hands behind her back and looks down at the dusty floor. "He is such a good boy. He always helps out whenever he can. Now I may lose him." Her lips tighten against the tears. A sun-worn campesina woman places her arm around her, then turns a hardened eye to me. "The doctor says he's bleeding inside. From the spleen." If a doctor doesn't do surgery and put a clamp on his spleen immediately, the kid may bleed to death from within.

"I hope that he will live," says the mother. She looks toward the ceiling. "Can you help us?" she asks.

"Yes, I can," I say, trying to make eye contact despite the piercing shame I feel right now. "Does your son need blood?"

"Yes." Bolivian hospitals don't have blood banks, so friends and loved ones must be present to donate. I guess motherless children bleed to death.

"What is your son's name?"

"Arturo Sanchez." I brought Gabriel to the orphanage. Not only did I bring him there, I cajoled him into coming. Then I left him to the counselors and assumed he had reformed when he made some little people out of clay. I searched him on the first day, so I assumed he wasn't packing a knife. But a steel blade ends up in the spleen of a boy. Arturo Sanchez.

I enter the phlebotomy room as the attendants discuss what they want to do after graduation while watching a soap opera on TV. "Hello, I was wondering if you could tell me how much blood Arturo Sanchez needs for his surgery."

"It's hard to say. They are doing an exploratory laparotomy right now, examining the abdominal cavity for organ damage."

"I heard his spleen was injured."

"Apparently the knife went through the boy's back, damaging two lumbar vertebrae, puncturing his small intestine, and lacerating the spleen. The boy is lucky to be alive."

"How much blood does he need?"

"He needs two liters of A positive." My blood is O positive. I can donate to anyone. I sprint the five blocks back to the church. The congregation sings another hymn. I tap the shoulder of an elder named César and tell him in three sentences what happened. His eyes widen. As I walk out of the church, the congregation continues to sing.

Upon returning to the hospital, I find Alejandro sitting in a green plastic chair.

"Alejandro," I say, "what type of blood do you have?"

"I don't know. I don't want to give blood."

"The boy needs blood," I tell him.

Alejandro cringes.

"Hey, it's just blood," I say. "You've faced worse."

"Chi, I don't like needles." Tears well up in his eyes.

"I'll go first. You'll see. You will be fine. The boy may die if we don't give him some blood. Did you hear me?" I ask. "The boy may die."

Alejandro's face clears. "Okay, I'll do it." We walk down to the basement blood lab. I lie supine on a stretcher. I turn and see the young phlebotomist holding a 250-milliliter plastic bag and a large eighteen-gauge needle. I see him neither take the needle out of a plastic bag nor clean it. He could have used that needle all day. All week. What are my chances of getting HIV? I don't want to die giving blood to someone who was stabbed by a kid I stupidly invited to stay at an orphanage because I wanted badly to change his life. Where did he get the knife? From the kitchen! I clench my fist. My arm veins bulge as if I'm holding the knife. Or am I the one being stabbed? A sharp pain runs up my arm and into my chest as the needle penetrates my vein. Dark maroon blood races through the labyrinthine tube and into the big bag, which grows fat and dark. Giving my blood doesn't make up for what I did. What if it were my son who got stabbed?

I walk out of the phlebotomy room to find twenty people from my church sitting in the waiting room. "Chi, we heard about the boy. *Pobresito.* We are ready to give blood."

The phlebotomist comes out of the lab. "We're ready for Alejandro." Alejandro clenches his teeth.

"You'll be fine," I tell him as he trundles in.

One of the lab technicians dashes up the stairs, carrying my blood in one hand and an IV line in another. My blood will soon course through the arteries of another human being.

Señora Lydia walks in. "Chi, Jessica told me what happened," she says. "How is the boy doing?"

"He's in surgery right now. You may want to talk to the family. They are right over there." She glances at the mother, who has just walked out of the phlebotomy room.

"Remember," she says, "Gabriel did not stay at Bururu. He only came to the orphanage to have lunch for the past few days. He is not our responsibility." I look at Señora Lydia with confusion. A prolonged pregnant pause, and my high regard for this courageous woman crumbles. None of us should be placed on a pedestal. The air is thin up there and your mind plays tricks on you.

"Maybe you should go and talk to them," I tell her.

"How is Tómas?" she asks.

"I don't know," I say. "He is upstairs. I am going to visit him later." I walk out of the hospital. It is 2 p.m. already. I walk down the cobblestone steps of the hospital. On the hospital veranda, women sell candy, soft drinks, toys, and trinkets. I walk up to one of the women and look over her wares. "How much is that play action figure? The one that looks like a professional wrestler."

"Twenty bolivianos."

Tómas, a ten-year-old boy, lies in bed staring out the window. He wears a hospital gown. His moppish hair looks as if it's been given a bowl cut.

"Hello, Tómas"

"Hello, Chi,"

"How are you feeling?"

"Fine."

"What happened?"

"I got hit by a car."

"Did you hit your head or lose consciousness?"

"No."

"Show me your leg."

"They took X-rays and everything. I don't think it is broken or anything."

I examine the leg to make sure he hasn't been neurovascularly compromised. He has full sensation and there is adequate blood perfusion. The X-rays hang from his bed railing. His pelvis and femur look normal, thankfully.

"I got this for you."

He cautiously opens the packaging, as if it might explode. His eyes don't light up, but he starts moving the hero's arms and legs around and making him fly and save people. Out of his mouth, he lets dribble a weak "gracias."

"I'd better let you rest," I say, pushing open the door. I glance back at Tómas. "Gracias, Chi," he says emphatically.

Later that evening, I hear that the surgeons removed Arturo's spleen and that he has awoken from the anesthesia. He will leave the hospital in one week. The next morning I visit him in his room. He is a fourteen- or fifteen-year-old boy.

"Hello, Arturo."

"Hi. Who are you?"

"I work at Bururu and gave you some of my blood yesterday. How are you doing?"

"Better. I still feel weak."

"I want to apologize for what happened. I know that does not make amends, so please tell me what else I can do for you."

"My father died when I was young. My mother sells candy in El Alto Obrajes. She's in debt to the person she works for. She works hard so that I can live a better life than she has. But we keep sliding backward."

"Did the director of Bururu visit you?" I ask Arturo. "She is a middle-aged woman with curly brown hair."

"No one visited me," says Arturo, "except you and my family."

"I will talk to Señora Lydia to see if Bururu will pay for your medical bill."

Arturo remains silent. He blinks slowly.

"What happened, Arturo? Can you tell me why this happened?"

Arturo folds his hands together. "I was in the park in the morning with my friends. This boy gave me this look that I didn't like. I demand respect. So I went up to talk to him. All his boys ganged up behind him, and all mine stood behind me. But before too many punches were thrown, I felt a sharp pain in my back. I fell to the ground in agony. I don't remember much after that."

"This didn't have to happen," I tell Arturo. "If someone gives you a look, you can walk away. Your mother has suffered a lot because of this."

Arturo's entire body stiffens, but he does not move. "You know I demand respect. That's all I want. Respect. I'd do it again if I had to."

"You mean you would die for respect."

Arturo blinks slowly.

9

Into the Night

12:30 a.m., November 7, 1997;
Alonzo de Mendoza

A child, having worked hard all day selling snacks and having made almost no money, gives in to hunger and eats some of his inventory. I finish treating a boy next to him with an infected cyst on his eyelid. Rodrigo whispers in my ear, "Guess who I found." I turn in the direction of Rodrigo's chin to see a boy with his fist to his nose, getting high. After wrapping up with my patient, I slowly walk over to the intoxicated boy.

"Hello, Gabriel." Three seconds pass.

"Hiiiiiyyyyaaa, Dooooocttor Cheee."

"What have you been taking?" Five seconds.

"Eevveerrythhinngg."

"Paint thinner?"

"Yep."

"Glue?"

"Yep."

"Alcohol?"

"Yep."

"Marijuana?"

"Yep."

"Cocaine?"

"Ooooohhhh nnooo."

"Why are you taking all these drugs?"

"Doctorrr Cheee, yoou shhhoould knooow theee answerrrr to thaaat."

"Actually, I don't. Why?"

"To escaaape thisss terrrriiiible exiiistence."

"Where have you been?"

Moving his arms in a sporadic manner, he replies, "Everrrywheeere."

"Where are you sleeping?"

"Heeerrrre aaand theeerrrree."

"Why so many places?"

"Oohh, Doooctooorrr Cheeee, yooou knoowwww whyyy."

"Why?"

He lifts his right arm up in the air and cocks his head to the left in the manner of a hanging.

"Beeecaaaause theeey aaaaare looooooking fooorrr meee."

"Why?"

"Beeecaaaause I ssstabbed a kiiid."

"You nearly killed him."

"Reeealllyyyy. Thaaaat's toooo baaaad."

I search hard for remorse in his eyes, in the way he holds up his head, in the twist of his torso. "You ruptured his spleen," I say, "and he bled into his abdomen."

"Hooooowwwww looooong diiiid heee staaaay iiiinnnn theee hooooossspppitaaal?"

"Five days." Gabriel shifts his weight, starts to limp away. "What's wrong with your leg?" I ask him.

"Anooooother boy staaabbbed meee iiiin the leeeeg."

"Do you want me to treat it?"

"Noooo, thaaat's okaaay."

"Okay then, be careful."

"Byyyye, Doctorrrr Cheeee. Yooou shooooould beee caaarefulll tooooo."

I walk away from Gabriel, and I stand before a large group of street children hanging out on several concrete benches. Some of them carry little babies by piggyback. All of them have their fists to their noses. I open my arms to get their attention. My heart jumps. Anger and sadness at Gabriel coalesce.

A teenage boy walks toward me. His body swings in semicircular motions as he attempts to maintain his balance. The fumes of his paint thinner penetrate my nostrils and cause me to get a mild high. He drops his ball of yarn into his pocket and attempts to gather enough neurons together to form a thought. "Chi," he slurs, "why are you here on the streets with us every night? Why would anybody in their twenties spend their weekend nights on the streets when they could go to parties or the movies?"

Silence. I don't respond to his question.

A boy shouts out, "It is because you are a Christian!"

"Yes, I am a Christian. My faith plays a major role in what I am and what I do." The children ponder this.

"So how do you tell who's a Christian on the street?" I ask them. "Does he have a big nose? Does he have long hair? Is he a good person? Is it a person who says that Jesus is God? Does that make him a Christian?"

There is no answer.

"What's a llama?" I ask the children.

"It's an animal that goes *uurruu*!" shouts out a boy. The children giggle.

"Where does it live?"

"In the mountains!" shouts a girl.

"Does it have fur?"

"Yes, it has fur," explains a boy. "That is why they can live up in the mountains!"

"Since you know so much about llamas, does that make you a llama lover?"

"No, they smell bad!" exclaims the boy. The children explode in laughter.

"It is the same thing with Jesus. Many people say that they know who Christ is. But they just know the facts. They do not really know Him. You can go to church every Sunday and still not know Him."

"So how do you know Him?" asks the boy.

"By praying to God, reading the Bible, and looking at myself honestly each and every day."

I think of Gabriel. "For many people it goes in one ear and out the other. In reality, it needs to go from your ear to your heart. I came to accept the presence of God in my life eight years ago. It changed me so much that it is my desire to live a godly life, even if it is at midnight on a Friday night. That spirit lives inside me and continues to change me. Because of this, I am just trying to do what Jesus asks: to serve my neighbors. That's you."

Glancing at my watch, I notice that it is 1 a.m. I look over to Rodrigo, who is explaining Christianity to one of the street girls. I unlock my backpack and dig for more songs. I ask the children if they would like to sing. Everyone responds with a fervent "yes." The children grab for song sheets. Rodrigo tunes his guitar, and we start with "Cuan Bello Es el Señor."

Cuan bello es el Señor, cuan hermoso es el Señor.
Cuan bello es el Señor, hoy le quiero adorar.

La belleza de mi Señor nunca se agotará.
La hermosura de mi Señor siempre resplandecerá.

Their off-key voices careen outward and upward like winged, uncoordinated chimes flying into each other. Police officers, soldiers, drunks, and prostitutes glance at the children momentarily and move on.

11:30 p.m., November 8, 1997, Bridge over Sewer System

Between the street and the sewer system fence, the twenty-four-hour vendors in their yellow metal stands busily grill hot dogs and hamburgers. A woman wearing a stained apron carries a bucket of dirty water from her burger stand and dumps it onto the street. The brown water hits the black street and ripples outward, then settles together to form a new puddle. A tiny foot skirts the puddle. The foot belongs to a small black boy wearing a dirty, grayish-white hat and dark, frayed blue jeans. He stands before the burger stand. He turns around and looks for something or someone. No one is watching him. He walks between two yellow stands. He crouches down and crawls through a hole in the sewer system fence that looks as if it were made for dogs.

"Mario," I call to the boy. He turns around, startled. He turns back and hollers through the hole in the fence, "Hey guys! Dr. Chi is here! Dr. Chi is here! Dr. Chi is here! Come here guys! Come here guys!"

The boy waves his arm, telling me to hurry. I place my medicine box on the ground and crawl through the hole in the fence. Five cement steps descend to a worn dirt path. Turning right on the path leads to a five-foot drop-off, at the bottom of which sits a rectangular cement box, open on one side. It is big enough to hold several street children but short enough to make adults uncomfortable. Small children tend to stay there.

The boy and I instead turn left and head down the steep path leading to the edge of a deep valley. Within this valley runs the gigantic
sewage canal, which carries the city's waste down into the La Paz
River. A misstep on the steep path means an ugly fall down a slope
lined with trash and excrement and into the valley of the sewage
canal. A bad way to die. But living twelve thousand feet up, and
among mountains, Paceños are used to climbing hills, and street kids
take this path several times a day.

We are now descending on all fours to keep from falling. It's hard
to keep my balance, as I am carrying a tackle box full of medicines.
Above me, I hear the sizzle of hamburgers; below, the roar of raw
sewage returning to nature. I look up at the fence. No one watching.
I feel silly even though I've done this many times now. Small rocks
tumble down into the valley, at the edge of which stand four boys
and one girl.

"Be careful. Hurry!" Be careful and hurry. A necessary contradic-
tion for the children's everyday survival. I get to the bottom of the
decline. The kids surround me and shout out their various ailments.

"I have a sore throat!" shouts Paola.

"Look here," says Enrique. "My cut. It has pus in it. Do you see?
Do you see?"

"My eyes. My eyes," whines Lupe. "They itch."

"I have diarrhea! Bad diarrhea," groans Jorge, holding his
intestines.

"Hello, Dr. Chi," says Gabriel. He is sober, in more ways than one.

"Hello, Gabriel," I say. And then I announce, "I can only help you
one at a time." The kids put their fists to their noses to inhale their
paint thinner–soaked yarn. A dog gingerly sniffs at my clean, soapy
odor and growls. Lupe bats the dog away. I examine eight-year-old
Mario's left hand. Eight razor blade scars in a crisscross design.
Last time there were seven.

"What happened, Mario?"

"It's a cut." He giggles.

"How did it happen?"

"I was drunk!" He stumbles about, and the kids laugh.

"What did you use?"

"A razor blade. It's because I am tough!" Again they laugh.

I clean his wound and move on to the next child. After taking care of all of them, I ask each of them how they are doing. Each child responds, "I'm fine." I ask them if they would like to sing praise songs. They say yes, but they don't mean it.

"Look, Dr. Chi." Gabriel points to the top of the hill. Two men peer down at us, their eyes narrowed. One man rests his hand on his club. He turns to his partner, who doesn't take his eyes off of us. Silly me; we were being watched all along. And now we are trapped. The two men stand before the hole in the fence, the only safe way out. These men will go to unusual lengths to "cleanse the streets" of the street children. I still have not figured out why. Why would anyone be so cruel? Why would anyone go out of his way to cleanse the streets? I am not oblivious to the other side of the lives of these children.

There remain two options. A small passageway approximately one foot in width runs along the sewage canal. The twelve-foot walls along the passage are smeared with the street children's own fecal matter to discourage intruders. Walking through there would be like passing through a large intestine. At the end of the walkway is a plank that we can climb to get to the top of the encased sewage canal. Once there, we can walk to an overpassing bridge and climb up. But if the violent men were even somewhat determined, they could easily meet the kids at this bridge. The other option is to walk down along the sewage system toward the river. The walk would be about one hundred yards, but at the end of it, we would have nowhere to go except to jump into the river along with thousands of liters of excrement.

The boys form a semicircle before me and Paola. They ready themselves to be beaten. I begin packing up. Mario's voice trembles.

"Don't leave! Please don't leave!" If I leave, the men will do whatever they wish, free from the eyes of any other adult.

"I won't leave," I assure them. I was never planning on it. The man who had his hand on his club—the senior, it seems—begins to descend the dirt path. The other follows, slipping slightly in his leather boots. The boys' bodies grow stiffer. Their brown eyes grow bigger as they glance back at me. What can I do? No one takes a step. No one says a thing. They'll be down here within a few minutes, even if they are careful and do not hurry. Gabriel looks around. His fifteen-year-old mind turns quickly. He knows how these men work. He knows that down here, where no one can see them, the men can do anything they want. Gabriel raises his hands to the sky. "Let's start singing!"

The five boys and one girl open their mouths and sing. In the beginning, the song is simply a collection of trembling voices afraid to offend the men, afraid to let the world hear them, afraid, perhaps, to be heard by their own ears. But the song grows stronger and stronger, until the tepid murmurs transform into shouts of courage and hope. They sing about a God they rarely see in their world. A God who is truly a far-off myth—a Being they know of only through nearly unbelievable stories. They sing of His beauty and His splendor, and how He protects the weak and the helpless. The voices bounce off the walls of the sewage canal—up, out, into unsuspecting ears. The vendors stop their cooking and peer down into the valley to witness—what? A miracle? I hope.

The two men finally step down to the edge of the sewage valley. They are on the same level as we are. I step forward and block their path to the children. Clocks throughout the city strike twelve. My heart starts to pound. Anger swells up within me. Such men are the enemies of my children. They rape the girls. Break the bones of children, leaving them crippled or limping. They kick boys in the crotch. I am ready to take the beating. The children's song has shaken the fear out of me. The men approach.

"Hello." I stick my hand out to shake. Nothing. I bring my hand back into my jacket and tightly grip my metal flashlight; if I can get in a hard shot or two, the children may have time to rush up the hill and escape.

"Hello," says the older man. "What are you doing here?"

Silence. We look at each other.

"What are *you* doing here?" I respond.

"It's none of your business what we do."

"I work with the street children from 10 p.m. to 2 a.m. Monday through Thursday. I also work at two orphanages."

The older man looks me in the eyes. "These children are criminals and drug addicts, you know." Had he heard a word of their song? Has he glanced for a millisecond at their faces? Our only chance to escape this beating is to make these men hear the inaudible, see the invisible. To transform, in their eyes, the children into children.

"Well," I tell the man, "some of them use thinner. Do you understand why? Do you know how these children become street children?"

The man looks surprised by my forwardness. "Their parents are alcoholics," he says, "and sometimes just abandon them." I cannot tell if he says this to express sympathy or condemnation.

"Yes," I say, "most of them are from El Alto. Poverty can cause mothers to abandon their own children, fathers to beat their sons and daughters. Poverty can lead to alcoholism. Some of these children have been molested by their own blood kin. They are running away from the worst things you can imagine. They end up on the streets, sniffing thinner, trying to forget their past, present, and future. Look at them."

Although this man no doubt makes less money than the poorest-paid illegal immigrant in the United States, he still may not understand the utter poverty these kids run from. He may never have been beaten or abused. He may not empathize at all with these children, whom he sees as animals. Nevertheless the man obliges my simple request. Look at them he does, and perhaps for the first time. He looks at them as if they were real—living, breathing. With some vendors watching us, with some passersby squinting down into our sewage darkness, and with the song of the children still echoing in all our ears, the man looks at the children and takes a lip-twisting breath. He swallows, the muscles of his jaws tensing up.

"Yes," he says. "It's sad." He glances back at his partner, who seems less than impressed. The two men start their ascent back up the slope. Behind me, the children sing another song. The men stoop through the hole in the fence and disappear. A feeling of relief floods through me. The children look around at each other, grateful that the men did not beat them on their own territory. The children place their fists to their noses and deeply inhale their thinner. Entering a state of oblivion, they look vacantly at me for a response.

"Listen to me, children. I don't trust these men to stay away. Even though one of them looked as if his heart turned tonight, they may return later. So you guys will need to leave immediately. Do you have a place to go where you'll be safe?"

Gabriel steps forward. "I have a secret hiding place." He does? He looks at me from beneath his raggedy red cap. Does he want me to stop him? If he shows the other kids his secret hiding place, it will no longer be secret. His enemies will be able to find him and stab him; malicious men may eventually learn of his hideout. "I know of this place," he says without reluctance, "down in the sewer system, toward the river. There's this little hole in the cement block where I sleep. No one can find me, and the sewage keeps me warm. There's room for all of us."

The kids stare at Gabriel. "Maybe all of you should go with Gabriel," I say.

The children all nod. Gabriel is their leader, and they will follow him to a hole in a sewage canal before they sleep in a strange orphanage.

"Very well, then. When I get to the top of the hill, I will check if the men are on the bridge, and then I will wave you clear. You can run to the hiding place undetected. Does that sound good?"

"Yes, Dr. Cheeeee," they sing.

The children sniff their paint thinner, loosening their grip on this terrible existence, as Gabriel calls it. Mario asks me, "When are you going to come back?"

"Tomorrow night. Don't worry. Be careful. But hurry. Good night." I climb up the hill, constantly losing and regaining my footing. I get to the top, and I look down at the kids, crowded together, a small choir, a chorus for their own tragedy. They look up at me for a sign. The only people on the bridge are street vendors. A taxi honks as it zips by. The children's eyes are fixed on me. I give them a wave. Five boys and one girl run across a field littered with trash and feces. They disappear into the night.

10

I'm Bleeding

November 9, 1997

Out of the night, from out of the far-off darkness, down the street, up the hill, springs forth a pubescent boy holding a clear plastic bag of thin, whitish water. Before my head can crane down to see under the boy's red cap, he is upon me. "Chi!" he says. "I've been looking for you!"

The boy in the red cap is Gabriel. I should have recognized him by his walk—the way he shifts his body as he gaits forth—long before he greeted me. He is my little brother, a brother who looks like a stranger tonight. His eyes are clear, bright, focusing on this and then that. And then back at me. "Chi, you must come quick," he says. "Anna is sick. She is bleeding. A lot." Besides the white water, Gabriel carries in the crook of his arm two rolls of bread.

"What's that for?" I point to his food.

"It is for Anna. She's really weak."

"What's in the bag?"

"Milk," he replies.

I cock my head to the side. "It doesn't look like any milk I've ever seen."

"A little bit of milk with lots of water and sugar."

"It's midnight. Where'd you get it?"

"I had to look for a long time, and then I bought it. I didn't steal it. I couldn't afford to waste any time."

My face flames red with shame. I had written Gabriel off as a juvenile delinquent. It almost shocks me now to discover that he is a human being with feelings of empathy. How am I going to help these kids if I cannot even internalize their essential humanity? I fought for his residence at Bururu, arguing that he could not be judged by his past, and then he stabbed a boy in the back. I felt like he owed me for "rescuing" him from the street, and when he made me look like a naive fool, I retaliated by defining him as a bad egg.

"Come on, Chi." Gabriel pulls my hand. "We must hurry."

We walk briskly to "Gabriel's house." I call it Gabriel's house because he is the only one who consistently sleeps here, and he takes care of the place. Gabriel lets any street children sleep in the shack as long as they leave room for him. The walls of the shack consist of wooden boards, corrugated metal, cardboard, and blue tarp leaning against each other. The roof is held up by six or seven wooden planks acting as pillars. The stone sewage canal provides the back wall. The house even claims a makeshift wooden door, tied to a post by ropes. As we approach the house, the two guard dogs bark at me. These two dogs belong to a pack of seven who rummage through trash and growl at passersby. They defend the children from strangers. They are loyal and stinky in the way only dogs can be. They sleep with the children, but tonight they wait outside. The sewage roars as it rushes by in the open canal.

I open the door to Gabriel's house and shine my flashlight into the darkness. Two bodies lie closely together, their backs toward me. His arm is around her stomach; his leg is over her leg. They breathe synchronously. Javier turns around, squints into the light. "Hello, Chi. We were hoping you would come tonight. Anna is bleeding. She is bleeding really bad. Can you help her?"

"Where is she bleeding?"

"You know. Down there."

"How long has she been bleeding?"

"Two days. I don't know what to do. Can you help her? Please."

"Why is she bleeding?"

"We got rid of the baby."

My heart sinks. Street abortion is a reality I have difficulty facing. "How did you abort the baby?"

"*Matte.*"

"Matte?"

Former street girls at Yassela have educated me on how to get rid of a baby. They cannot go to the "doctors" because they cannot afford them. So they go to the witches. Oh yes, there are witches every-where, with all types of medicinal herbs and teas and llama fetuses. The underworld will take care of your problems in life. "The witch mixes the matte for us from her many glass containers filled with leaves and powder," the girls explain. "We drink the horrible tea and within a day we start to bleed. It's a horrible bleed. A bleed that you cannot believe. But it does the job. It does the job good."

"Yes, matte," Javier tells me. "It's over there in that bucket."

"I mixed it with hot water," mumbles Anna. "And then I drank it. And then I started bleeding a lot. The baby started coming out."

I walk outside with Javier and see an old, rusted coffee can, the *M* of "Maxwell House" the only letter not completely rubbed away by time. I recall the Maxwell House slogan—"Good to the last drop"—and wince. I look inside the bucket. Different colored flowers with petals big, small, and weird. Green weeds, too. Boiling has muted the colorful flora.

My heart aches. Was her only company a street mutt? I picture Anna drinking the bitter concoction from this bucket. Gulp. Gulp. She shrieks in pain. Dogs bark, sewage roars. The remains of a human fetus separate from her body. I can only imagine her pain, its depth and breadth, the way it reaches into every corner of her soul, how it curls in on itself and feeds itself infinitely. I don't need to tell her what is right and wrong. She knows by the pain. I cannot help but understand why Anna and other street girls abort their babies. Right now, the only thing I can do is support her.

"Where did you place the baby?"

"Right here." Javier points to the ground right beneath my feet. I take a step back.

"You buried the baby right in front of your house."

"Yes," he replies. "Where else would I bury it?"

So the fetus has been buried in the sewer, joining so many others. One third of the street children's children are aborted, another third die in infancy, and the rest are street babies. These infants do not know beds or bathtubs. My tears fall gently on the ground of this sewage cemetery. How many more things can these children endure before they give up? I wipe the tears from my eyes and walk back into the house. Javier hunches protectively over Anna, whispering to her.

Anna turns and looks at me, and then my tackle box. "Oh, no," she says. "It's better now. I'm fine, Chi."

"She's still bleeding, Chi," says Javier. "She is just afraid of needles. Give her a shot or something to stop the bleeding." I am impressed by this boy's sense of compassion for his lover. He even seems to feel responsible for her well-being.

I dig deep into my fishing box and find the brown vial labeled "ergonovine." My last vial. With this vial I am supposed to treat a street girl named Vera later on tonight. But Vera may not show up, and Anna is here, in pain. Ergonovine will contract the uterine arteries, the arteries that have been ripped open after the abortion.

Two-tenths of a milligram of the drug will stop the bleeding for the night, buying me enough time to purchase more the next morning. Holding the vial inside my fleece jacket, I crack it open and withdraw 0.2 milligrams into my syringe. Anna looks at the 22-gauge needle, cringes, and hides her face in her blanket.

"Okay, Anna, we are ready for you." Javier giggles in delight.

"Where are you going to put that?" she asks.

"Where else?"

"I'm not getting a shot in the butt!"

Javier looks at her and laughs hysterically, rolling on the cardboard. "You're not helping," I tell Javier, so he composes himself and then cajoles Anna to let me give her the shot.

"Oww!" she yelps. She rubs her buttocks in a circular motion and has a distinct look of disapproval.

"I will be back tomorrow to check and see if you are all right."

"No," she pleads. "I will stop bleeding by tomorrow."

"I'll see you tomorrow." I stand up, stooping to avoid hitting my head on the roof, a problem I had never foreseen myself ever having. Javier and Anna resume their usual sleeping position, one arm over her stomach and one leg over her legs. I walk out into the night. Gabriel walks over and asks me seriously, "How is Anna?"

"She is fine," I say. "If she continues to bleed, you need to take her to the hospital."

He nods. Both of us know that even if Anna had the audacity to go to the hospital, this Aymaran street girl might not even be treated.

"Don't worry, Chi. I will take care of her." Gabriel holds up his plastic bag of milk-water as if it were a talisman against all one's ills. The longer children live on the street, the more they realize the meaninglessness of words. They don't say things such as "Thank you" or "You are my friend." They'd rather show through actions what is inside. It is more difficult for these street kids to speak than to act. The plastic bag filled with milk-water represents a covenant between Gabriel, Anna, Javier, and their family of street children. The one part milk and six parts water means, "Anna, you are my blood."

The Next Day

I return the next morning to Gabriel's house and find Anna dozing in and out. Gabriel wakes up and rubs his eyes. In her semicomatose state, Anna opens her eyes and recognizes me. There is something not right with Anna, but I cannot put my finger on it. "What happened, Anna? Why did you get rid of your baby?"

She looks away and toward the ground. She has always been rather quiet, oftentimes sad. She says nothing. I wait for a long time.

"It was Javier," she says.

"What do you mean, it was Javier?"

"Javier was able to get a hundred bolivianos. I don't know how he got that much money, but he did. He told me to keep it safe. Somehow I lost it. I looked everywhere for it but couldn't find it. I was so scared that I shook all over. So I just waited and waited for my punishment to happen. When I told him that I lost the money, he went into a rage. Uncontrollable. He yelled and kicked. He kicked me in the stomach over and over again. I wanted him to kick me in the back or in my legs. Anywhere but my stomach. I just lay there until it was all over. Until his temper subsided. My baby was dead by then. Dead forever. Never to cry. Never to smile. I was in a state of shock. I don't even remember if I cried or not. All I knew was that it was all over. Done." Anna's triangular face is blank. No anger. No sadness. Nothing.

"Then what happened after that?"

"Then I started to bleed slowly. Part of my baby came out bit by bit, but not all of it. I needed to find a way to take care of it. So I went to the witches and they gave me matte. I drank it and it hurt tremendously. I started to bleed a great deal after that. Afterward we buried the baby in front of the house. I continued to bleed. Then Gabriel went to look for you."

Javier killed his own unborn child. The sun comes up only half-way on the street. There are no hard divisions between light and shadow. All is washed over by a gray moral ambiguity. The kids live in a violent and desolate world where right and wrong are often interchangeable, and their souls end up matching their environment. They become gray. Like Anna's face as she cries. The forces of good and evil have fought their war of attrition within her, and she is left with nothingness. She turns over on her cardboard bed. I cannot see her face anymore. "Why do you still stay with Javier?" I ask her.

"Because I love him, and he protects me from men and other street boys. He is good . . . and bad."

11

Lice

November 10, 1997;
The Hole, beneath a Busy Overpass

I look down into El Hueco. The Hole. A dozen street children sleep
in a twelve-foot-deep concrete "hole" located beneath a downtown
bridge. This architectural appendix of sorts is walled in on two sides
by the stairwell down which I am walking. I sit down on the steps
next to El Hueco, and I wonder why street children rarely snore.

To the south, rising above the petty edifices of man, Mount
Illimani's four snowcapped peaks glisten in the moonlight, singing
their crescendo at twenty-one thousand feet and tickling God's feet.
I breathe in slowly. Cold air burrows beneath the mists of Illimani
and seeps into the alveoli of my lungs, invigorating me.

I hear footsteps. A boy swaggers down the steps from the bridge.
His hair flows down to his nape once again. Where has Gabriel
been? He sits down beside me.

"What's up?" I ask him.

"Nothing."

"I have been looking for you," I tell him.

"You can't find me. I am invisible." He gives me a coy smirk.

"Why are you invisible?"

"You know why." Gabriel tilts his head to the right, sticks out his tongue, and pulls up an imaginary noose. "They are after me."

"You almost killed the boy."

"I know. It's too bad he got hurt," he states nonchalantly.

"Why did you stab the kid?"

"Because I had to protect my own people."

"But why did you have to stab him?"

"Either you get killed or you kill others. That's survival on the streets. That's how it is on the streets. I want to survive. Either you get killed or you kill. And I kill in order to survive. I want to live. That is the law of the streets, Chi. You know that."

"You should be in jail."

"I know," says Gabriel. "But they will never find me."

"Maybe I should turn you in."

"You won't though. You understand us."

Silence. I make no reply. "I like your shoes," I say, reading the faint words in black marker across their sides: "Gabriel Garcia."

"Yeah, these are good shoes." He smiles.

We look to Mount Illimani. We breathe frigid breaths.

"Chi," says Gabriel, "my hair itches." He looks at me with quiet eyes.

"Hmmm," I say, "take your cap off."

Lice and their eggs entangle the twines of his head. I open up my medicine box and shuffle through the various bottles. Found it. Permethrin.

"Lean your head over the railing."

I squirt the medicine onto his head. A quarter liter flows down his long tangles and into the La Paz River. I rub the medicine into his scalp. With his eyes shut tight Gabriel asks me, "Do you think this will work? Will this kill the bugs?"

"No," I say, "but it is worth a try. Otherwise, I will need to cut your hair off and make you a monk."

Gabriel does not want to be a monk. He lets his head hang over the railing for a few minutes, the dead lice tumbling down into the river.

"Here." I hand Gabriel the bottle of permethrin. "Keep it. Wash out all the medicine in ten minutes."

"Thanks, Chi." Silence. Illimani calls to us. Her icy breath roars in our ears. Gabriel looks up at the top of the bridge. We will need to leave El Hueco soon.

"Hey, I want my friends in the United States to know about you. I would like them to know your story."

"Why would anyone want to know about me?" He is sincere. I look him square in the face. "You have an important story to tell."

"Really?" he asks, understanding the mysteries of my world as much as I understand the mysteries of his. Why would well-off people want to know about him? He trusts me; if I ask him for something, it must be for a good reason.

I take the tape recorder out of my jacket.

"Why are you recording us?"

"Because I am old, and my memory is terrible." I tap my temple.

"You are not going to make me look bad, will you?"

"No, because I understand you. I will tell the truth though."

"Promise?"

"Promise." We hook our pinkie fingers together.

Gabriel looks at the tape recorder and then at me.

My name is Gabriel Garcia, and I have been on the streets for the past eight years. My house is in El Alto. I was sad during most of my childhood. I left my home due to the abuse from my family. My mother and father would beat me with sticks. On some days, I came home from school with my clothes dirty. My mother would be angry and beat me. Then she would make me wash clothes, oftentimes until one in the morning.

I like the streets more or less. I have many friends on the streets. We help one another, especially when we need to defend each other. To eat. To drink. I helped Anna when she was bleeding. Anna is a little bit crazy in the head. When she uses drugs, she says crazy things. Overall, the street children are a bad lot. They drink and use drugs.

I stabbed the boy because he was bothering and taunting my friend from the orphanage. He started the fight. At that time, I was cutting an eraser in half with my knife. The boy was bothering everyone. He was saying things that were incredibly ugly. Then he started to call his friends to join him. That is when I stabbed him.

I admit it was a bad thing to do. It was a bad thing because I could have gone to jail. I am sad for that action, because I was living at the orphanage at that time and I had many things going well for me. Yet a street boy often does not know what he does. He does not realize the possible consequences until after the action. On the other hand, I steal and rob from women in the streets so that I will not die from hunger. I need to survive.

The older men on the streets are stern, evil, and corrupt. Just the other day, I had my radio. They beat me and tried to steal my radio from me. But I would not give it to them. Oftentimes, they take money from me, five or twenty bolivianos. They often beat me. I am not afraid of them, especially when I am high or drunk.

I always change the location of where I sleep. They are always looking for you. Looking to steal from you. Looking to beat you. Sometimes when we don't give them money they spray gas into our eyes.

I think the streets have changed over the past eight years. Everything is changing. There are more children on the streets now. There used to be only forty or fifty children. Now there are many more.

However, I do not want to sleep in the streets for the rest of my life. I want to learn and work because I am tired of begging and shining shoes. I want to become something else in my life. I want to leave the streets, but it is very difficult. It is difficult because I am used to the life of the streets.

Some of the orphanages for street children are terrible. They are terrible because they abuse us. They make us work day and night. A home for street children should give us support and help us. If I were a counselor for street children I would tell them to change their lives. You can only accomplish this by talking to them. Tell them to return to their families.

The most important people in my life are those who have helped me and continue to help the children on the streets now. You have helped the street children with your medicines and by bringing materials to us. You cure our wounds and stabbings. You encourage us to change and move forward. But it really depends on us. We are changing in very small ways.

My dream is to get off of the streets. To change. How do I change my life? I change my life through work and stopping my thievery. However, I will stop stealing when I do not need any more money. I know it is wrong to steal, but I have no choice.

I want to be a mechanic. In five years, I will have a job and some money to feed myself.

Nine years have passed. I have lost Gabriel, my friend, my child. That interview was the last time I ever saw him. Rumor has it he traveled south to Cochabamba for the warmer climate and better economy. Some children tell me he died in a fight. No one knows, except Gabriel and God. Sometimes not knowing is best. In the end, I am disappointed in Gabriel the Criminal, and I am proud of Gabriel the Survivor. I can say this now because I do know him. I understand him.

12

Fatso

95°F, Summer 1980, Texas

Humid air slaps my face as it blasts in through the car windows. We're driving to Houston, and my head hurts because my father is driving. He slows down when he is talking and speeds up when he remembers he's driving. I lay my head down on the seat and perch my legs on top of the Styrofoam ice chest filled with Mountain Dew and *ba zang*, our lunch. Ba zang is rice with pork and peanuts wrapped in banana leaves. I love filling my stomach with ba zang.

Mingfang sleeps next to me, clinging to her gigantic teddy bear. I hate my little sister. She's fat. She's stupid. She's ugly. I don't know why my parents still call her Cutie. When we lived in South Carolina, Mingfang went to the hospital because she was sick, and when she came back she was bald and skinny. But Mom made up for it by feeding her like there was no tomorrow. Mingfang stayed inside and away from germs and did nothing but eat.

Now we live in College Station, Texas, where my dad studies computer science all the time. He's so busy it's hard for him to stay around the house. He comes home and doesn't say much. My mom tells me he is under a great deal of stress. I stay out of his way and keep quiet.

I open the ice chest quietly and dig up a few pieces of ice. *Plunk. Plunk. Plunk.* And one! The ice hits her right nostril! She flinches and changes positions. Okay, it is time for Dr. J to hit the right ear and win the NBA Finals. *Clunk!* Oops. The ice misses the rim and hits the right eyeball.

"Yannnnn!" my sissy sister cries. "Mom! Chin-chin is throwing ice at me!" Oops. Technical foul.

"I am not throwing ice at you, Fatso," I tell her. "Maybe if you weren't such an oink-oink you wouldn't sweat so much. Isn't that right, oink-oink?"

"Mommy! Chin-chin is calling me a pig again!"

My mother turns around and glares at me. "Stop it!"

Every year we have to take this stupid vacation down to Houston in the yellow Ford Maverick. "This stinks, Mommy. I hate the banana car. We need air conditioning." My mother doesn't reply. "And why does Mingfang always get presents when we go to Houston? She goes into the room, she comes out, and you buy a gift from the gift shop for her. You favor her. I hate you!"

A tall man in a long white coat finally comes into the office. A silly yellow mask hangs from his ears by white rubber bands. "Hello, I'm Dr. Jacoby," he says to me in a deep, baritone voice. He peers down at me.

I look over to my mother. She has a tear in her right eye. I think she might have dealt with him before. I tug on her shirt. Mom! Why don't we get out of here? I will just punch Dr. Jacoby in the stomach, and we'll run.

"Mingfang, how are you today?"

She starts to cry and whimper. How do you think she's doing, mister? She clings to her teddy bear. "No, Mommy! No, Mommy!" The bear is lying on the ground now, and she uses both of her hands to cling to Mommy.

"Let's bring her to the examining table and start the conscious sedation," Dr. Jacoby tells the blonde nurse. The nurse injects some liquid into a tube that's connected to Mingfang's arm. Whoa! What's going on? Mingfang's eyes just rolled up into her head. Her arms are like Jell-O. Gee whiz!

They lay my limp sister down on the cushioned table. Her right buttock is showing. I have never seen it before. Boy, is it white and fat. I hate her. She's spoiled.

Everyone is quiet now. Dr. Jacoby brings forth a shiny silver box. Inside the box are long metal rods with sharp points. He places brown liquid on my sister's buttocks. A uniformed woman holds my sister down. My mother looks on, resigned.

"Are you ready, Mrs. Huang?"

"Yes," she replies. Ready for what?

"Are you sure you want your son to see this?"

"See what, Mommy?" I pipe up.

She nods. "He needs to see."

The doctor takes a metal rod, about the thickness of a pencil and really long, and slowly punches it deep into my sister's butt cheek.

"Yeaaowww," my sister whimpers.

"Can we have a little bit more fentanyl?" he tells the nurse. The rod goes deeper, and I just wish it would stop, but it doesn't stop until the whole thing goes inside. Hasn't it hit a bone? Hasn't it ended up on the other side of her body? Gee whiz. I want to scream. I want to jump up and pound the freak for hurting my sister. I don't know why I am not doing anything. Maybe this is supposed to happen. Before I can do anything, the freak takes out the rod.

"Mrs. Huang, I will know the bone marrow biopsy results within the next week. At that time I can tell you if your daughter's leuke-mia is in remission," he states without emotion.

Leukemia? What's leukemia? Whatever it is, I don't want it, especially if I have to see the freak again.

I squeeze my sister's arm. "Don't be afraid, Mingfang. Things will be all right."

My sister is in her room drawing animal pictures at her desk. I walk up to her, and I smirk in her face. "Hey, Fatso. Do you know what day it is?"

"What day is it?" she asks, falling again for a trick question.

"It is report card day."

"So?"

"So? What did you get, Mingfang?"

"None of your beeswax." She covers up her animal pictures.

"C'mon, my little piglet sister. Let me see your grades."

"No."

"C'mon. I'll let you see my report card."

"You're so stuck up, Chin-chin. I already know what your grades are."

"You don't know that."

She considers for a moment. She's not that stupid. "No," she says. "Mind your own business."

"C'mon. We can play carnival or obstacle course tonight with prizes and everything." Carnival is a game we play where Fatso has to throw balls into small boxes and form three in a row in a tic-tac-toe grid.

"What type of prizes?" she asks.

"Hmmm. Stickers. Erasers. Pencils. Pens."

"Those are prizes? Those are things left in your desk."

"C'mon. I'll bring something back from Games Galore for you."

"Okay. You promise that you won't make fun of my grades?"

"Sure," I say. My sister hands me her grades. B. B. B. C. D. B. "Dang, Fatso. You're not only fat like a hog—nrook, nrook—you're also stupid!"

She snatches her grades from my hands. "I hate you!" She stands up and stomps out.

"Same to you and more of it," I spit out.

"I hate you!" Fatso shouts through tears. "I am never going to let you see my grades again!" Mingfang runs into her room and slams the door. A second later, she opens her door and shouts out, "I didn't need that!" She always says that. As if I was worried about what she needed.

I stand before the door to my sister's room. "C'mon, Mingfang. It's time to go through the obstacle course."

"No! I hate the obstacle course," I hear through the door.

"I've got prizes from Games Galore." The local arcade hands out free game tokens for good grades, and I spent mine on Skee-Ball and the skill crane to win prizes for Mingfang.

The door opens a crack, then swings open ever so slightly. "What kind of prizes?" asks Mingfang.

"They're in my backpack. You have to earn them."

She opens the door all the way, and she beams forth an angelic smile. I almost want to give her the prizes without making her earn them. We walk into the living room, and I explain the situation. "Okay. You need to finish the course within sixty seconds. If you finish in world-record time, you get to blindly pick out of the treasure bag."

"You have to promise that you won't hit too hard," she says. "The last time we played obstacle course I bruised my elbow."

"I can't help it if you couldn't handle the linebackers." She gives me a sad look. "Okay," I say. "It'll be a level-one obstacle course. Promise."

"Okay," she half smiles and then gets a hard, determined look on her face.

"Ready," I say. She leans forward. "On your mark. Get set. Go!" Mingfang hops over the pillow hurdles. "Go! Run!" I shout. "Now zigzag between the cones. Underneath the piano bench. Careful! If you touch it you'll burn to death! Okay, now jump over the moat filled with alligators. Okay, now comes the hardest part." I pick up a big pillow. "The linebackers of doom." Mingfang tries to run past me as I pop her with the pillow. She falls, gets back up. "Time's running out! C'mon, you can do it! *Boom! Boom! Boom!* Beat those football players up!" She crunches into the pillow with her shoulder and dashes over the finish line.

"And in first place! Mingfang Huang in fifty-five seconds! A new world record!" My sister doubles over, panting. She smiles with glee.

"Okay. You can pick out of the grab bag of treasures." She reaches into the backpack. She feels pencils, papers, little pinball games, key chains, but I know what she'll take out.

"Look what I got! Look what I got!" she shouts.

"A puppy stuffed animal. Good job."

"Thanks, Chi." She beams. "You're the best."

October 1985, College Station, Texas

It's 7:05 a.m. My sister's leukemia is in remission. I'm not sure what that means, but we don't have to go to Houston anymore, and everyone is real happy about it.

I have a math exam today. "Dad!" I holler from the foyer into the hallway. "Hurry up! We're going to be late again." Gee whiz. "Dad!" I holler. Out hops my sister. I can't stand Fatso. She needs to exercise more and eat less. It's all supply and demand, simple as that. "Hey, Mingfang! Hurry up!"

"Leave me alone," she says perfunctorily as she walks past me into the living room.

"I don't have to leave you alone if I don't want to, so just shut up!"

"Leave me alone," she says again, as if I were a machine needing clear, repeated vocal commands.

"Hey," I whisper to her, "you need to know something."

"What?" she snaps at me.

"Abnormal fat distribution throughout your body will cause you to fall and lose your balance."

She steps toward me. "What are you talking about?" Before she can finish her question, I stick out my leg. She trips and smacks her face on the tile floor.

"Waaaannnnnn!"

Shoot. Blood flows from her mouth. Did she lose a tooth? Shoot! "Chi! What did you do?" My dad mysteriously appears.

I hate my sister. She always gets me in trouble. She should have known I was going to trip her. She should have kept her face from hitting the floor. Why can't she be more resilient? I wish I had a brother so we could wrestle and play.

"Chi! Get in here."

It is 7 p.m. now. I thought my dad would forget what happened. I broke the golden rule in our family: no violence against anyone. As I walk into the living room, I remind myself that he's never spanked me. My father is standing up. That's a bad sign.

"Chi!" he shouts down at me. "You lied to me this morning!"

"I did?" Did I?

"Yes, you did," he says in Taiwanese. "You tripped your little sister. You know that you are not allowed to hit or hurt anyone."

"Yes, Father."

"You could have caused her to lose her teeth."

"Yes, Father."

"You could have scarred her face."

His face is beet red. My father is so angry. And he keeps glaring at me. "Go outside and get a stick!"

I look at him as if he was kidding.

"Get outside and get a stick!"

My mother runs over to me in a panic. "Just go outside," she whispers, "and don't come back for a little time. Let him cool down."

"Okay."

I leave the house. It is dark and cold outside, and I notice various sticks lying on the brown grass. None of them look very good for hitting, except for a thick plank with nails sticking out of its end, which sits quietly against the foundation of the house. My father has never hit me or my sisters—not even spankings.

I don't know what to do. Just wait around here? I feel so alone suddenly. I walk to Thomas Park, where I stand around on the basketball court without a basketball. For a couple of hours, I look up at the sky, and then I study the basketball hoops. How do people do this? Live alone without a family or home?

I know I can always go home. I might get hit a few times, but it'll surely be the last time I get hit. I'm never going to hurt my sister again. This really stinks. I'd rather take a stick back and let my father hit me than have to be out here another hour. I look around for appropriate sticks. What would it be like to get hit with a stick? Maybe I won't go home just yet.

Another half hour, and I walk back home. I open the front door, and my mother and father look at me silently. I turn down my eyes and walk to my room. I can tell by the look in my father's eyes that his fury has cooled and he will not hit me tonight. I lie down on my bed without changing clothes. My father has taught me nonviolence. Violence is wrong. I fall asleep knowing this, and I sleep well knowing it.

November 1987, College Station

I'm a junior in high school, and I am finished studying for tomorrow's advanced biology exam. I walk into my parents' bedroom and see my sister lying on her stomach, studying on the bed.

"What are you studying?" I ask her. "Maybe I can help you."

"Yeah, right," she says, rolling onto her back. "Every time you help me, you make fun of me."

"Okay. I promise that I won't make fun of you this time."

"Promise?"

"I promise."

"I have a spelling test tomorrow," explains my sister.

"Okay, I want you to do three things for me. I want you to spell each word by mouth, write it down on paper, and then use the word in a sentence."

"But it's just a spelling test."

"I know it is just a spelling test, but you will remember the word better this way in the long run. Besides, I want you to get a hundred on tomorrow's exam."

"Okay."

"The first word is *logic*."

"Logic. L–O–G–I–K."

"Try again. Think."

"Logic. L–O–G–I–C."

"Very good. Now write it on the piece of paper."

I watch her carefully inscribe the word on her paper. "Great," I say. "Use it in a sentence."

"Ummm. I don't know what it means."

"Look it up."

"Gee whiz. You make more work for me. It's just a spelling test."

"Look it up," I insist. Two hours later, around midnight, we've

gone through each of the twenty words. At times, I don't understand my sister's poor memory. A part of me is embarrassed by
her. The fact that she is not athletic or smart or artistic does not
sit well with me. A failure in all three areas. And yet she studies
harder than I did at her age. My mother tells me that it is her cancer that made her this way, but how can a disease make you stupid?

"Okay," I announce, "it is time for the speed rounds!" I shoot out
the words as fast as she can handle them, and she spells every one
of them correctly.

"Great. You can go to bed now. Review the words tomorrow
morning and you will get a hundred."

The next afternoon, Mingfang comes home and I ask her what
she got on her spelling test. "Seventy-five," she tells me. "I got ner-
vous and couldn't spell the words because my mind went blank."

Several days later, after everyone else has fallen asleep, my father
calls me out to the living room to sit and talk. We never sit and talk.
Usually he commands and I do. My father leans forward and clasps
his hands. "We need to talk about Mingfang."

"It wasn't my fault. I was only playing."

"What wasn't your fault?" he asks. "We must talk about
Mingfang's future."

"What about it? She's going to be a big, fat pig for the rest of her
life. Ba ha ha ha!"

"No. Chi. This is serious."

"Sorry, Dad."

"You will need to take care of her when you get older."

"Me?! Why me? I am only a teenager. Why not Chiufang? She's
the oldest, and she's in college already."

"Why? Because you are the eldest son."

"And? She is the eldest daughter. What has that got to do with anything?"

"As the eldest son, you will need to support your younger sister."

"Why can't Mingfang support herself? She's got two legs. Maybe she can go to the Houston Zoo and be a part of the petting zoo as a piglet. Ba ha ha ha!"

"Chi. You need to treat your sister with respect. I will not tolerate this."

"Sorry, Dad." A dead-serious look washes over his face. "Okay," I say. "What do you want me to do?"

"Well, I would like Mingfang to go to college after high school. I sincerely doubt that she will get into a university with her grades, but Regents College is a viable option."

"Sure. How much does that cost?"

"Your mother and I will pay for the tuition. But when we retire, we would like you to support Mingfang."

"Gee, that's pretty big stuff. I guess I better earn some big bucks."

"You need to find an occupation that can support you, your future family, your sister, and us too."

"Who am I? The Social Security system? What does Chiufang do? Hang out at Club Med sipping piña coladas? This isn't fair."

"That's life, Chi."

"Man. I better enjoy my childhood freedom, because it looks like I'll be thrown into adult slavery."

"Don't be silly. It's called growing up."

"No, it's called growing poor!"

"One possibility is that you give your sister enough capital investment so that she can run a gift shop. She loves the Hello Kitty paraphernalia and would really excel at sales."

A gift shop. She would like that. She'd be happy doing that. Not a bad idea. "Okay. Okay. Can I leave now? You put me in a bad mood."

"Respect, Chi."

"Yes, Father."

Mingfang does not speak in public. I do not know why. Is it because she has nothing to say? Does she think people will think she's stupid? Or perhaps that nobody will listen? I've never asked her why, but one day I will. We're siblings; we don't really talk like friends.

Right now she's doing ballet, and I'm sitting at the kitchen table eating a bowl of cereal. Every Saturday morning my two sisters do ballet along with three other girls. First they do the stretches, which seem to go on forever. And then they do the real thing, little dances and routines. My mother teaches. She used to dance ballet in a studio in South Carolina.

As I crunch on my Frosted Flakes, I watch Mingfang make her chubby body into shapes that I figured were impossible. It's like she's a completely different person. Mingfang loves ballet. She hangs her ballet shoes up on the wall of her bedroom. She happily wakes up early every Saturday morning, takes those shoes off the wall, and launches her body into rigid movements that seem to set her free. She flies in those shoes.

I am in high school now, and she is in junior high. After ballet, we're all going to practice Chinese, reading and reciting from elementary school textbooks. I'm looking forward to that like a cat does a bath. I finish my bowl of cereal and prepare to walk through all their uppity ballet dancing to get to my room. Boy, am I glad my mother doesn't make me dance. Look at Mingfang. She's making her leg stick out, straight out. It's unnatural. It's beautiful. Yeah, I hate to admit it, but it is. I bet it hurts like a dog. There she is, quietly prancing across the floor, her whole body, round as it is, somehow transformed into a set of straight, fluid lines. Standing on her toes and keeping her head straight, she's got to be screaming inside. And yet she doesn't let out a peep.

13

Christmas Eve

December 24, 1987;
College Station, Texas

It's the morning of Christmas Eve. I am sixteen, and Cutie is thirteen. I am a senior in high school, and she is a freshman. I stand behind Mingfang as she sits at the coffee table making Christmas cards out of construction paper, Hello Kitty stickers, and colored ink stamps. She seems a bit old to be playing with this kind of stuff; Chiufang, who's now a psychiatric intern in Dallas, says that Cutie is "socially regressed." But I suppose what matters is that she's a sweet girl and a good sister. I wish I were a better brother. "I'm sending these to my friends," she tells me with a sniffle. She's recovering from a cold.

I sit down behind her on the couch and read. Spring semester starts after the Christmas break, so I'm getting a head start on all the other nerds by reading *Hamlet*.

I get through the first act of *Hamlet*, and then I go out to play tennis with fellow tennis team member Chris Dinkel. The day is bright, dry, spectacular, in the high 60s. The tennis ball whistles through the air.

I come home after tennis. Mingfang is still making Christmas cards.

"Hey, Mingfang."

"What do you want? Leave me alone."

"Who made you so grumpy?"

"I know you are up to something mean." She squints her eyes at me.

"It's almost Christmas. Would I do something mean to you on Christmas Eve?"

"Okay, okay. What do you want?"

"Nothing. Do you want to go to College Hills to play on the swing set and slides?"

Her eyes light up, and her pale, round face produces a smile. "Sure," she says.

Mingfang attended College Hills Elementary School, which is just a couple of blocks southwest of our house. Its playground has a swing set with slides and bridges and monkey bars and a swinging tire, and it also has a basketball hoop that's only eight feet high. We drive there in the banana car. I hop out of the car and dribble my red, white, and blue Dr. J basketball to the hoop and dunk. My sister follows me. "Okay"—I turn around and face her—"you can play on the swings after you run five laps around the playground."

"What?"

"Five laps."

"Why?"

"Just because."

My sister is fat. She needs to lose weight and grow strong physically and mentally. The world has little patience for the weak. I guess my being mean to her doesn't help her confidence much either. Maybe I'm jealous; my parents ignore me, but I'm still expected to take care of Cutie when I get older.

"Because why?" she asks me.

"Because it's good for you. If you don't run laps, I won't let you play on the jungle gym."

Mingfang pouts. She looks at the same track I used to run around as a kid. Five laps is a long way. But it can be done. "Okay," she says. "I knew there was a trick."

Mingfang walks toward the track as I slam-dunk the basketball a few times, and then I stand there and watch her run. She takes a slow pace. She is in no hurry. She knows she will get there. It's just a matter of time. And whether it takes her twenty minutes or an hour, it doesn't seem to matter. I love her simplicity. I can say that sincerely. I admire her. With her simplicity, she makes life good. If she can make her banners and cards, if she can play with her Hello Kitty, if she has her ballet on Saturday, she is happy. I wish I could be more like Mingfang—content with the simple things in life.

Twenty minutes later, Mingfang walks up to me, huffing and puffing, her hands on her knees. "Okay," I tell her, "you can go play on the swing set for twenty minutes. Afterward, I'll let you drive the car around the parking lot."

Mingfang stands up straight, and she tilts her head to one side as she searches my face for signs of trickery or mental illness.

"What are you talking about?" she says.

"Do you want to learn how to drive the car?"

She realizes that there are no conditions attached, or rather that she has already met the conditions. A small smirk precipitates beneath her nose, and electricity courses through her body. "Sure. Are you sure Mom won't get mad?"

"Mom won't need to know."

A smile stretches from cheek to cheek. "Okay," she says. Mingfang skips to the swings, and she swings, kicking her feet up high in the sky. Christmas brings out the best in people, even mean older brothers.

Some twenty minutes later, she stands at the door of the banana car. She looks at me through the driver's side window. I am sitting in the middle of the front seat. She is still not sure if this is for real, and if it is, if it's okay. But if it isn't okay, I can see that makes her even happier. No one but her big brother would let her do this. And even he is acting strange. She opens the door slowly, as if it were the lid to a magical treasure chest.

"Okay, go ahead and sit in the seat."

She giggles as she settles down on two pillows I have set up on the seat. She is only four and a half feet tall, and without the cushions, she wouldn't be able to see above the dash. She grabs the steering wheel with both hands and peers through the windshield as if she were already driving. "Start the car by turning the key," I tell her. She turns the key slightly. "No," I tell her, "you need to turn the key harder." She puts her shoulder into it as I pump the accelerator.

Vroom! "There you go," I say. "Okay. Now I have my feet on the accelerator and brake. I'm going to reverse the car first, and then after that, we'll drive." I maneuver the car into the center of the kindergarten parking lot. Good thing there are no kids here. I put the car in drive, and Mingfang lets the car coast in a straight line until we reach the edge of the lot. And then she tries to make a left by turning the steering wheel ninety degrees. I step on the brake before we hit the curb.

"It's hard to turn the steering wheel," she says. The banana car has no power steering. I rotate the steering wheel all the way to the left. "I didn't know you had to turn the steering wheel so much to make it turn," she adds.

We turn to the left and keep turning to the left, and we make slow doughnuts in the middle of the parking lot. Cutie giggles with glee, "Heeheehee!" The sun shines brilliantly, and the sky sings a true blue. On the faint smudge of the moon, I can almost make out the innocent face of Hello Kitty.

"Watch out!" We're about to smash into the kindergarten. She arduously turns the wheel, and we roll alongside the kindergarten and not into it. She kicks up her feet and bounces on the pillows. We turn again.

"Wow," she says. "It's really hard turning the steering wheel. I thought you just needed to turn the wheel a little bit."

We turn the wrong way down a one-way street, and we pass the front pavilion of the school. We turn into the parking lot next to the gym and cruise around. "This is neat!" She smiles at me. We drive a few laps in the parking lot before I put on the brakes for good. She turns to me. "Thanks, Chi. That was so fun! Can we do it again?"

"Maybe tomorrow, on Christmas Day."

"Okay. You're the best." She sniffles and smiles.

"Let's go home. I don't want your cold to get worse." I sit down in the driver's seat. "And please don't tell Mom about this."

"Okay." She beams. "I promise."

Wake Up!

Christmas Morning, 1987;
College Station, Texas

I launch out from beneath the covers, and the cold hits me. I shiver all over. I walk into the living room, hoping, just hoping. Wiping away the condensation on the window, I peer outside searching for a white ground, a patch of white, any fleck of white. The Bermuda grass of our front lawn is dry and wilted. Another brown Christmas morning.

I turn around and look at the two handmade red and white stockings pinned to the living room wall. Mine will be filled with what I get every year: long tube socks and a red and gold Chinese envelope carrying one twenty-dollar bill.

I walk into the kitchen. My mother is rolling bean paste into balls, then wrapping dough around them. We can't afford Nintendo, but time is free, and my mother gives all of hers.

"Merry Christmas, Mom!"

"Merry Christmas."

"What are you making?"

"Bean cakes."

"You mean bean grenades. They are just the right size to pound Mingfang's head with. They smell so disgusting. You know that I've never eaten one. Besides, don't we have the bean grenades from last Christmas?"

"Leave me alone to do my work. Go wake Cutie up. She's usually the first person to open her presents."

"Oh, let me guess, Mom. It's socks and a twenty-dollar bill!"

"Leave me alone," says my mother, having not changed her tone the entire time.

I carry the "bean bombs" to my sister's bedroom door. I tap lightly on the door. No response. A sign on the door shouts, "Stay Out!"

"Mingfang," I say. "Mingfang. I have your Christmas presents for you. They're nice and tasty." No response. The door opens on its own. I stick my head into her room. "Wake up! It's Christmastime."

She is lying on her side with her back facing me. "Wake up, Mingfang," I say mischievously. "Don't you want to eat these bean grenades? Come on, wake up, sleepyhead." I shake her shoulder; she falls supine. Her hands and face are light blue. The bottom half of her body is a dark blue. Horror wrenches my body. My hand carefully touches her face. It is icy cold. I jerk back. "Mom!" I scream. "Mom! Come here!" My mother's feet pitter-patter across the linoleum floor, slide against the carpet as they run into Mingfang's room. Chinese bean cakes make a dull thud on the ground. A scream reverberates within the four walls of my sister's room. My eyes dilate. Shock anesthetizes my mind. Like a forklift, I stick my arms under my sister's icy body, and I carry her into the living room.

Fwuoooo. Fwuoo. Her lips are cold and pasty. Her chest rises with every breath pushed into her lungs from my own, just like the mannequin Annies in our high school health class. My hands push into my sister's chest. "One. Two. Three. Four. Five."

She died hours ago. I knew that as soon as I touched her face. The breath of life that blows into her chest is my own, filling a hollow cavity to circulate meaninglessly. I am breathing for myself, for my mother, for the appeasement of our souls, to let us know we are doing something, so that we may more clearly hear ourselves screaming, futilely, at God: No!

Fwuooo. Fwuoooo. "One, two, three, four, five . . ." Sirens knife into my ears. The red lights of the ambulance shine like a beacon, leading me where? I fear to tread this path. I stare into Mingfang's eyes, and she looks deeper into my eyes than she ever did alive.

Two men and a woman in white jumpers walk into our living room. The woman and a tall man lay out a stretcher. They look up at the chubby man, who says, "Let's resuscitate her here. Please step aside, son." I step back and sit on the couch. Can't stand.

Shmack! My sister's body lurches up as if she might burst through the ceiling. The defibrillator jolts artificial life into her small body. "Turn up the joules," says the woman. "Clear!" says the chubby man. *Shmack!* My sister jolts up again, possessed by the spirit of medical technology. The woman places a plastic mask over Mingfang's face and pumps air into her mouth. "Clear!" *Shmack!* She is still limp. Still cold. Still blue.

"Okay, let's take her to the hospital," says the woman. She turns to my mother, who has remained standing, with the same expression on her face, unburdened by fear or despair but taut with readiness. Just tell me what I can do, her face says. "Ma'am," says the female medic, "we are going to take your daughter to Saint Joseph Hospital. Do you want to ride in the ambulance with us?"

"No. I go by car," my mother replies, and she runs into Mingfang's room.

The two men strap Mingfang onto the stretcher and carry her out the front door. Sirens fade away. My mother comes back into the living room, holding a bag.

"What's in the bag?" I ask.

"Mingfang's clothes. I am going to the hospital," she tells me in Taiwanese. "Call your father and older sister and tell them to come home." My mother hops into the banana car and drives away. My father is visiting his parents in Taiwan, and my sister now lives in San Antonio with her husband. I am alone now.

What just happened? I want to be a little ball, curled up like a roly-poly bug shielded from the world by its exoskeleton. I sit in shock for a long time.

I switch on the television. The Green Bay Packers are playing in one foot of snow at Lambeau Field. The snow falls quietly on the players and the grass. The game of moving a piece of leather one hundred yards to an end zone is oddly soothing. I cling to my sister's favorite animal, a life-size teddy bear. Time passes. Passes.

The doorbell rings, and I nearly jump off the couch. Who is here on Christmas morning? I open the door. A big-boned policeman introduces himself and says, "Sorry to disturb you, but I need to investigate the house."

The policeman walks into Mingfang's room and looks at the homemade banners on her wall and the jumble of stuffed animals on her shelves. He picks up a bottle of amoxicillin sitting on the desk. The pediatrician had prescribed the antibiotics for her cold. He opens the container and sniffs at it. "Did your sister take any illegal drugs?"

"No, sir."

"Did she ever tell you that she wanted to kill herself?"

I think about this question. Was Mingfang happy? I don't know. "No, sir," I say.

The policeman wants to know why Mingfang died. Yes, why did she die? This man is probably a Christian. Officer, please tell me why your God chose to kill my sister on Christmas morning.

He opens each drawer of Mingfang's desk, inspecting the Hello Kitty pencils I gave her for suffering through obstacle courses. We walk into the living room. The Packers just scored a touchdown.

The wide receiver showboats in the end zone. I take a seat on the couch and hug my sister's bear. The officer looks at me. "Would you like me to stay for a while?"

"No, sir. I will be fine. Thank you though."

The door shuts and I am alone again. I make a call to my older sister. The answering machine picks up. "Zee-zee!" I say. Big sister, where are you? Tears stream down my face. "Zee-zee! Zee-zee! Are you there? Pick up! Cutie died. Mei-mei died. Zee-zee, where are you?"

I sit on the couch again. My lips continue to tremble as my eyes soak Mingfang's teddy bear. I want to wail. I want to wail from the pit of my diaphragm. But what good would it do? I flip the channels: MTV, ESPN, CNN, ABC, NBC. I don't want to be alone.

Hours later, I call my buddy Chris Dinkel. "Hey, Chris. I was wondering if you could drive me to get something to eat. My sister just died and I am hungry." I state my sister's death as a matter of fact. I am full of emotion at one moment and devoid of feeling at another.

After lunch with Chris, I sit on the couch again, staring off into space. Another knock on the door. A stout man with a peppered beard stands before me. He carries a black leather Bible. "Hello," he pronounces slowly in a Texas twang, "my name is Pastor John." He hands me a card:

> Pastor John
> 2nd Baptist Church of College Station
> In the love of Jesus!

I gaze into his eyes as I consider how utterly cheesy his card is. "May I come in?"

Sure. Why not? At least he'll talk. The next twenty minutes are a blur. Pastor John speaks of love and Jesus' concern for us during times of tragedy. His words sink in as deeply as an echo does into the Grand Canyon. Finally, he asks me, "Is there anything else I can do for you?"

I want to tell Pastor John that the bubble that was my world—a world that made a little sense, a world of some minimal pretense of justice—has popped. Don't waste your time on me, I want to tell him. Maybe you can ask your Jesus why He kills innocent kids.

"Yes," I say to Pastor John. "Can you take me to Saint Joseph Hospital?" Pastor John graciously agrees, and we climb into his Ford Ranger truck.

Mingfang lies on a white hospital bed, and my mother sits at her feet. I hand the bear to my mother and stand before Mingfang's face. A thick crust of blood stains the left side of her mouth. Out of her nose sticks an offensive tube leading to a suction container, wherein percolates green mucus. Her frozen chest, her slackened face, the pall of death veiling her undramatically—seeing all this, I know for sure now. Christmas brings no miracles.

My mother does not take her eyes off of Mingfang. She cares for Cutie more than me or Chiufang because Mingfang is the weakest of her three. Mothers protect the most vulnerable. The ones God has determined to die prematurely. The mothers of the world universally scream, "No!" But today, my mother wasn't strong enough to defy God or fate or whatever it is. Mingfang's spirit was stolen away in the night. Why He would take my sister instead of taking me I do not understand. My life has been blessed in so many ways. Take me. Take me. Take me instead! Yet I am still here, and she is gone.

A nurse enters. "Ma'am, we'll need to use this room for trauma cases."

"Oh." My mother looks confusedly at the nurse. "Sure. Um. We will leave as soon as my daughter wakes up."

15

Just One More Time

December 26, 1987;
Rider Funeral Home, College Station, Texas

The mortician is a little middle-aged man wearing a suit from the 1960s. His skin is a jaundiced yellow, exposed to too much artificial light. He is developing a small hump on his upper back. My father looks at the mortician, wondering how to broach the subject. He has just flown in on the red-eye from Taiwan. He was there visiting his parents, whom he hadn't seen in years. Sheepishly, my father asks, "Um, can I see my daughter?"

Embarrassed, I tell him, "Dad, I thought we were going to pick out a casket."

He waves me off.

"Well," says the mortician, "your daughter has not been removed from the refrigerator." Refrigerator? She must be cold. No. I am being silly. She is dead. I just keep forgetting.

"Uh, Dad," Chiufang says, "I don't think it's such a good idea. Mingfang's body is still blue in some areas. The morticians haven't done the cosmetic work yet."

My father ponders this for a long moment. "Okay," he says, "we will wait until the funeral."

"How much cost—box?" my mother asks.

The mortician jerks his head toward my mother. He is caught off guard. My mother has changed the tone. It is time to get things done.

"Well"—the mortician points at a shimmering hardwood casket—"this fine model is airtight, and it is five thousand dollars."

"Too much," says my mother. She leads us to a Ford Escort–type casket. "How much?"

"That one is two thousand dollars."

"Okay, we take," my mother replies. "We go now. You prepare everything."

I sit, hunched over and limbs cramped, at Mingfang's desk. This rickety old hand-me-down is where Mingfang studies. Sticky contact paper covers the desktop, and atop it resides a panoply of trinkets and small toys. On the right side of her desk stands a picture of Mingfang wearing a tutu, standing in a ballet pose. And on the wall behind the desk is taped a newspaper clipping of me winning a ribbon for my science project, which addressed the effects of aspartame artificial sweetener, as a possible neurotransmitter, on the heart rhythms of cockroaches. The project won second place in the Life Sciences category at my high school. I cut open roaches and placed NutraSweet directly on their hearts. It all seems so silly now. Even perverse.

Mingfang idolized me. She couldn't excel in school, so she did it through me, posting every clipping on her bulletin board. From me, any bit of warmth expanded in her heart exponentially. Instead of warmth, I gave her help. What I thought she needed. I made her run laps in the cold.

I pick up her Cabbage Patch doll. She got it last year despite my mother's reservations. I don't even know its name. A silvery, aerodynamic Matchbox car sits precariously on the base of the study lamp. Its windows are tinted, and the small doors open and shut. It's odd that Mingfang, a girl, collected cars. This was her dream car, this silver Mazda RX-7.

I tilt the desk drawer up in order to open it. Tucked squarely in the back right-hand corner of the drawer is a stack of worn blue playing cards. It was a part of her ritual at night to play cards, usually by herself and sometimes with my mother or me. Crazy Eights. Hearts. Twenty-one.

I look around her room. I read the banner above me: "Mingfang's Room." She will never again shout out from behind this door, "I didn't need that!" What if I had studied less, played less tennis, and spent more time with Mingfang? What if we all acted like we loved the ones we claim to love? What would the world be like? There'd be less technology, less production, fewer things, but used for better purposes. We'd all know the names of each other's Cabbage Patch dolls.

Mingfang lies before us in an open casket, watching heaven. In the front row of pews sit my father, my mother, Chiufang, and me. My father sits stone still. Then he doubles over, and a terrible sob throbs upward through his body. Tears spray the floor. He shakes. Gee, I have never seen my father cry. I don't like it. Fathers are not supposed to cry. Stop! Stop your crying. You can't cry and break down. We need to be strong.

To divert myself, I look behind us. Every pew is packed. All three

aisles overflow with people. The throng stretches through the
church doors and out onto the lawn, all the way to the walkway. I
never knew Mingfang was so well loved; I don't think she did either.

Chiufang's husband begins reading the eulogy. I've been in no
shape to read anything, so we asked him to do it. As I listen to my
brother-in-law speak, I hear my own words echoing from the past:
"Mingfang, you look like our national bird. Yep, the bald eagle."
"Hey, roly-poly, you better stop eating or else you'll become just a
poly and won't be able to roll any longer." Perhaps the simplest one
was the most powerful: "Retard!" I was young then. I didn't understand why she was treated the best even though she wasn't good
at much. I was so mean, such a jerk, until the last hours of her life.
Now it's too late to make it up to her.

My brother-in-law is still talking. I wait nervously to sing
"Amazing Grace." My family rarely goes to church, and when they
do, it's for the free lunch afterward and the ESL classes. Most of the
time I go to church only because of David Ray Wright. He is one of
my best friends and one of the few Christians I respect. He doesn't
shout at me and tell me I'm going to burn in hell. No, he actually
cares about people. Nevertheless, I usually fake a stomachache just
to sleep in on Sunday mornings.

Mrs. Johnson, the Sunday school teacher, plays a nice, easy opening on the piano. I take a deep breath. I stand next to Mingfang, facing the funeral audience. Mingfang loved this song. I will sing it for
her for the last time.

> *Amazing grace! How sweet the sound*
> *That saved a wretch like me!*
> *I once was lost, but now am found,*
> *Was blind, but now I see.*

I don't know if my sister knew God. What does God do to those
children who do not have a chance to live?

'Twas grace that taught my heart to fear
And grace my fears relieved.
How precious did that grace appear
The hour I first believed.

If there is a hell, is Mingfang there right now? Is it the way those fire-and-brimstone Southern Baptists describe it? Or is it the "Jesus loves you" stuff Pastor John talks about? Are they one and the same?

Through many dangers, toils and snares
I have already come.
'Tis grace hath brought me safe thus far
And grace will lead me home.

Did I escort my sister to her death? I made her run laps. The next morning she's dead.

When we've been there ten thousand years
Bright shining as the sun

Maybe if I sing even louder, I really will believe God exists. And that He is a good God, not one who snatched Mingfang from this world. How can God be so cruel? I have to sing louder so even those in the back can hear.

We've no less days to sing God's praise
Than when we'd first begun.

The processional has started. My father walks up to Mingfang and looks at her for a split second before walking past her. It's as if he refuses to let this image of his daughter be implanted in his memory. He will remember only the living Cutie. Now it is my mother. She has such a kind face as she looks at her baby for the last time. Her hand reaches toward Mingfang's hand as if it might bring her back to life.

And now I am standing by my sister. She lies so peacefully in the coffin. I place her Cabbage Patch doll next to her hand. And then I give her the silver matchbox car to remember our last happy day together. Lastly, I hand to her my high school letter, the "C" I wear on my school jacket; it was awarded for tennis and academic achievement. She lived through my success. Now she can have the trophy.

I look at her face. Mingfang. Cutie, I wonder if you knew. Did you know that I really cared about you? Those brief moments when I would help you with your spelling or give you a small present, and even when . . . even when I made you run, those were an adolescent male's way of saying, "I love you."

My friends—Chris, Josh, and Irwin—and my brother-in-law and I lift the coffin out of the hearse. I am the right rear pallbearer. Mirrored in the surface of the lacquered, mahoganylike casket are the puffy cumulus clouds hovering above, and yes, that face—my face. We walk in cadence toward the grave. We lower the coffin onto three longitudinal belts over the grave. A man slowly turns a crank, and the coffin descends gradually into the ground. *Wait! Wait! Wait! I want to see my sister. Open the box one more time! I won't get to see her ever again. Can I please see my sister? Just one more time, please.* The words never leave my mouth. Of course I don't say anything. Not even a whisper. I don't even cry. I watch the coffin as it is consumed by the shadow of the ground.

16

Red January

3 a.m., One Year Later

I am standing in a red room. Actually everything is red, not just the room. Other than that it is a plain room. I don't even think there is a door in here.

"Hello, Mingfang. Why are you back? You came back to say hello?" Wait. It's been over a year since she died. Why does she still look thirteen? Why hasn't she grown? Her hair hasn't gotten longer; it still scratches the nape of her neck. She sits quietly in the corner, her back to me. "Mingfang," I whisper to her. "Mingfang! What are you doing?"

My baby sister turns around for a brief second. Her big, brown eyes peer at me like the eyes of the woman in Diego Rivera's *Panchita* painting. But. But her eyes grow larger every second. *Stop!* I want to yell it out, to scream it out, but . . . but nothing comes out. I want to walk up close to her, but my legs won't move. Paralyzed.

She returns to staring into the corner. I lost my chance. Wait. I feel my voice coming back. "Mingfang. Cutie. Hey, you!"

No response.

"Why are you here?" I ask her, pleading for an answer. "Why are you visiting me every night?"

Nothing. She is done with me. Mingfang rocks back and forth now, mindlessly. I'd always called her retarded. Now she is. *Boom. Boom. Boom.* She bangs her head into the corner of the red room. *BOOM. BOOM. BOOM.* Louder and louder. Harder and harder.

"Stop hitting your head," I demand. "Quit it."

She turns around and looks at me. Her black eyes stare at me with anger. I hate that look. She has never said anything to me since she died. Almost every night she comes to me, and she never says anything. *BOOM. BOOM. BOOM.* I want to place my hand between her head and the wall, but my feet won't move.

The room recedes. Red turns to black. I might be awake. But I won't open my eyes. I don't want to see where I am now. Only a couple of hours left before the test. The verbs. The conjugations. Think about *that.*

Vine. Viniste. Vino. Venimos? Venieron?

Is that right? I knew the conjugations five minutes ago.

Hablé. Hablaste? Habló? Hablamos? Hablaron?

I have twenty minutes left, three pages of verbs to conjugate. Hurry, Chi. Hurry, Chi. Gonna get my first F. Fail college. Think. I can't! I can't remember anything!

I am back in the red room again. How did it happen so fast this time? Everything is speeding up. I have my rose-colored glasses on again. The redness is darker now. Almost maroon, like blood. I can't focus on anything, but I know she is here. I can hear her. *BOOM. BOOM. BOOM.*

"Hello, Mingfang. You are back in your corner again. What did you do since I last saw you?"

She turns around and her stare eats into my eyes like acid. I'm

falling out of the red room again, but I can still hear it. Like the
drum of a marching band, the sound is monotonous, constant,
deafening. I hear her in the day, too. The sound lurks beneath my
thoughts, in between the words I speak, in the air between exhala-
tion and inhalation. During any downtime, I hear the booming, the
booming, the booming, so I try not to relax, keep myself constantly
studying at school. I'm on the run. But eighteen credit hours and
multiple student organizations cannot stave off what I still hilari-
ously call "sleep."

I try to take a deep breath, and my throat shakes. How did this
happen? Everything was normal after the funeral. I wrote thank-
you cards to all the families that gave us food and support after her
death. But I never finished. I couldn't. After writing fifty long personal letters, I ran out of steam and simply quit. I did not send out
one card. And then I decided to say thank you over the intercom, at
school. I started saying it, and then the intercom broke up, and I had
to say it again.

After that, things just got busy. Before Mingfang died, I was
going for valedictorian, but afterward it became apparent that
Christina Laane had wrapped that up. I mean, how does a person
score one hundred on everything? So during the final semester of
high school, I studied even more diligently, studied every night until
I passed out, so that I might get second place. I graduated last May
in third.

I chose Texas A&M in order to continue living with my mother,
who still suffers. And so I went to my college classes. I did not think
about my sister. Her funeral was months ago. Yes, she would pop
into my mind occasionally, but she would never wrest over my consciousness. Don't get me wrong. I visited her on her birthday and
on Christmas, the day she died. I made sure that she had fresh flowers at her grave and that the tombstone was free from bird drop-
pings. I never knew how much birds liked to perch on tombstones.

The point is, I've changed. I am not a negligent brother anymore.

But it's been over a year since she died, and there is nothing I can do to bring her back. It doesn't matter how much crying or wishing I do. She is not coming back. My sister is in the past. I need to move forward. I've got to get things done.

I pull the covers over my head. I should get up and study, but who am I kidding? I can't study. All I hear is the booming. It's seductive really, the way it crept up. Before I noticed, my fourteen-hour study days dropped to eight. The gym workouts lasted forty-five minutes instead of an hour. Before it all started, I could recall ten pages of notes verbatim. Now I can't remember the beginning of a sentence at the end of it. My sentences don't come to a right ending. Professors' words? Incomprehensible.

At first it was kind of nice to "see" her again. I miss her dearly. But something bad always happens in the dreams. She dies at the end of every dream. Always in red. But now it's worse. It's the corner. The stare. I wish she would scream at me to leave her alone! To say how mean I am! But she looks inside me with disgust, pity, loathing, what? She never tells me.

I just need to motivate myself and work harder. I don't have time to worry about minor nuisances.

Chiufang has nice dreams about Mingfang. "I took Mingfang to SeaWorld," she tells me. "Mingfang got all excited when she saw Shamu the whale, and then we went to the gift shop and I got her a stuffed Shamu. When I woke up, I just had this warm feeling inside. Mingfang was telling me that she is okay in heaven." Chiufang is a Christian with a capital *C*. Then she told me about her shrink's interpretation of her dream. I wanted to laugh at all that psychobabble, but I just told her I had a Spanish test to study for.

I close my eyes. I think I can sleep now. Thinking about Chiufang's dream is relaxing. I walk into the red room. "Stop hitting your head against the wall," I plead. "Please, please stop. You are making me sad. Very sad."

All is silent now. She lies on the red floor in a fetal position. Her back seems huge now; it is all I see of her. I dare not walk up to her and look at her face.

"Mingfang. Get up. Please sit up! Mingfang. Cutie." I crouch over her. I wish I could give her a prize, to entice her to open her eyes. "Please sit up. Please wake up. Please." I reach out to her, but her body retracts into the redness; she's falling away. I'm rising from the red room. No. I have to tell her something. I have to tell her—

I open my eyes. I'm back in my own bedroom. I roll onto my stomach and cover the back of my head with my hands. Tears soak my sheets. I flip over, stare at the ceiling. I can't tell anyone about this. They'll think I'm crazy. But I am! I've lost my mind. So I'd better not tell anyone. How can I be living in the middle of a town, in a house with my parents, and be so alone? I used to never cry. Now I cry every night. After every nightmare. I need to study. I kick the covers off of me. You're going to fail. You can only remember things in the distant past, things you don't even want to remember. Everything else is scratched out by a red marker—you can't connect two thoughts. It's hopeless. I'm going to drop out of college if I can't think straight. I don't care anymore. I'll do anything. Anything to stop this. I'm so tired. I just want to go to sleep. A sleep without dreams.

17

Magic Juice

November 12, 1997;
Yassela Orphanage, La Paz, Bolivia

It is almost ten years to the month since my sister died. God creates life circles. Events repeat themselves in almost mystical, déjà vu–like ways. Some people learn from their past and handle their present in a more sanctified, mature manner. Others fall into the life circle and disappear into the black hole of despair, reliving their past suffering and injuring themselves in the present. Will I come full circle, or will I fall into that black hole? Ring around the rosy, pocket full of posies. Ashes to ashes.

I stand on the roof of Yassela orphanage taking in the sky above me. Below me, on the second level of the orphanage, girls stand around the outdoor cement basin scrubbing their clothes. The crunching-scrunching noise of the scrubber against the hand-me-down clothes is almost hypnotic. I see an older girl washing her clothes. I don't know her name. Her hands are pruned and covered with soapsuds. I walk down the stairs to the second level. Her wide, round face frames her almost Asian-looking eyes. Her face, wider than it is long, is almost a caricature. A simple pug nose dots the space between her eyes. Having been separated by several thousand years, two continents, and thousands of miles, the Asian meets the Aymaran. I find my ancestors, my sisters, my brothers, my blood in these indigenous Americans, for I am more related to this Aymaran than my Caucasian friends in Boston, Massachusetts. *Aymara* even sounds Taiwanese to me.

She works diligently at her duties, washing baby clothes and hanging them on the clothesline. She glances at me as I walk down the stairs to the first level of the orphanage—the kitchen—where four girls are cooking lunch. A little girl, her cherubic cheeks aglow and her thick dark hair tied back in two matching ponytails sprouting sideways out of her head, skips up to me. She hands me her doll and runs away quickly. The doll sees out of only one eye and suffers from severe balding. Funny, isn't it? The only opportunity to see golden hair around here is on the movie screen or on the heads of Barbie dolls.

"What's the name of that little girl?" I ask a girl named Diana as she stirs a pot of soup with an oversize spatula.

"Her name is Natalia. She's four," she tells me.

"Natalia? I don't think I know her. Who does she belong to?"

"She is Daniela's."

"Who is Daniela?"

"Daniela. You know Daniela. The big girl upstairs washing the clothes." The girls giggle silently among themselves.

"Why isn't Daniela playing with you guys?"

"You know. She's different." She tips the end of her nose up. A cacophony of cackles emanate from the group.

"You mean she's stuck up."

"Yup. She does not like us 'kids.' "

"Why?"

"I don't know. She keeps to herself. She does her chores, washes her kids' clothes, meets this man at the door every day at three o'clock, and goes to bed early."

"Natalia." She magically reappears, peeking around the door frame of a dark room.

"Natalia, don't you want your doll back?" I ask her.

She takes a tentative step toward me. I take the doll and make it walk along the cement ground. "Hola, Natalia. Me llamo Raquel. Me gustaria tener una amiga. Puedes jugar conmigo?"

Her eyes grow bigger and she tilts her head to the left. She hops up to play with her new friend, Raquel. She lifts up the doll and takes it to a nice warm spot on the cement floor outside, well within a spotlight of Andean sun.

"Hola, Raquel. Vamos a jugar 'la casa.' " A little girl who may have never lived in what you and I would call a home still plays house.

"I think Natalia likes you." I hear a teenage voice from behind me. "She usually doesn't like new people. Especially men. You must remind her of her father." I turn around to see the older girl. "Hello, my name is Daniela," she says, "and you must be Dr. Chi."

"How did you know?" I ask.

"There aren't too many men working in this girls' orphanage, and besides, how many Chinese men do you know in La Paz?"

"I guess you are right," I say. "I see you washing clothes a lot."

"I wash clothes every other day."

"Every other day? Why don't you just wash once a week and save time and effort?"

"Because we only have two pairs of clothes. One is worn and getting dirty and the other is dirty getting clean."

"Oh. I see," I say. "So, why are you here?"

"Why am I here? Because I live here. Why would I be here if I did not live here?"

"I mean what brought you here?"

"Oh." She turns, deflecting my gaze. "You mean why am I a street child?"

"Yes, if you want to put it that way."

"Because my mother beat me," she says, puckering her lips. "She used to beat my younger sister and me every single night, so we left home. We lived together as sisters on the streets for a long time—two years."

"Why did you leave the streets?"

"We got tired of the streets with the drugs, beatings, pimps, drunks, cold, and hunger."

"Do you like it here?"

"Yes," she says, "and no. I don't want Natalia and Maria to grow up and live the life that I have. We have food and beds so I cannot complain, but I feel that they don't want me here."

"What do you mean, they don't want you here? Isn't it a home for street girls?"

"Yes." She nods and straightens up, arms akimbo. "I am not a young street girl, innocent and cute. You see I have scars on my face. The badges or 'medals of honor' that say that I am a veteran of the streets." She pauses to see if I comprehend, then says, "The administration doesn't like us because we are difficult to deal with. No one likes an old street girl. The heart hardens as we get older. We go from innocent little children to little punks and criminals." She crosses her arms. "At least that is what most people think."

"Have you ever committed a crime?" I ask her.

"Crime? No, not really. Never stole anything from anyone. The only crime I committed is that I am not a better mother."

"What were the streets like?"

"Been cut. Been punched. Been robbed. Been kicked. Haven't been raped. Not yet, at least. That's one good thing, I guess. I have to thank Pedro for that."

"Who is Pedro?"

"Pedro is my *marido*." Marido, she says, meaning "lover."

"Lover," I say. "That's kind of a weird word to use."

"I guess you would say he is my husband, the father of Natalia and Maria." I suppose most street children don't hold a traditional wedding ceremony.

"So Pedro protected you on the streets," I say.

"Oh, yes." She nods fervently. "He protected me from the other street boys, the adults, and the pimps."

"Do all street girls have 'lovers'?"

"If they are smart, they have one. Otherwise, they are going to get gang-raped." She gives me a look that tells me it is important to understand this fact. "Without a lover, it is going to happen, sooner or later."

"So, do you love Pedro?"

"Oh, yes." She walks outside to see what Natalia is doing. I follow her. "Pedro and I met when we were first on the streets, and then we both ended up in the home I lived in before this one. I am one of the lucky ones who actually loves my lover, my protector. Other girls just find the strongest street boy and become his. I guess it is better to give it up to one person than to give it up to dozens. Besides, what's love all about anyway? You need to survive first before anything else." We look down at Natalia, who is looking down at Raquel, who swims in an imaginary river.

"Where is Pedro now?"

"Oh, he sells gum on the streets near the hospital and then goes to an adolescent boys' home at night."

"Do you miss him?"

"Oh, he visits me every day and gives me money."

"Where is your sister?"

"She is staying at another street girls' home uptown."

"So how long are you going to stay here?"

"As long as they will let me. I try to do my chores and stay out of trouble. Hopefully Pedro and I can make enough money to rent a small room somewhere nearby."

"Great. Maybe I can help you a little when you make that decision."

"That would be good. Ummm. Dr. Chi, can you take a look at my baby? Her name is Maria. She has liquid poo-poo."

"Oh, you mean she has diarrhea."

"Yes, diarrhea."

We enter into a dimly lit room on the first level. Posters of Latino pop singers with coiffed hair decorate the walls. In the far corner of the room lies a little ball of wrapped cloth. I unwrap the cloth and a tiny baby appears. She gives a small whimper. Dark grayish blue bags surround her eyes.

"When was the last time she cried for food?"

"She hasn't cried in a day or so. She is not her usual self anymore."

"Has she had a fever?"

"She has been warm and sweaty."

"Warm and sweaty?"

"Yes. We don't have a thermometer."

I give Maria a thorough examination, and I tell Daniela that her baby daughter is suffering from gastroenteritis and mild dehydration.

"What's that?" she asks me.

"It means she has too much diarrhea, causing her to lose too much liquid from her body."

"Is that bad?"

"It could be if we do not treat her."

"What are you going to do?"

"I'm going to take her to the hospital and run some tests."

"No," she says emphatically. "I don't want her to go to the hospital."

"I can't take care of her here." I don't understand why Daniela wouldn't want the best for her baby.

"I don't like the hospital," she says. "Because they don't like us."

"What? Who is 'us'?"

"You know." She tilts her head, frowns. "Us. They usually kick us out."

"Well, I'll go with you," I assure her. "It won't be a problem." By the look on her face, I can tell she doesn't believe me. "Listen, it will probably be fine, but she may die if I don't take her to the hospital. I don't know if she has an infection elsewhere, and we can only tell at the hospital."

"Dr. Chi," she pleads, "they may take my baby away and never give her back to me because . . . because I am a street girl. Is there any other way I can take care of her here?" Daniela holds her clasped hands to her chest. "I will stay up all night if I have to and watch her to make sure she is breathing."

If I were in Boston . . . but I am not. I am in Bolivia with no lab, no scanners. Just me and a tackle box of medicines. Without a hospital lab, I can't take blood to rule out bacteremia, I can't analyze urine to rule out a urinary tract infection, I can't do a lumbar puncture to rule out meningitis, and I can't do a chest radiograph to rule out pneumonia.

"Please, Dr. Chi." She places baby Maria in my arms.

I measure Maria's rectal temperature: 39° Celsius—too high. I walk to the pharmacy and spend my entire monthly food allowance on drugs for Maria. I'll freeload lunches and dinners from the orphanages. When I return to Yassela, Daniela refuses to let me place an intravenous line in Maria, so I give Daniela specific instructions to feed her one liter of oral rehydration therapy solution every hour. I tell her that I will inject Maria with an antibiotic once a day for fourteen days. Daniela takes this all in earnestly.

"I will see you tomorrow then. Let me know if you want someone to look after Maria during the day while you work. I have a friend named Laura who likes to care for children. Don't worry. She can't take your baby away."

"Why doesn't she have her own baby?" Daniela asks.

"Because she is not married."

She laughs a hard, deep laugh.

"Chi. Babies are not made from getting married."

"Well, she doesn't believe in having kids before marriage."

"Oh. That's weird. Why doesn't she just get married?"

"She cannot find the right person."

"Why? Is she ugly? Is she a bad cook?"

"No."

"Hmmm. Then what is wrong with her?"

"Nothing is wrong with her. I met her at church and she was interested in my work on the street with all of you. She's a good woman who's willing to help. And she *would* probably adopt Maria, given the chance, but she's willing to just help you in any way. So that's just another option. Just to let you know, I think that keeping a mother and her child together is extremely important."

"Okay, I will think about it."

"Remember, call me if Maria doesn't drink."

"Okay, Dr. Chi."

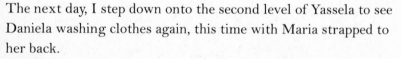

The next day, I step down onto the second level of Yassela to see Daniela washing clothes again, this time with Maria strapped to her back.

"How did Maria do?"

"Great, Dr. Chi. I gave the magic juice just like you told me every single hour, and she got back to her normal self."

"What is her normal self?"

Daniela wrings out the baby clothes, takes Maria off her back. She holds Maria up before her. "Her smile. Look, she is smiling again. Look, she's looking around. She knows her mommy."

"That's great, Daniela. I am proud of you."

"Thank you." She smiles at me.

"Okay, I need to give her a shot."

"A shot? Why does she need a shot? The juice made her all better."

"You don't know that it was only the juice."

"Sure I do." Daniela holds Maria against her chest. "I gave her the juice, and she got all better in front of my eyes. I was up all night with her. It was the juice."

"It may have been the juice in part. But it may have also been the shot."

"No shot," says Daniela authoritatively.

"Daniela," I say, matching her stern statement with doctorly seriousness, carefully enunciating my syllables, "I have to give the shot in order to prevent her from possibly getting sicker. Let me give her the shot."

"Okay."

I administer a shot to Maria every morning for fourteen days. "Daniela, we are finished with the shots."

"Good. My poor little baby was like a pincushion."

"Well, she is back to normal now."

"Yes. Thanks to you."

"No, actually it was you who saved her life."

"Maybe . . . with your help."

"Daniela, I am going on a vacation."

"Good," Daniela says. "You need a vacation."

"Why do I need a vacation?"

"Because you work too hard," she says.

"I work too hard. Umm, you are the ones who work too hard." She does not respond. "I'm going to Peru, to Machu Picchu," I say.

"So are you going to take the bus? There are bandits along the road. They stop the bus and rob each passenger."

"Actually, I am going to fly. The ticket's only a hundred dollars."

Daniela's eyes widen with astonishment. "ONE HUNDRED DOLLARS! Wow, you are rich!"

"Well, I will see you in a week, okay?"

"Okay," says Daniela. "Be safe."

"I will. You just take care of your kids."

I am on the plane to Peru. I will be gone for one week. I'd always dreamed of hiking to Machu Picchu, one of the seven wonders of the world. Now is my chance. I suppose I really am rich. But is money important in the big picture? Absolutely. Upon walking the streets of La Paz, I shed both my liberal leanings and the "blind faith" that God provides. Children die on my streets, babies cry for food every night. Does God provide for our needs? Yes, but money helps a whole lot.

A vacation might help even more. I'm snapping at the kids, losing patience. I'm burned out. Spent. I don't have time to pray. Too many one-hundred-hour weeks in the orphanages, on the streets, writing reports back to Park Street Church, and holding Bible studies at church. I understand now how some doctors can be so inhumane to their patients. After spending one-hundred-plus hours in the hospital, the enemy suddenly becomes the ones you treat. It's only been four months here in Bolivia; I have four more to go. I need to go away to replenish my soul and spirit. Yes, but I know already: There is a fine line between self-preservation and self-indulgence.

18

Not in Any Hurry

30°F, 2 a.m., November 23, 1997;
El Hueco
The graffiti on the wall reads:

> Drugs and alcohol may kill me slowly
> . . . oh, s—, but I'm not in any hurry.

The poets sign their verse with their bodies. Fifteen little children and teens slumber in a huddle beneath the words. One large sheet of blue plastic tarp is their blanket. Corrugated cardboard is their bedding of choice. I shine my flashlight on the ceiling, and the kids' brown golden retriever–type mutt—balding, mangy, and emaciated— lifts his bony body and growls. I reach over to wake a boy, and the dog barks. The boy grumbles, peeks out at me from beneath the blue tarp, then jumps up and shakes the other children.

"Wake up! Wake up! Chi is here."

The children begin to call my name—and their ailments. Three societies of street children are sleeping here tonight. I begin taking care of a group of kids on the left side of the alcove.

Alejandro walks around and talks to kids, seeing what medical problems they have, while I treat them. After cleaning and dressing a leg wound from a beating, I feel a tap on my back.

"Someone wants to talk to you," Alejandro tells me, and leads me to a disheveled girl. She has the eyes and shoulders of a lost child, the anxious wrinkles of a thirty-year-old. She seems to wait for me to make an announcement about her future. And then her eyes topple some barrier in my brain. This girl is Daniela. My own stubborn hope wouldn't let me recognize her.

I smile for her. "How's it going, Daniela? I haven't seen you in a while."

"Oh, it's going okay," she says.

"Heard you were on the streets."

"Yeah."

"How come you're on the streets? How come you left Yassela?"

"They kicked me out. I missed curfew on a Saturday. I had to go to my aunt's birthday. It was very important to her and to me. And so I did not have a choice. I left at 1 p.m. and I hurried back at 3:30 p.m. And the door was locked. And Señora Lola would not let me back in. I really did not want to leave Yassela. She won't even let me back in to wash my clothes in the basin."

Daniela looks far away, into the wall, into the words: "Drugs and alcohol may kill me slowly" . . . Her matted hair looks like that of a cocker spaniel that has lived in the woods for a year. *Drugs and alcohol may kill me slowly. . . .* The words seem to draw her in, as if her soul were being suctioned into the letters themselves. "Daniela." I try to make eye contact with eyes that simply are not there. "Daniela, what have you been doing?"

"I just walk and walk and walk."

"Where are you going, Daniela?"

"I just feel like walking. I just walk all day. I walk everywhere." Daniela's eyes do not move; they do not twinkle, they do not blink. They try to hold in what her entire body—which is so dead, so much more like a pile of matter than an upright human being— despite its limp weight, screams out to release. Street kids don't cry. No, it doesn't matter if you are a boy or a girl, old or young. Four months on the streets and I haven't seen a single kid cry. As if spontaneously generated, a tear grows from her unmoving eye; it grows and washes a path down her dirty face. "All I can think about all the time is . . ."

The Andean wind sends her fleece jacket floating like a cape. The bags under her eyes look as if they are about to crack open and bleed.

"What's wrong, Daniela?"

She looks around. She takes three steps away from everyone else. I follow. I whisper to her, "What's wrong?"

"Maria's dead," she says.

Maria. Who's Maria? For ten seconds I rack my brain to remember Maria. Two hundred and fifty kids I deal with. Which one is Maria? Maria, Maria, is she a girl at the orphanage? Maria is Natalia's baby sister, Daniela's youngest child. Five months old. She looked so healthy when I left. How could she die in two weeks? Was it because of the cold on the streets?

"How'd she die?" I ask.

"Maria got a lung infection while I was still at Yassela, and then I was kicked out. Then she choked on her milk," says Daniela, "and had a worse infection in her lungs."

"Wait. Start from the beginning."

"A few days after you left for your vacation, Maria started to breathe really fast. Her chest went up and down. Sometimes I felt that she could not catch her breath. It all started when she was lying in bed and I was feeding her milk. All of a sudden this gush of milk spurted out of her mouth and shot across her body. I did not think she could spit that far. After that she was never the same. I wish you were here, Chi. You could have made her better."

I want to kill myself for going to Machu Picchu. "Then what happened?" I ask.

"Well, then I remember that you said Maria was very sick last time and that she needed to go to the hospital. She looked sicker this time, so I knew she needed to see a doctor, even though I hate that place."

"Which place?"

"The hospital. I took Maria up to the floor and they told me that I needed to get her some medicine to kill her lung infection. Of course, I did not have any money."

"Did you go to Yassela?"

"Yes, Señora Lola started shouting at me and made me feel bad. I did not cry in front of her. I will never cry in front of her. She called me a bad mother. Yet she gave me money to buy the medicine that Maria needed. The doctors gave her the medicine, and she got better. I visited her every day."

"And then what?"

"And then I got kicked out of Yassela because I missed getting back at 3:30 on a Saturday afternoon. I had to go to my aunt's birthday party. You know she is very important to me. Señora Lola did not make an exception in my case."

"So where did you go?"

"Where else do I go? I went to the streets to live and sleep."

"Did you still visit Maria?"

"Yes. And then she died. She just died."

"When did she die?"

"She died on Sunday morning, 2 a.m."

"So it's been two days. Where's the baby?"

"She died in the hospital, and she's still there."

How can a baby die in two weeks in a hospital? "How come you didn't get her body?"

"They won't give me my baby until I pay all the bills."

"So where's your baby?"

"In the hospital, I suppose, in some dark room all alone. They won't even let me see her."

"Have you gone to Yassela to get some money from Señora Lola?" There has always been a silent tension between Señora Lola and Daniela. Maybe Señora Lola thought Daniela did not "rehabilitate" the right way. But people never fully heal from childhood trauma. You twirl around the life circles. On the last day of your life the wounds still hurt. Maybe Señora Lola does not like Daniela because of her strong will toward authority. That same fortitude has allowed her to care for two children on the streets, even as she herself grows up.

"I ring the doorbell and Señora Lola tells me to go away. My mother does not have any extra money either. Can you help me? There's no one else who can help me."

"I can help you. Meet me tomorrow morning at the hospital at 8:30. You should go to sleep. It's already 3:15."

"Okay," she says.

"Okay, remember, 8:30. Don't be late."

"Chi," she says, "there's something else."

"Where's Natalia?" I ask her.

"She's with my parents."

"What is it you want to tell me?"

Daniela looks back at the words. *Drugs and alcohol may kill me slowly.* . . . "Nothing," she says. "Nothing." *I'm not in any hurry,* say her eyes.

19

A Way of Life

4 a.m., November 24, 1997;
Obrajes District, Church Construction Site

She is dead now. Maria, and my sister. What did they do in their
short lives to deserve such cruelty? If anyone should die, it should
be me. I have treated people poorly at times. I have greed and
extreme anger, lust and temptation, selfishness and material desires.
And yet these two girls die. How could God let this happen?

I just spoke to Daniela. Now I am back at the half-built church
where I sleep. I am washing the excrement off of my shoes, a nightly chore. And now I hose off my body. I set my alarm for 6:30, and
I lie in bed. I close my eyes, and I see things. I don't want to bury
Maria. Someone else will have to go get her body at the hospital. Go
to sleep, Chi! It's not Christmas.

I don't want to see a dead baby. I don't want to have to pick up a
dead baby. I will do anything to avoid being in that room. But I am

Maria's only hope. Maria must have a proper burial. If she is left in the morgue, they will throw her away or incinerate her with the medical waste.

The last chapter in Maria's short life has closed. The possibly long epilogue of the story is how Daniela will live the rest of her life and how she will raise Natalia. She must move forward and become a better mother. But she can't start the epilogue until she buries and mourns Maria properly. I could not start my new life without burying my sister, without mourning the loss of her life, and without healing. Maria deserves a respectful burial. A respectful burial would be a statement to Daniela that street children are children. This statement I'll make to anyone who'll listen.

For six months before I came to La Paz, I studied hermeneutics in Boston. Hermeneutics: the theological analysis and investigation of biblical text. Sitting in the safe confines of Boston, where I was never hungry, cold, or in danger, I made a commitment to a more godly life. I was prepared to make the sacrifices and take the hardships related to humbly living such a life. Now I lie here in the dark, in a cold unfinished church, just a step or two off the La Paz streets. I've been asked to bury a baby girl. And this simple request has me scared of sleeping, nay, of dreaming.

The boys of Bururu, dressed in aprons, stir dough in large silver pots. "Why are you here at seven in the morning?" Jorge asks.

"I . . ." I hesitate, "I have to do a few things with Alejandro."

Every two or three blocks, Alejandro and I walk past a coffin store. The market for coffins is large because Bolivians die at an exceedingly high rate. The infant mortality rate is 90 per 1,000 births (nearly one out of ten); in the United States, the rate is 7.1 per 1,000 births (less than one percent). In shantytowns such as El Alto, the rate tops 200 per 1,000 (one out of five), and among the street community, babies die at a rate of 300 to 500 per 1,000, based on anecdotal evidence. In Bolivia, death is a way of life.

Alejandro and I walk in silence down the city sidewalks. I dig into my pocket and make sure I have my weekly income: five hundred bolivianos, or about one hundred dollars. I never have enough money to care for my children, so I kick myself when I spend two dollars on a café au lait. How many meals for street kids could I buy with that?

Alejandro and I step into a coffin store. Thirteen coffins stand against the walls in this nine-hundred-square-foot room. There are deep brown mahogany coffins, silver-gray metallic coffins, white wooden coffins, and coffins-in-progress. "This old woman who sells baby coffins is a Christian," Alejandro says. "She'll most likely give us a good price." I nod my approval. Saving a few dollars on a coffin means more food and medicine. "Hello?" Alejandro calls out.

A short, elderly woman dressed in a gold business suit waddles out from the back room. Her face is marked with lines of wisdom, and her deep black, dyed hair is neatly tied in a knot. She wears black shoes one size too small for her, and the dorsal parts of her feet stick out.

"Buenos días," she says.

"Buenos días," says Alejandro. "We need to purchase a coffin for a five-month-old baby. She is about this big." Alejandro holds his hands about twenty inches apart. "We don't have too much money."

The old woman squints at us. Why would two young men purchase a baby coffin at seven in the morning? She walks around her store. She picks up a fifty-inch hardwood coffin and carries it toward us.

"This is too big, madam," I say, "and it is probably too expensive."

She walks into the back room. We wait five silent minutes. The lady reenters with a small wooden hexagonal box, white and riddled with globs of dried paint. Two silver cloth flowers decorate the top of the casket. I turn the casket over and rap my knuckles against it. The wood is thin but solid.

"How much?" I ask.

"Two hundred bolivianos," says the old woman.

I give Alejandro a look.

"Madam," he says, "the coffin is for a street baby. We work on the streets at night trying to recover children and give them a place in our two orphanages just up the street. This baby girl died two days ago, and we need to bring her out of the morgue."

She looks at us with slackened, watery eyes. Her shoulders slump, and she stares at her feet sticking out of her shoes. She waddles into the back room again and brings out a cream-colored dress. Pinned to the chest are two little angel wings. Paper flowers decorate the skirt, and the hem is crimped.

"Your baby needs a funeral dress. I sell the coffin and the dress for 150 bolivianos."

"Thank you for your kindness." We walk outside and hail a taxi. The driver steps out and notices the casket. "I won't take dead bodies."

"We don't have one yet."

It's 9:30. Alejandro and I sit in the first-floor waiting room. Daniela's an hour late. I dread she might not show up. Was all her anguish just an act? How could she be so irresponsible as to not even bury her own child? Ten minutes pass, and I check my watch every thirty seconds. My heart has sunk so low, my intestines are beating. Like some character in a Kafka story, am I waiting for something impossible?

Daniela rushes through the door, out of breath and wearing the same outfit she had on last night. Beads of sweat pimple her tanned forehead. "I am so sorry that I am late. Please don't be mad at me. I woke up and started to walk to the hospital immediately."

"It's okay. You tried your best. Okay, Alejandro is going to get the paperwork, and you and I can have the doctor sign the permit to release Maria from the morgue."

Daniela takes a small step backward, and we lose eye contact.

"What's wrong, Daniela?"

She does not respond.

"Would you like me to talk to the doctor by myself?"

"Yes, if possible."

On the second level, next to a file cabinet, I study Maria's charts. Her electrolyte (sodium) levels skyrocketed over the last days of her life. Was she not drinking? Eating? Receiving any hydration?

I walk up to a nurse. "Hello, may I see Dr. Rico Velázquez?"

The nurse looks at me with mild suspicion. "I am sorry, but who are you?"

"My name is Chi, and I work with some of the children on this ward. I would like to see Dr. Velázquez."

"Okay, I will overhead page him."

A young doctor with wire-rimmed glasses and gelled-back hair enters the room. The nurse scurries over to him and points to me.

"Hello, may I help you?" he asks.

"Yes, I would like to know how Maria Moreno died."

"And who are you?"

"Does it matter who I am?"

"Yes."

"I am a medical student from the United States who took care of Maria."

"Maria died from dehydration and pneumonia."

"How does a baby die of dehydration in the hospital?"

"The baby wasn't fed for two days."

"What do you mean she wasn't fed?"

"I am sure in America it is different, but at this hospital, we cannot afford to feed the patients. It is the responsibility of the mother or the caretaker to feed the child and purchase medication. The mother never came to buy intravenous fluids or feed her baby."

"And so you let her die."

"Listen, we tried to enroll Daniela in an alcohol rehabilitation program. She never showed up to the meeting, nor did she attend to her baby. For a couple of days, another Aymaran mother breast-fed this baby out of pity. But when the mother took her baby out of the hospital, Maria remained, and Daniela never came to feed her. She let her own baby die, not us."

"I did not know that Daniela had an alcohol problem. Regardless, you are a doctor, and this is a hospital. You let a baby die in a hospital."

"Maria was a street baby. She would have grown up to be a little criminal anyway."

"So this is your way of justice. Exterminate the homeless. What if someone let you die?"

"I don't need to hear this." The doctor turns to leave.

I follow him. "If I ever hear that you allowed this to happen again, I will try my best to make sure that you never practice medicine in Bolivia again." I stop in my tracks, as he walks on. "Besides, you'd be a better mortician than a doctor." With my face red and sweaty, I hand the nurse a hundred bolivianos for the medications and IVs used on Maria.

I head down the stairs to see Daniela. What will I say to her? She helped kill Maria. Do I confront her with her failure as a mother? She already knows. The street children know the difference between wrong and right. They love their children and their street families. Daniela spent days walking already, numb and self-destructive. The Lolas of the world will ingrain her failure further into the lining of her soul.

I am Daniela's advocate. No one besides Pedro encourages her. With street children, there are times to be strong, and there are times to be kind and gentle. This is a time to be caring. Daniela knows more than anyone else her wrongdoing; she has lost her daughter as a result. What she needs, like other street children, is the social tools to prevent tragedy from recurring. Hopefully, I can help her find a new way of living.

As Daniela and I stand quietly in the hospital lobby, I act as if I haven't learned anything about her role in the death of her daughter. Daniela says nothing. She examines a scar on her hand for a long time.

We get more stamps. We pay more fees.

Finally, the social worker in the basement asks for us to pay a morgue fee: one hundred bolivianos. I reach into my pocket. Nothing. All we need is a lousy twenty bucks, and we don't have it.

I ring the doorbell to an upstairs apartment attached to La Iglesia de Dios. Laura opens the gate and, without asking any questions, says, "I don't have much, but you can have all that I have." She examines my face. "It was Maria, wasn't it?"

"Yes," I say.

"How did she die?" she asks.

"Daniela let her starve in the hospital; the doctors did too; the father wasn't there; society and the government let Maria live on the street; the orphanage kicked her out; and I left on vacation. It took a village to kill Maria."

We watch Mount Illimani, allowing silence to supersede words. I want to scream out at the mountain: Why? But the only answer I'd get is the echo, Why?

"I'm sorry, Chi, about little Maria," she says. "How's Daniela?"

"Keeping it inside. She doesn't ever say anything about Maria. When I ask her if she's okay, she always says she's fine."

"Come on in," she says. "I have another visitor—Señora Nuñez."

"So what are you doing here?" Señora Nuñez asks me.

"I came to borrow some money from Laura to get a baby out of the morgue."

"Oh, that is so sad. Whose baby is it?"

"A girl I have known for the past four months."

"Is she from church?"

"No, she's from the streets."

"From the streets." Her maternal facade melts away like wax, revealing a cosmetics-caked volcano. "Let the baby die!" she demands. "They are just street children. They're drug addicts and thieves! Let them rot! Don't waste your money. They are not worth anything."

Daniela, Alejandro, and I have been waiting for an hour now in the hallway of the morgue. We know which room we need to get into by the smell emanating from the gap beneath the door. A large-set janitor walks up to us and asks us for our papers. He glances at the rainbow of stamps and unlocks the door. The smell of formaldehyde and rotting flesh eats at our nostril linings. Alejandro picks up the casket.

"I can't go in there," says Daniela. "Can you take care of Maria for me?"

"Sure."

Alejandro and I walk in and shut the heavy door behind us. A humid breeze blows across my face. The window is open, but the view is striped by four rusted bars. The walls are tiled by light brown ceramic squares. Atop a lonely steel surgical table sits a small package wrapped in cream-colored cloth.

Alejandro pulls on the casket's lid, but it doesn't budge. He doesn't notice the painted white nail heads along the coffin's edge. I take the coffin from him and try to pry the nails loose with my

Swiss army knife. My hand trembles. Pain blazes, and I watch blood drip from my right index finger. Alejandro takes the knife from me and opens the casket. The tiny space within it is barely enough to bury my arm.

I open up a fresh pair of gloves. The snap of latex on my skin echoes off the walls. With my bloodied index finger and thumb, I slowly peel the cream-colored cloth off the small package. A grayish blue doll lies supine before me. Maria. Her glassy, glazed eyes look straight into mine. Two big green-black flies buzz out of her nostrils. My heart races. I try to catch my breath and breathe slower at the same time. Calm down! Three thin red scratches mark her left cheek. Her front incisors clamp down on a wad of cotton. I try to open her mouth to take it out, but her jaw is locked. Suddenly I feel as if I am watching myself from the ceiling. I see myself running away, but I can't. My legs can't move. Mouse or lizard fecal matter sticks to her skin. I brush it off of her. My nostrils flare and my stomach turns. Her face is turned stiffly toward me. Those black, beautiful olive eyes of Maria . . . Mingfang? I slip my hand under her. Her back is icy rubber; her hands are cold as mountain stones. I rush Maria into the coffin. Alejandro nails the lid down.

20

The Wake

4 p.m., November 24, 1997;
Yassela

Señora Lola barks in Daniela's face. "This is all your fault. You killed your baby! The only reason I am letting you have the wake at the orphanage is because of Chi. And because Maria is a baby angel. She was too young to be impure."

Daniela is just standing there without expression as Señora Lola continues her tirade. Daniela shows no anger. No sadness. Señora Lola is talking to a brick wall. Daniela does not want to fight. She just wants to hold the wake for her baby.

Minutes later, Señora Lola finishes, "I never want to see you again! This is the last time, Daniela!" Señora Lola takes a breath and turns to me. "How much did you spend on this girl? I hope not too much!"

Señora Lola and I walk to a corner. "Daniela's drinking again," she whispers to me. "She can't stop it. So irresponsible. I knew that she couldn't make it. How disappointing. She killed her baby because she is still a child."

"Señora Lola," I say in a soothing voice, "I'll take care of everything from here. Just give me a room for the wake."

"You can have the room on the roof."

Up on the roof, the sky above is blue, and the tile floor beneath is magenta with white speckles. From the edge of the roof, I study the huge "Disfruta Coca-Cola" sign to the north and the blue neon beer billboard next to it. Down on the street, little white taxis bob and weave through traffic, past a 1960s Tortoise bus. Colorful bundles of babies bounce up and down as their mothers piggyback them zigzag across parallel lines of moving metal. Mothers and fathers here work eighty to one hundred hours each week so their families can build a red mud-brick shack in El Alto.

I step along a small plot of rich brown dirt on the roof. Plants and vegetables sprout from the soil, their leaves still too young to be differentiated from each other by species. In one corner of the roof is the room for the wake. Its old door, warped by rain, can never close. The room is six feet by six feet, with a view of the city through a broken window. Serrated chunks of glass litter the stained green carpet, inviting soles to open up. An uneven wooden table holds up a black-and-white television.

Sara pokes her little brown nose into the wake room. With my torso, I block her view of Maria. "Chi, Chi," she says, "here are the bedsheets you asked for. Can I come in, Chi?"

"No, Sara. That's not a good idea."

"Why not, Chi?"

"Sara, I have to do a few things today that are not good for you to see."

"What happened, Chi?" asks Sara. "Did Maria die? Poor little baby."

"Yes, Maria died."

"Why?"

"These things sometimes happen. I don't want you in here because I have to wash her and dress her in new clothes."

"But, Chi . . ."

"You will get nightmares."

"Okay," says Sara. I look at Sara in her dirtied pink dress. Sadness swells in my chest. Sara unpokes herself from the room.

I retrieve some towels and a basin of soapy warm water. Daniela sits on the steps near the exit, quietly explaining what is happening to one of the older girls. I find a few rusted tacks on the floor and pin the bedsheet over the window.

I look at Maria once again. The three distinct red scratches on her left cheek are the only color on her pasty face. My chest tightens. With her lungs full of fluid from the infection, did she flail about as she gasped for air? Did she scratch herself in a final attempt to let air into her lungs?

I dip the towel in the water. Twist. Twist. Water trickles into the basin. I wipe Maria's face, hoping it will bring back some color. It doesn't. Maybe the angel dress will make her look more alive.

Alejandro whispers to me, "What are we going to do with these red marks, Chi? Daniela will be quite upset if she sees this."

"Do we have makeup of this color?" I ask.

"I don't think any of the girls have white makeup."

We maneuver the funeral dress over Maria's stiff arms. Two semitransparent paper wings extend from her chest. I tug the wings upward but cannot make them cover the scratches. I hear voices. Startled, I turn around. Five little faces peep through the curtains in the front window. I throw open the door, slamming it into the wall. "How many times do I have to tell you to go downstairs?"

The little girls fly down the stairs. They have never seen me angry before. Shock paralyzes Alejandro. I offer him no explanations.

I watch night fall. The cloudless sky fades away, from brilliant red to pink to dark purple. Blink, blink, blink go the neon lights of Plaza San Francisco. Downstairs, the girls clink and clank plates, clang and bang pots as they prepare dinner.

With night comes the Andean wind. At eleven thousand feet, heat dissipates rapidly, and wind kicks up in a hurry and gets into everything. The wind whistles in through the broken window before me and tickles the candle fires that glow softly on the closed coffin, within which lies Maria, cloth flowers tied to her collar to hide her death scars. Daniela, who has been waiting for four hours, walks cautiously into the room, taking in every detail, her mouth agape. She has never seen this room so clean, and rarely has anyone prettied anything up for her.

"Do you want to see Maria?" I ask Daniela.

She nods apprehensively. She shuffles to the rigged-up table. I lift the lid of the casket. She lets out a gasp and jerks her head downward. Her body shakes as she weeps. Her sobs fill the room quicker than the wind ever could.

A knock on the door. Three of the older Yassela girls approach the casket. These girls fed and changed Maria when Daniela was busy or away. I lift the coffin lid. One girl manages, "Pobresita, pobresita," before they sit down with Daniela.

Minutes later, the Yassela social worker crosses herself and walks

with a respectful slowness toward the coffin. I remove the coffin lid.
Her brows curl inward. She steps backward, step by step, into the
doorway, crosses herself again, and leaves without having spoken a
single word.

Silence. Brutal quietness.

Another knock. I open the door and see a young man. He is short
and thin, yet strong looking. He wears a striped shirt and cheap
dress slacks. "I am Maria's father."

He walks up to the casket, and I take off the lid. He looks at his
daughter. His right hand goes to his face. His eyes narrow. His fingers tighten over his face. He looks up toward heaven with his hand
over his mouth, as if keeping himself from speaking. He looks back
down, between the candles, at a photograph: Maria is being blessed
by a priest as Daniela and Pedro watch with young smiling faces.

Where were you, Pedro, when your baby was at the hospital?
Where were you when your baby was dying and gasping for her
last breath? Are you a man or a child? You are both, more child
than man.

Pedro sits down next to Daniela.

"Did you call my parents?" Daniela asks.

"Yes," I answer.

"Are they coming?"

"They didn't say."

Silence. We sit and ponder for another hour or two. Some time
after midnight, I say a prayer for Maria Moreno. I ask God to protect her soul and to lend us strength and wisdom to honor Him with
our lives.

Daniela looks up from her bowed head. "Thank you for the prayer,
Don Chi."

"You are welcome," I say. "I know what you are going through."

"How do you know?" she asks.

I had not meant to bring it up, but perhaps some part of me wants
to talk about it. "My sister died," I state concisely.

A quizzical look flashes across her face. "She did?"

"Yes."

"How?" It seems by Daniela's questions that she believes no one dies in the United States, that it is an Eden of sorts.

I sit down next to Daniela. "A virus killed her on Christmas morning. For most people, this type of virus causes the common cold, but we learned from the autopsy that this virus attacked her heart and killed her. I had a very difficult time for the first two years after she died. I missed her nearly every day. An emptiness lay inside of me and nothing could fill it up. Not work. Not family. Not entertainment. Not even God."

"What did you do?"

"I worked hard to forget the past. To put it away in a dark corner of an attic."

"Did it work?" she asks, perhaps considering this route.

"No," I tell her. "It never does."

"So what did you do?"

"I prayed and got help with my sadness."

"And . . ."

"And even though the pain and emptiness never fully disappear, the nightmares eventually stopped. I finished living the past in order to walk into the future. You need to do the same thing. Let's make this a proper wake and burial. Find friends or even me to talk with. Mourn together. Mourn alone. But you must mourn. And then you must focus on the future. The future is Natalia. The way you can redeem yourself is to make sure Natalia grows up to be an adult."

"Yes, Don Chi." Daniela nods.

The rest of the night is a long, slow hypnotism by flickering candlelight. The dark yellow flames dance in all directions. We wait for Daniela's parents, but they do not come. For most of the world, Maria is just a street baby, a small part of one statistic that shows up on a World Health Organization chart in Geneva. We doze off here and there. The candle flames finish their dance together, still far apart, and the light goes out.

The next day, a dozen street boys carrying plastic cartons full of water stand around the front entrance of the cemetery. As an elderly woman approaches the entrance, one of the boys escorts her, saying, "Señora, would you like me to water the flowers at your husband's grave? I am sure they would look a great deal better next week when you come see him."

"I am sorry," says the old woman, "but I promised another boy that he could water the flowers for my husband."

"Please, Señora."

"I am sorry, my child." She pats him on the back and moves on. These are the cemetery kids—street children who live among the dead. Eerie. They sleep in unoccupied graves, and they rest in peace. Neither the dead nor the living bother them here. Are they preparing for their own early exit? They sleep two to three in a grave, to keep warm.

A man sits at a table, an accounting notebook and bureaucratic forms strewn before him. "Good morning, sir," I say to him.

"Good morning."

"The mother of this baby wants her to be blessed before she is buried."

The man looks at Daniela and Pedro. He can tell they live on the street. "It will be ten bolivianos for the blessing." He looks at his ledger sheet filled with numbers and figures and furiously pencils in debits and credits.

"What do you mean ten bolivianos?" I ask.

"Ten bolivianos for the blessing. This is what we charge."

"Since when do we sell God?" I ask.

"The priest needs to feed himself, you know. He is supported by offerings."

Alejandro nudges me gently, to no avail. I say as calmly as I can, "These street children have no home, no family, and no money. I can't believe you have the audacity to ask for money from these youths. If the priest wants to charge, then I want to talk to the priest."

"You can't see him right now. He is doing a mass."

"Then I can wait."

"Okay, okay. You don't have to pay this time."

"Or ever."

Daniela and Pedro look at each other; as street children, they fear all authority. They are amazed that I challenged this clerk for their sakes.

Daniela and Pedro walk out of the church carrying Maria, now blessed by the priest. The caretaker leads us into the cemetery. "Maria is to be buried at site G-3."

Three orphan girls carry bright flowers as we walk past cement block after cement block. Each block, two stories high or so, contains a couple of dozen coffins. Embedded in each block is a plaque stating who is buried within. Most of these dead come from families too poor to bury them underground. The spaces are leased by the year, and if the lease is not renewed, the dead person is incinerated.

"G-3. Hmmm. G-3," mumbles the caretaker. We make a turn here, a turn there. "I'm sorry," says the caretaker, and we backtrack. "Ah, yes. Here it is." A three-story block.

Daniela and Pedro look spent but resolved. "The workers will arrive soon," says the caretaker.

We wait in the quietude between G-3 and G-4, in some windless corridor within the card catalog of the deceased. I am about to black out. Daniela looks at my weary eyes and says, "Chi, can you pray for Maria?"

Thank you, Daniela. And yet I don't feel I should be the one to pray. "Maybe Pedro or a priest would be better," I say.

"No," she says, "I want you to pray." We bow our heads and face the ground, even as the thousands of dead surrounding us face upward to the clear sky. "Heavenly Father, Lord, Holy Spirit. We are gathered here to bury Your child, Maria Moreno, who died too soon. I don't understand why she had to die, but I pray for protection for this baby and comfort for Daniela and Pedro. I trust in You. Fill us with the Holy Spirit and give us wisdom to continue on after such tragedy. In Christ. Amen."

Two elderly men in cement-stained overalls lean a ladder against block G-3. I climb the creaky ladder and look down into a hole in the roof of G-3, and I see caskets. Alejandro passes me the casket holding Maria, and Daniela watches me intently. Using pulleys, I lower the casket through a hole in the roof, down into the cement block, slowly laying the body of Maria on the cement floor. I step down, and the two old men fill in the hole with a cement slab that is broken in two. They mix cement dust with water and fill in the cracks around the slabs. G-3 is sealed.

Daniela hands me a stick. "You have the best handwriting."
I climb the ladder. I press the stick into the layer of wet cement:

Maria Moreno
Descansa en Paz

Daniela sobs.

21

Batir

Batir: to beat; to batter; to beat down.

A group of schoolchildren jostle for a soccer ball on the corner plot of Plaza San Francisco. But none of these children are from the street. No facial scars. No missing teeth. No furtive glances or meandering walks. My subcortical street child radar is completely silent. Weird.

And then I feel it. Beatriz. The young street mother rumbles toward me from Alonzo de Mendoza, where she spends her nights. Her large body jiggles like Jell-O. Beatriz rarely acknowledges my presence, except to ask for sore throat medication. I scare her away with my songs of God.

"Chi, I have been looking all over for you. You must come quick."

"Why? What's wrong?"

"It's a *batir*."

"A batir. What's a batir?"

She drags me up the street with the full two hundred pounds of her strength. At a street corner, seven child mothers, their babies in ahuayos on their backs, stand around a small child sitting on his shins, slumped over, his back forming a soft tortoiseshell and his bent elbows moving like the wings of a bird. His hands, I see now, wipe his eyes over and over again. He screeches like a cat. I run to his side. The child's name is Christopher Chávez. He is nine years old.

His younger brother Daniel runs up. "We've been looking for you. Some men gassed Christopher in the eyes. We didn't know what to do." Christopher and Daniel inhale paint thinner almost every minute of the day, which is an anomaly even for street children. Their alcoholic mother used to beat them with whips, chains, belts, and steel rods. They left their El Alto home a year ago to look for a better life on the streets.

"Who is that?" peeps Christopher.

"It's me. Chi."

"Chi, my eyes! I can't see! They burn, Chi! I can't see!" Christopher lets out a horrendous scream. It is as if he'd been waiting for someone to listen. He rolls from side to side, and I put my hand on his back to calm him down.

"What is a batir?" I demand.

"The violent men," explains Beatriz. "Every month or two, they round up a bunch of street kids to take to dark places. If we resist, they beat us and spray gasoline in our eyes." The "gasoline" Beatriz speaks of is actually a Mace-like chemical sprayed from an aerosol can. "They are 'cleaning' the streets of all undesirables, and that includes us."

"Where are they now?"

"They are gone for now, but they'll return. You'll see. Ten to fifteen men. They take us away, where no one can see, and they beat us and rape us. This is a batir."

"If they're coming back, maybe you should all leave," I suggest to the child mothers.

"We cannot leave Christopher here. He is part of our family."

I leave for Bururu orphanage and return within a few minutes with a silver kettle of water. A couple of the violent men have returned too. The street mothers argue vehemently with them. "Leave the boy alone!" Beatriz snaps. "We haven't done anything to you. We have a right to stay in this park just like anyone else."

"You can't loiter in the park!" barks the enraged man.

"What about that man drinking over there? Or that couple over there kissing? Aren't they loitering?"

"We are cleaning the streets." The man calms down. "You need to leave. We will take care of this boy."

"We are not going to leave Christopher and Daniel," shouts Beatriz. "What wrong did they do?"

"He talked back," says the man, "and he received the consequences."

I lead Christopher to a nearby bench, whereupon I guide him onto his back. I tell him to stop rubbing his eyes, and then I let the water pour. The boy closes his eyes and turns his head away. "Christopher, you need to keep your eyes open so that I can wash all the chemicals out."

"But it burns, Chi."

"I know, but I have to do this." I pour the entire kettle of water into his eyes, and he breathes easier. "Why did the men spray gas into your eyes?" I ask him.

"Because I talked bad to them," he says guiltily.

Suddenly a hush falls upon the mothers. A large, dark-skinned man walks drunkenly toward me and Christopher. His stomach pro-trudes out of his suit jacket. The street mothers rush over and stand around Christopher, ready to defend him with their own bodies. The big man walks up close to me and speaks down into my face. "You know these children?"

"Yes."

"These children should not be on the streets."

"These children have no home, sir."

"That's why there are orphanages."

"I know. I work at one. Unfortunately, some of these orphanages are as dangerous as the streets. On the streets, they don't risk living in the same building as abusive adults, and they avoid stabbings and fights within closed quarters. Better to risk the streets than to live with the guarantee of physical and sexual abuse."

"Who are you?" The large man falls to one side, then catches himself.

"My name is Chi Huang. I am a medical student, and I work with street children."

"Where are you from?"

"The United States."

"Oh, yes. The great country." He smiles. I project a calm face. He turns away. Not one of the street mothers or the children back off. A bead of sweat drops from his brow. He talks to the young mothers and girls. "The streets are no place for children, especially girls. You should come with us to a place where you will be cared for. There is even a television there for you." The girls stare blankly at him.

A van screeches to a halt twenty yards away. Ten men sitting in the van gaze at Christopher, Daniel, and the girls. The large man approaches the van, and the van door cracks open.

I whisper to the children, "Go south near the river. They never go past the downtown area. Go and sleep in the woods by the soccer fields. You will be safe there if you stay together as a group." Watching the violent gang of men carefully over the months has finally paid off; I know how they operate.

The dozens of street children begin to run and walk en masse down the street as the men step out of the van. I urge the last stragglers to hurry; some street children buy into a fatalism that tells them that since they will be killed eventually, they might as well let it happen sooner than later. Christopher and Daniel deftly weave between pedestrians, and the men only halfheartedly chase after them, knowing that the boys, who play fútbol every day, can outrun and outmaneuver them.

It is 1 a.m. now, and I walk down the street toward Plaza San Francisco. Without the street children, Plaza San Francisco is deathly peaceful. I will get an early night's sleep tonight.

A group of young men stand on a large median. They appear to be gang members who roam the city communicating with each other by their signature whistle calls. One of these young men crouches over his knees and holds his head in his hands as if his cranium might fall apart. Between his feet, a pool of bright red blood expands with each drop of blood. "Ahhh!" he yells in pain. As I approach, two grown men—who apparently beat the young gang member—glare at me.

"Hello," I peep timidly to the pained one.

"Who is that?" screeches the boy in agony.

"My name is Chi," I reply.

"Chi, thank God that you are here," he declares. "It's Pedro. Daniela's lover."

"What happened to you?"

"Those men," he whispers. "Are they still around?"

"There are two of them about ten feet away watching us."

"It's a batir, Chi," Pedro gurgles. "They beat me over the head with their clubs. Because I was drunk."

He attempts to lift up his head to give me eye contact. His neck goes into a spasm and his head jerks downward. "Because it's a batir," Pedro says, his voice clogged by agony. "It's a batir; I live on the streets."

Pedro refuses to go to the hospital, so I examine him on the street. I palpate his head to determine if any portions of his skull have detached. He sees clearly and responds appropriately. Despite his yelps of pain, it appears that he suffered no severe neurological damage. But his intracranial bleeding could quickly intensify and kill him. I clean his head with water, peroxide, and antibiotic cream. I implore him to go to the hospital. He refuses again.

Demonstrations of open defiance, however slight, are some of the only ways street children can express their dignity and power. They refuse to let go of their defiance; it is one of the few remaining aspects of their lives that is both human and completely under their own control. They are shouting fervently to society, "I am not a dog that you can abuse at your whim. I am a person."

"Hey, Chi," says Pedro as I walk off.

"Yes?" I turn around.

"Thank you." He twists his head in an uncomfortable angle to give me eye contact for the first time. Despite the heavy bleeding, I am confident that Pedro will survive this beating and those to come. I hope that I am right.

"You're welcome, Pedro. You're welcome." I walk a few steps, turn around, and add, "Please make sure Daniela watches you carefully tonight. I'll see you tomorrow."

Several days later, I walk around Plaza San Francisco, and in one corner of the plaza, I spot Pedro and Daniela sitting among a group of older drunk men. Why am I not surprised that Pedro seems to be nursing a severely bruised right leg?

"What happened to your leg?" I ask him.

"Violence," he states—the one-word answer to a variety of questions. "They wanted my money."

"Did you give it to them?"

"I told them to f— off."

"That was really smart. What did they do after that?"

"They pounded my leg and took my money." He looks down at his leg, remembering the beating.

"Pedro," I say, restraining my exasperation, "do you enjoy bringing violence upon yourself?"

"No," he says. "But they can't break me. They may see me as a worthless street boy, but I am worthy of respect. I have pride."

"Yes, I agree that you are worthy," I say, "but now you are *crippled* and worthy."

His drunken friends laugh without reservation. "Yes, we have our crippled Pedro, but he's a man! Hear him roar!"

"He's stupid," Daniela retorts. "Ever since he got his head beaten, he has lost a few of his marbles."

"And he only started with a few to begin with!" a drunk man chimes in. "Baahh! Baahhaaaa! Baaahhaaa!" the men laugh.

"I am a man with rights," Pedro contests. "You may laugh, but I know that I am right. They can beat me all they want, but I will not be broken!" He sticks out his chest as much as he can without moving his outstretched leg.

"Okay, Che Guevara, I respect you. The only thing that is broken is your leg."

"It is?!"

"Yes. How did you not know?"

"Oh, Dr. Chi. The beauty of alcohol. You drink until you can't feel!"

"You need to go to the hospital."

"No. No hospital. I don't go to hospitals."

"You need to go to the hospital," Daniela says flatly.

"No." He lashes out with his arms. "You can take care of me, Dr. Chi."

"No, I can't. You will need a cast. I can't do that here."

"Do whatever you can."

"The two of you make my job so difficult sometimes. Okay"—I point at three of the drunkards—"Larry, Curly, and Moe in the peanut gallery, find me some cardboard boxes."

"Yes sir, boss. We are on our way, boss." Ten minutes later the young men bring back several boxes. I pull the cardboard apart and fold the sides longitudinally to form hard planks. I show Pedro the splint. "You see how hard this is? Try to break it with your hand."

Pedro attempts to punch through the accordion cardboard splint. "Oww!"

"I guess your drinking doesn't take away all the pain."

I wrap the splint around each side of his leg and tape the leg to the splint tightly, using four feet of surgical tape.

"Hey," says Pedro, finally realizing this: "I can't move my leg."

"That's the idea."

"Oh. Okay." Pedro smiles. "Thanks!"

"And the next time you run into trouble"—I stand up and wipe my hands—"will you please call me first?"

Over the next ten days, Pedro lies on the pavement of Plaza San Francisco as Daniela brings him food and medicine for his pain. She takes care of him through the day and the night. During this time he makes several attempts to walk around, but she forces him to rest his leg. This is not the best beginning to the epilogue to Maria's life, but I can tell Daniela now considers her actions seriously before she acts. She conscientiously cares for Pedro. She leaves Natalia with Grandmother, who treats Natalia better than she ever treated Daniela.

On the streets, the struggle of life versus death is paralleled by the struggle of the desire to live against the desire to die. The death of Maria could have killed Daniela. But Maria's death, and the way we all handled it, has only strengthened Daniela's love of life—and the living.

22

Merry Christmas

11 p.m., December 23, 1997;
Plaza San Francisco

Ragged Christmas gift wrap skirts across the plaza like red and green rats. Stalls line the plaza, with vendors selling Nativity scenes and steroid-pumped action figures. 'Tis the season to celebrate the birth of baby Jesus by selling Christmas trinkets in order to survive, commercializing Jesus so that food can be placed on the table. Is that so wrong? Give me the bowl instead of the soul, no?

"Joven. Joven." A cholita waves at me. "Come here. Do you want a three-gallon water gun that can shoot thirty yards? Guaranteed! You look like a good, caring father wanting to buy a gift for your son."

"I'm sorry, but I am not married and I do not have children."

A mustached man bellows over to me, "How about this Nativity scene with a beautiful baby Jesus and real hay? You seem like a devout Christian."

"No, thank you."

I turn away and make eye contact with a large young woman walking carefully down the steps, one step at a time. She carries a plastic meshed bag across her right forearm, and a checkerboard apron accentuates her pear-shaped figure. I have not seen her face in nearly one month. She has aged a couple of years since that time. It is Daniela.

"Hello, Daniela," I say to her.

"Hello," she responds in a despondent voice.

We have developed a special bond since Maria died. She can now show emotion around me.

"What are you doing these days?" I ask her, nodding at her plastic bag.

"Selling Christmas cards," she says.

"Can I see them?"

"Sure." She hands me three cards. "You see the nice quality of the paper? On the front is the baby Jesus lying in the manger with a star hanging up high in the sky."

"You are a good salesperson, aren't you?"

"It is all about the presentation," she informs me.

"How's business?" I ask.

"Terrible." The despondent voice comes back.

"Why?"

"Competition is fierce this season. The other vendors have nicer cards and sell them for a cheaper price."

"Are you making enough money to survive?"

"You know. You make do. I still have enough money to feed myself and Natalia."

"Hmmm," I ponder.

"How can I compete?" she asks me.

The obvious answer is to get better cards and put some of the other street children out of business. Maybe then you will make two dollars a day, Daniela.

"I purchase them in bulk from vendors uptown," she tells me. "I wish I could get a better price, but times are tough right now."

"How did you come up with the idea of selling Christmas cards?"

"I don't know. It just seemed like a good idea. More profits than selling gum or juice. There are so many shoe shiners that it is hard to earn a living in that business. Not many people were selling Christmas cards three weeks ago. But now everyone is."

"What are you going to do after Christmas?"

"I don't know." She purses her lips. "Find something else to sell, I guess."

"Where are you living now?"

"On the streets," says Daniela. "But Natalia is staying with my mother. I am not welcome in the home. Besides, we fight too much." Silence. "I left Pedro," she says, watching a stylish young woman walk past. "I left him because he is an alcoholic. I left him last month. I miss him though." She looks down at the empty space within her palms as if she had dropped something.

"How did the two of you do after Maria died?"

"We were sad, both of us. Sort of lost and unable to move past her death."

"Did it affect your relationship?"

"I don't really know. . . . It doesn't really matter now. Does it?"

"Are you still drinking?" I ask her.

"I'm cutting down," she says.

"So you are all alone now on the streets? Isn't it dangerous for you?"

She smirks a shaky smirk. "Don't worry, Chi. I am an old woman for the streets. I know it too well. I can protect myself easily."

Silence.

"Daniela, I want people around the world to know your story. I want you to tell them who you are."

"Why do you want my story? Mine is not a good story."

"We want to hear your story because you are important."

"I am important?" She laughs, her hand on her chest. She doesn't want to believe it. She cannot believe it. Street children are never asked for anything but their money and their sex.

"Yes, you are important."

She brings three more cards out of her plastic bag. "Buy my cards, Don Chi."

"Sure, I will buy your cards."

"Why do you want to know about my story?"

"Because I want to learn from you," I tell her. "You need to teach me."

"Okay, but will you buy my cards?" she asks, making sure.

"Daniela, I will buy your cards regardless," I tell her.

Silence.

"Okay, what do you want to know?" she asks.

"Tell me about your home," I say, pressing the record button on my tape recorder, "and why you decided to leave."

Daniela settles her body, as if doing so might snuggle her mind backward into the past. "I have been a street girl for the last six years. I used to live with my grandmother, but she died. My mother drank quite a bit and would beat me. She would hit me all over my body with cables, *chicotes* (whips), knives, fists, and sticks. The only time I was a happy child was when I left home. I went to live with my grandmother when I was ten years old. I was so happy because she understood me and did not abuse me. Then she just died on me. I know it sounds selfish."

"Where is your father?" I ask.

"I never knew him," she says.

"Do you have brothers and sisters?"

"I had an older sister, but she died two years ago."

"How did she die?" I ask.

"She was in prison and got very sick," Daniela laments. "I have a younger sister. She is the same as myself. She went to the streets because of physical abuse from my mother. She lives in an orphanage right now. I think that she is doing well."

"Do you see her much?"

"Every once in a while."

"What happened after your grandmother died?" I ask her.

"I left home six years ago and went to the streets. I met this lady, Valeria." Daniela looks up, as if the name itself uplifted her. "She told me that the streets are dangerous, and she allowed me to live with her. But Valeria eventually had cancer and took too many pills. I was so happy when I was living there, but then she died."

"What is it like being a street girl?"

"Life on the streets is bad," says Daniela, her mouth twisting. "We, as street children, have been abused throughout our entire lives. But people never listen to us. People just look at us and see dirty kids; they treat us poorly. I admit that street children use drugs and steal sometimes. But people don't understand our situation on the streets. They don't realize the problems. It is not necessarily the problems on the streets that make us do bad things. Oftentimes, it is our families; we have bad parents. But people don't *listen*. They never *listen*."

"What do you want for yourself?" I ask her.

"My dream is to leave the streets," she says. "I want to move forward in my life. I want to sell things. My girlfriends changed their lives, and so can I. I took a wrong turn and went down the wrong path. I want to change because of my little girl, Natalia. I want to go to a program where they can give me money so that I can sell material—to allow me to help my baby. Everything is in God's hands."

In God's hands. Trite. Concise. Do I believe it? At times my belief in God is so weak that it frightens me. After months of walking the streets and knowing that the hungry mouth today will remain hungry tomorrow, I wonder. "Do you believe in God?" I ask Daniela.

"Yes."

"Why do you believe there is a God?" I find it strange that a girl who lives in hell on Earth believes there is a God in heaven.

She looks at me quizzically. "Of course there is a God, Don Chi. Don't you believe in God?"

"Yes," I say. "Of course I do." I take a deep breath. "Tell me about Maria," I say.

"Maria died because she was sick," Daniela states. "We went to the hospital, but she died anyway. I miss her so much." Daniela cries. "When I got kicked out of Yassela, she was well. We went to live on the streets, and she got sick. She got sicker and sicker on the streets, so I took her to the hospital. She was ill for nearly one month. And then one night she just died." Daniela lets out a sob. "I just walked and walked the streets that night. I was looking for help because I did not have any money. I found men and women who were kind, but they had other responsibilities. . . ." Daniela gathers herself. "Then I found you. We spent all day in the hospital trying to get my baby out of the morgue. We had a wake, and then we buried her. I miss her so much. Natalia is all alone now with no one to play with. I never want Natalia to live on the streets."

"What do you want for Natalia?" I ask her, not skipping a beat.

"I don't want her to be mistreated like I was when I was a child," Daniela says, her voice strong again. "I want everything good for her. I want her to work and study. I don't want her to turn out like me."

"What would you say to the president of Bolivia?" I ask Daniela.

"The children of Bolivia are the most important people because we are the future. When you have more street children, Bolivia will fall. Build more schools. Protect us from violence."

"How can I help the street children?"

"Build a home for us, Don Chi. We need a home where they understand us. Please don't misunderstand me. Most of the people in the homes do not treat us poorly. Overall, they treat us quite well. There are counselors who understand us. But there are other counselors who treat us poorly and cause us to return to the streets. Build a home for us, Don Chi."

Build a home? Is she crazy? How am I going to build a home for the children? I don't even have a job. I don't have any money. I can't speak the language fluently.

"Daniela, there are plenty of homes in La Paz that you can go to."

"Yes, I want to live in the home that you build."

"Why? What is so special about the home that I build?"

"You. You understand us."

"You know I am pretty strict on the children, and some people say that I am hard on you guys."

"I know, but that is okay because you want what is best for us. The kids listen to you."

A home? It is an impossible dream. Who is going to take care of the children when I am gone? Who is going to put food in their mouths?

"Do you want to buy some Christmas cards now?"

"How much are they?"

"One boliviano for every card, and six bolivianos per pack. There are ten different cards per packet. Each card celebrates baby Jesus." Daniela searches through the motley assortment of cards. She picks out a packet that is not bent on the edges and has the clear wrapping still intact. "They are beautiful," she assures me.

"I will send them to my friends at Park Street Church in Boston," I tell Daniela. "They will receive them just in time for Easter."

"Why don't you buy two packets?" she suggests. "I am sure that you have lots of friends." She gives me a smirk and a wink.

"Sure." I take an extra packet. She really is a good salesperson.

"Thank you, Don Chi," she says to me. "Are you going to celebrate Christmas?"

"Yes," I tell her.

"How? Are you going to have a big feast and sing songs?"

"No," I say.

"What do you do for Christmas?"

"I go and pray," I say. "I think about Christ, birth and death, and other things."

Daniela looks at me and with great care asks, "You think about your sister, don't you?"

"How do you know about my sister?"

"You told me about her during the wake. Remember?"

"Oh, yes." I don't usually tell strangers that story. But Daniela is a stranger no longer. I am glad that she remembers my story. The night is silent. People walk by quietly, and the Christmas vendors pack up for home. "Yes," I say. "Christmas is a hard day for me."

"Yes, it's hard," she admits.

"Take care of Natalia, okay?" I stand up to leave. I have more work to do. "You are doing much better than one month ago."

She looks into her bag and heaves a heavy sigh as she counts dozens of Christmas cards. "Thanks. I have to go sell the rest of these cards. Merry Christmas, Don Chi."

Daniela walks slowly down the stairs into the darkness. I was probably her last sale for tonight. She is caught in a system of economic Darwinism. The unskilled, the homeless, the inefficient are thrown into a pool of poverty and forced to compete against each other for a tiny pile of bolivianos. Many of these competitors die, others are imprisoned, and some fit into the mainstream economy as low-skilled, low-paid workers. Through this system, society rids itself of its less productive members for the relatively cheap price of prisons and incinerators.

I cannot change Bolivia's economic system. I am not even Bolivian. Instead, Daniela has made a simpler request. She wants me to build a home for street children. One where people will understand street children. One where people will be patient with them. One where people will teach them skills so that they may compete in more lucrative markets than shining shoes or selling gum or begging. One where people will appreciate them even after they grow out of their cute "Little Orphan Annie" stages. One where people will give wings to their better angels.

But how can I do it? I need money. I need people to volunteer their money and their time and even their hearts. I need life efforts. Everything, like you said, Daniela, is in God's hands.

23

Vicki

January 7, 1998;
Alonzo de Mendoza

What happens to street children when they grow up? Obviously some of them do not grow up. Some die on the street, their spirits going, we hope, to a better place. Some of them survive. Which is better, dying or living? An argument can be made for either side.

Little is known about what happens when street children grow up. Researchers do not follow individual street children over the years of their lives. Researchers take collective "snapshots" of the population of street children. They interview them about their pasts sometimes. They watch them over a period of a few days, a few months even. But the world really does not want to know how many of them are killed by the elements, by disease, by other street people, by adult perpetrators; how many commit suicide; how many become street adults; how few survive and find a home and a sustainable role in the world.

I stand in the middle of Alonzo de Mendoza. Over the months,
I have come to think of these children as "my" children; will I watch
over the years as my children grow into adults? Will they survive
that long? Will they still retain their humanity while crawling
through the concrete gauntlet? Alejandro taps me on the shoulder.
"Do you see those men over there?" Alejandro points to the far end
of the park. "They used to live at Bururu. Many years ago."

"What happened to them?"

"They prefer the 'freedom' of the streets," Alejandro says, sup-
pressing his own disdain. From my own research, I estimate that
about 10 percent of street people in La Paz are adults. And most of
them are alcoholics. I approach the twentysomething young men
and introduce myself. After hearing that I am the Bururu "doctor,"
one of the men says to me, "I used to live in Bururu. How is Señora
Lydia?"

"She is doing well," I say. "Why did you leave Bururu?"

"I left eight years ago," he says. "I lived at Bururu for a few
years, but I had to leave when I turned eighteen because I wasn't
an orphan child anymore. I was an adult. I live on the streets now."
Daniela's plea for a more understanding orphanage echoes in my
mind.

The clock strikes eleven. A teenage girl approaches me. I recognize her but can't remember her name. She shows me a five-day-old
cut on her left arm. "How did you get wounded?"

She looks down and to the left. "I cut myself by accident." I estimate
twenty older razor blade cuts on each arm. No one is that clumsy. Five
children have crowded around us. We walk away. The crowd follows.
"You are going to have to wait at the other end of the park," I tell the
bunch, and they grumpily oblige.

"What happened?" I ask.

She continues to look down and whispers, "My boyfriend got mad
at me."

"Why?"

She looks away and acts as if she doesn't hear me.

"Why?" I repeat.

"Because he wanted me, and I refused."

"What happened after that?"

"He took out a razor blade and tried to cut my face."

"And?"

"And I shielded my face with my left arm." We sit down on the concrete, and she shows me her arm. I push down on her six-centimeter cut, and thick white pus spurts out. She winces and jerks her head away. I thoroughly wash her wound with sterile water and swab on topical antibiotics. I hand her antibiotic pills with the hopes that she will be compliant.

Directly Observed Therapy—watching patients to make sure they take their medication—has been proved to work well with tuberculosis and HIV patients. Direct observation is a little more difficult when your patients can't be found. Street children. Visible one moment. Invisible the next. Dead. Sleeping. Looking for food. In an orphanage. Who really knows? Who really cares? I sit down on a bench among four street boys.

From the corner of my eye I notice a thirteen- or fourteen-year-old girl I've never seen. She is unusually slim. Her elliptical face—not round like the others—is clear of scars and bruises. Her neatly combed curly hair lies black and shiny upon her shoulders. She sports eyeliner and red lipstick, and she has donned a black leather jacket to match her black boots. A black scarf, fashionable among the wealthy high school girls, warms her neck.

Perhaps she has just recently come to the streets; no girl sleeping on the streets can maintain such a look for long. And yet she seems to be friends with all the street children; in fact, she is a social butterfly, moving from one group of children to another, laughing, flirting, and gracefully bowing out. She approaches.

"Dr. Chi," she says, "I have this terrible pain in my stomach."

I guess they all know my name now. "What's your name?" I ask her.

"Vicki," she tells me.

"Vicki, I need to ask you a few questions first," I say. "I'm collecting information on the street children in La Paz. Would you like to participate in my survey?"

"Sure. Sounds like fun."

"How old are you?"

"Thirteen. Almost fourteen," she states, arms akimbo.

"How long have you been on the streets?"

"Seven years," she says, standing squarely before me.

"Why did you leave your house?"

Vicki crosses her arms, looks down. "Because my parents were alcoholics."

"Where do you sleep?"

"Eturades neighborhood. Northeast."

"Do you take drugs?"

"Yes. Paint thinner, glue adhesive, and alcohol."

"Anything else?"

"Marijuana and crystals."

"Have you ever had sex?"

"Yes." She nods.

"Have you ever been raped?"

Looking down with uneasiness she replies, "Yes."

"By whom?"

She points at the bench I had been sitting on some twenty yards away. The same four boys sit there as before.

"Which one of them?" I ask.

"All four of them," she says, her voice unwavering. "A few days ago."

The only words I can muster are, "I'm sorry." What else can I say? Does she need someone to listen to her? Does she need a counselor? Does she want me to exact justice? Cowardly, I say nothing else. She waits for me to change the subject. "So, tell me about your stomach pain," I say.

"It has been hurting over the past three days."

"When was your last period?"

"A week ago."

"Do you have diarrhea?"

"No."

"Does it hurt when you urinate?"

"Yes."

"Do you have frequent urination?"

"Yes."

I open up my medicine box and hand her pills for her urinary tract infection. "So," I say, "what do you do for money?"

She looks at me as if I were cracking a joke at her expense. "I sell my body," she explains.

I'm shocked. I shouldn't be, but I am. She's a child. I maintain my cool. "How long have you been doing this?"

"One year," she states as a matter of fact.

"How much do you make each time?"

"Six bolivianos." One dollar. If I practice medicine in the United States, I will make in a matter of seconds what she earns surrendering her body to a stranger. The value of innocence? Inexpressible. The price of it? On a street in the developing world? One dollar.

Vicki changes the subject, going on about whatever comes to mind. I hear spunk in her voice. Confidence. Irrepressibility. She moves from one subject to the next, not out of anxiety but simply to move on. She walks over to a group of street mothers and asks them about their children; she strolls over to the boys. The way she stands, horses around with the boys as if she were one—she's tough. Her square shoulders shout it: Get off me, world, I'm a salvageable one. Salvageable.

She walks to the bench of boys who raped her. She sits among them. She chatters with them for a spell, and then they all inhale together, drifting off to sweet oblivion.

24

Not All of Us Children

1 a.m., January 15, 1998;
Alonzo de Mendoza

I find Vicki sitting on her own on a bench in Alonzo de Mendoza park. In one hand she clutches her thinner-soaked yarn, and in the other she holds what looks like a beef sandwich. "Dr. Chi," she says to me, "what are you doing here tonight?"

I'm not sure I understand the question, since I am here most nights. "I came to see you," I say. "How are you? Have you been taking the medicine? Is it getting better?"

"Yes," she says. "It doesn't hurt like crazy anymore. Are you hungry?" Vicki offers me some of her sandwich.

"No, thanks," I say. I sit down on the cold concrete bench next to her. She's wearing another relatively fancy outfit, and I can smell perfume blasting past my face as an Andean gust blows her black scarf at me. "I also wanted to make sure that you were okay, you know, because you were attacked by those four boys."

"If I was okay?" she asks. She looks at me for some clarification, but the subject is awkward for me, too. "Yes, I am okay," she says. "It's over now. It was horrible when they raped me, but it's finished now. We are getting along again."

"Getting along?" I ask. "How can you get along with them? I mean, because of what they did to you."

"Dr. Chi." She puts down her sandwich and takes a deep breath of thinner. "Look around you here. This is Alonzo de Mendoza."

I look around. Street mothers stand around talking about their kids. Street girls inhale thinner together and speak gibberish. Groups of boys stand against the walls, some of them gesticulating about last night's violence. Most of the street boys and girls have finished working for the day—peddling gum or drinks, stealing, washing cars or windows, singing on the buses, reciting Bible verses, shining shoes, watering graves, or just begging.

"Everyone here either rapes or is raped, Dr. Chi," she says to me. "Or both. Even some of the boys have been raped. Men on the street rape us, our parents rape us, our relatives rape us, strangers rape us, whatever. After I talk to you, I will go sell my body for six bolivianos anyway. So do you understand why I am not going to tell those boys—those boys who protect me from other men—you see why I don't tell those boys to f— off? They are my friends. All of us here, we are family. We have to be. We have family fights, but we can make up under the right circumstances."

I try to hold my breath, to not show any emotion; if I act shocked, Vicki might be offended or hurt. And then I ask a stupid question. "How can you sell your body for six bolivianos?"

"That's the going rate. You see those girls standing over there?" I look over to a group of thirteen-, fourteen-, and fifteen-year-olds. "That's what they charge too. It's our best way of making money. Some of them take more than one trick each night, but I prefer to only take one a night. Most of the men are drunk so if they don't pay, you just steal it from them. Some of them are so drunk, they can't tell the difference between men and women, and they go to a hotel with a transvestite. The transvestite beats them up and steals all their money." Vicki laughs.

"So," I clarify, "there are hotels that will rent a room to a man and a thirteen-year-old girl."

"Yes, of course," she says, as if I have a hard time understanding how the world works, which I do.

"I suppose it makes sense," I say. "If stores are willing to profit from selling thinner to street kids, somebody's going to make money off of child prostitution. That's sad."

"Yes, but how else are we going to survive if we don't have the thinner and the cheap hotels?" She takes a snort of her thinner.

I realize that I am not going to win an argument with her when she is in this state of mind. Not that she can't think while she's on thinner. There's another mind-altering drug she's addicted to: the drug of self-worthlessness. And yet how can I erase the lifetime of degradation and abuse that led to her self-devaluation? I sit and shiver for a moment, as my rear end has now iced over from the cold concrete bench.

"I'm going to go now," she says. "I have to make money."

"Wait," I say, "don't go," offering no reason.

"Why not? I don't have much choice. Um, do you understand? I have to make money."

"Why not sell candy or colas? Or shine shoes?"

"This is what I do," she says, presenting her outfit to me.

"I understand," I say, "but why not skip a night? I want to hear about your life."

"My life? I am thirteen. And I am a street child. What else do you need to know?"

"I need to know the details."

"No," she tells me. I can tell I've offended her.

"I want the world to know your life, to understand your struggles. Your life is just as important as anyone else's. Just as important as mine or the president's."

"No, it isn't," she insists. She doesn't want to hear my words. "Stop tricking me." She starts to walk away.

"I will give you fifteen bolivianos for an interview."

Vicki squints her eyes at me, as if I might be a mirage. Why would anyone pay money to hear her talk about her life? I can tell by the look on her face that she is internalizing this; perhaps her story is worthy of being heard. She wants to take me up on the offer, but she waits a moment, perhaps hoping I'll up the amount to twenty or twenty-five bolivianos. Realizing that she truly wants to talk anyway and that the money is pure gravy, she sits down. I take out my tape recorder. She takes a deep breath, and I soon realize that Vicki can talk. She can really talk, which is wonderful.

Since I was seven, I have fled and returned home several times. My mother used to beat me too much.

She used sticks, sometimes a belt. . . . My father was an "anti-social" and a thief. They used to fight a lot. Some days my father would ask me to pass him a pair of scissors to cut down my mom. I said, "No!" while he was brutally beating her. I said, "No, please," and he pushed me away. I was crying in a corner. That is why I used to escape from home, far from home.

My father kept a pair of scissors to cut my mother's face. That scared me a lot, and that's why I used to escape from home. "What am I going to do?" I would say. Then some time passed, but my mother would still beat me. So my sister took me into the streets. So then I was alternating between the streets and my house. Then I traveled to Cochabamba and came back to La Paz. By then it was already a lot of time I was in the streets. After that I returned to my house.

But my father divorced my mother and married another woman. So my mom married another man, who was very kind with us. But after that my mom broke up with him and started hanging out with another one. Meanwhile my father had children with this other woman. That is why he did not give us any money. That's why I was very sad. Moreover, my mother did not take me to school. Although my mother did not take me to school, my grandmother took care of me. My mother used to beat me a lot, and that's why I escaped many times. One day a woman stole from me two hundred bolivianos' worth of merchandise, and my mother beat me until I wet my pants. So I fled and started living in the streets. I started stealing and inhaling rubber cement. I used to sleep in *torrantes* (small and warm nooks) and abandoned rooms.

When violent men caught me, they usually beat me, and when I didn't want them to beat me they would say, "Let's go to a dark corner to have sex." I would always tell them that I was going to scream. So they would start to beat me harder, and only after that would they release me, and also because I would scream sometimes and some street boys would come to help me.

That is why I fled again. I traveled to Cochabamba again, but I received the same violence there. Now I am here. I was once in an orphanage, but my mother used to come to bother me. She took my clothes. That's why I occasionally left the orphanage.

My mother has beaten me a lot. . . . She even wounded my hand with a knife. After that my grandmother sent me to my father's house, but he was a drug addict and tried to abuse me sexually because I upset my stepsister. He wanted to beat me, but I asked him not to do it. Then he took me to the room and asked me to take my pants off. I told him, "No, Dad, please. No, Dad, please. No, Dad, please." And then he told me, "Okay, but forget everything I said."

That's why, fearing him, I left this house. This happened in Santa Cruz. My father then found me and sent me to live with my grandmother again. My mother was then with another man, who was very evil. He fondled my sister and me in Cochabamba and abused us. Since that moment I did not want to return to my house ever again.

I would cry a lot, and my mother was bad. She would say, "Cursed be the hour you were born, because it was because of you that I separated from your father." She would still beat me a lot and insult me. I would leave my house and come sleep here on the street, and she would find me. When she was high or drunk, she would beat me, pull me by my hair, and wound me. My grandmother would always tell me, "Do not approach your mother." I would try to avoid being around my house, but my mother would always find me and beat me.

Since that time I would not go home because my mother would come home drunk and beat me until I wet my pants. My stepfather gave me a radio, an iron, and a blender for Christmas one year. But then he came back with my mother and they were both drunk. So he told me, "Lazy *imilla* [girl], why don't you work?" and took my gifts. I answered, "But you gave me those for Christmas." He replied, "You should work, lazy imilla; buy your own things." Then, full of anger, I threw the radio toward him and almost hit him. And my mother threw some *moroko* [big milling stones] at me. I dodged them, but one of them hit my grandmother in the hand. She said, "Don't do this to your daughter." And my mother answered, "Why does this witch imilla do this to me? Why doesn't she work?"

That is why I started going to the streets, where I met boys and girls and started inhaling thinner with them. My mother would come and say, "Share with me." I would deny her, and she would beat me. Sometimes she would even drop her baby daughter.

Of course if my mom hadn't beaten me, I wouldn't have left my house. She beats me, insults me, and even has beaten me here in the street. She pulled me by my hair and soaked me in blood. She was drunk. Some ladies helped me escape. When my mom is not drunk she apologizes, but when she is drunk and even sometimes when she is not drunk, she shouts at me.

I sleep on the street now.

Vicki punctuates the story of her thirteen years with a concise sigh. We let the sigh settle in our ears as we watch three teenage girls walk out of the park to sell their bodies.

"Would you consider living in an orphanage again?" I ask.

Vicki speaks into the tape recorder as if it were a microphone at a UN assembly. "Many street children fear the orphanages because they don't trust the people who work in those places. They might hurt us or steal from us or shame us for what we are."

"Are *you* afraid?" I ask her.

"I am afraid," she says, untying her scarf quickly, as if it had been suffocating her. "I am afraid my mother will find me. My mother came to me each time I was in an orphanage. I've been in two orphanage houses, and I am scared to go to another one."

Should I bring up Yassela orphanage? Would Yassela be good for Vicki? Mercedes ran away from Yassela. Daniela was locked out. Many people are to blame, but that doesn't change the end results: two girls back on the street, one dead baby.

"Besides, Dr. Chi." Vicki interrupts my thoughts. "I am addicted to thinner, to taking drugs. They will never let me into an orphanage. Those places are for children whose parents drop them off there or who recently lost their parents. They don't want children who've lived on the street for a long time like me."

"Do you think you can stop using drugs, Vicki?"

"Dr. Chi, don't you understand?" she implores, begging me to see things through her eyes. "You have been out here long enough to know. We take drugs because of the deception we feel. I take drugs to forget the problems I have with my family, with my home. I won't lie. I have to take drugs because they let me forget the sorrows. I know the drugs damage me, but I want to forget the sorrows. Without drugs, I will cut open my wrists and die."

"So are you happy on the streets?" I ask her.

"I'm happy when I have food and don't have needs. When I am supported. I don't feel happy when I feel alone, when I feel that I don't have support, and when I don't have anybody. That's how I am feeling now: lonely and without support. I feel lonely always." Vicki looks at me with matter-of-fact eyes. She wants me to understand that this is simply the way she feels. She seeks no pity, nor is her spirit broken.

"You say you're lonely, but you seem to have a lot of friends," I say.

"I have friends, but sometimes they are evil."

"You know," I say to her, "if you leave the streets, you can still keep your friends and make new friends, and maybe find friends who won't be evil to you. And you won't have to deal with violent men."

Again, Vicki has a point to make: "On the streets, there is no lack of men who say to us, 'Let's go.' We don't want to go, and sometimes they take us by force and try to abuse us in large groups. Sometimes, if we don't want to give them money, they say, '*Vamos!*' So we say, 'Joven, we'll give you the money in a while.' Then they make an appointment, and we give them the money there.

"I would like to leave the streets," she continues. "I don't have a birth certificate because my parents have never taken care of it. If I had a birth certificate I could work, even washing dishes, but I don't have a certificate or an ID. Sometimes I look for a job as a servant, but they always ask, 'Do you have a birth certificate?' I say, 'No, but I will work. Don't distrust me.' But they always want a certificate or any guarantee. I don't have guarantees."

Vicki takes a deep breath. She wants to round out the picture of her life. She knows nothing of books, of research papers, of publicity campaigns, but she knows that someone, maybe just a handful of people, might someday read her words, listen to her voice. So she concludes, "The most important things in my life are my sisters. My sisters still live with my mother, so I don't see them much."

"Vicki," I say to her, "you are like a sister to me. You are my younger sister. I want to help you to get off the streets. How can I help you, and how can I help all the street children?"

"How you can help us?" she echoes. "Some people used to come and hold activities sometimes. That's what I would like. They would help us with various activities, and with food, because sometimes we don't eat. I would like them to help us with medical care, because we don't have the money for that."

She looks down at her hands, turning her scarf around in a circle like water in a mill. "Also"—she looks at me, still thinking about how to word this—"you can help by explaining us to the people, trying to communicate with them. There are always people like us, who need help."

"Why do people think that street children are evil?"

"Because we are always dirty," she says. "We don't have a place to sleep. We inhale, and they see us when we are high. Moreover, some people from the streets attack them, and they think we're all the same. I think that there are good people and bad people who don't understand us. I would like them to understand us and not think, because we are street children, we are evil. There are some bad, but also good, street children. They must know how to understand us." Vicki hangs her head, looks up from the shadow of her own face. The lights of her pupils scratch their way through the darkness. "Not all of us children are bad, are we?"

25

Dance with Me

11 p.m., January 25, 1998;
Alonzo de Mendoza

Vicki really is like a sister to me. She asks me about my life; she
looks after me. It's strange. Most street children are concerned only
about themselves and talk about their own problems, which is natu-
ral when you are at the bottom of the food chain.

Over the months, I tell Vicki about my life. That I grew up in
a Taiwanese household, about what my parents do for a living. I
tell her about growing up and trying to get the best grades and
then going to medical school. I tell her about Mingfang. But just
as if she were my real sister, I don't tell Vicki everything. I keep a
little to myself. I don't tell her what happened after my sister died.
I don't tell Vicki that she is the same age as Mingfang was when
she died.

As I walk the streets at night helping the children, I try to make each one understand that he or she is special, but no matter what craziness is going on, I keep one eye on this little sister of mine, Vicki.

Vicki and a dozen other street children have just finished playing *choro-moro*, a bizarre Bolivian children's game. One team of children line up, each with his head in between the legs of the person in front of him. They are all facing the same direction, and the child in front holds on to a pole. The other team takes turns leaping from behind the child in the rear and landing on top of one of the bent-over children in this snake of humanity. The more children on the leaping team who can land and remain on the snake team, the greater the accomplishment. Meanwhile, however, the snake team is shaking their backs, trying to make the leaping team fall off. When one of the leapers falls, the two teams switch roles. It is a testament to Vicki's spirit that she plays this boys' game.

Vicki and I sit on a concrete bench in Alonzo de Mendoza. "You know, Chi," Vicki tells me, "you're stupid."

"Excuse me?" I ask.

"You heard me. *Tonto*," she repeats emphatically. "You understand the Spanish, don't you?"

"Why am I tonto?" I ask.

"You could be having fun all these months, but you are out on the streets with us."

"You're here too, aren't you?"

"Yeah, but I don't have any other options," she argues. It breaks my heart to hear her say this. Her hopelessness coupled with her self-loathing means she may never escape the streets.

"You have other choices," I tell her. "You just don't see them right now. Besides, it's not so bad to hang out with you."

"I would think it would be boring," she says, concerned about the entertainment value of my walking the streets.

"Why do you think in the 'prime of my life' I would spend so much time with the street children?" I ask her.

"I don't really know." Vicki turns toward the wind to let it tousle her hair.

"Think about it," I say.

"Chi, I can't think clearly with the thinner."

"Then stop sniffing for a few minutes and think." I've been trying for weeks to get her to stop sniffing.

Vicki stuffs her ball of yarn into her sleeve and takes a deep breath. "Is it for the sex?"

"Pardon me?" I try to repress my own useless indignity. "Do you think I am a john?"

Vicki looks at me and tilts her head. For too many sad and twisted reasons, it may be more comforting for Vicki to think of me as a john than as an adult male who simply cares for her well-being.

"Why are you here then," she asks, "when you could be partying with your friends? With a girlfriend?"

"You tell me," I say.

"You want to help us?" she asks.

"Yes," I say. "That is part of it."

"Ummm." She takes out her yarn and breathes in the thinner deeply. "It is that Christian thing."

"What is 'that Christian thing'?"

"That Christian thing"—she exhales, her words forming a white cloud in the cold air—"is you need to do good works in order to have God look favorably upon you."

"Sort of," I say. "But my works do not buy me a ticket into heaven, you know."

"They don't?" she asks.

"No."

"So you are here because you want to be here. Because . . ."

"Because what?"

"Because you love God?"

Is she repeating a cliché? Something she heard another street child recite on a bus for tips? "Yes," I say. "That is the underlying reason for most of what I do in life. I'd rather be here than anywhere else in the world. Because I like to see children enjoy being children again. Because I see the face of God in every child."

"You're not only stupid," she pronounces in her drugged drawl, "you're crazy."

"Maybe," I peep out. "But I am happy. Happier than ever. This is one of the few places in the world that I feel truly alive, where I feel closest to heaven."

Vicki lets the matter go. She will think about it later, after it sinks in. She chatters on. And on. She talks so much that sometimes I tune her out. Sometimes I think she talks just to hear herself. It's like she is saying, "Yes, world. I exist." Maybe the world should tell her to be quiet sometimes. No, I don't mean that. The world has shut her up far too many times.

"If someone helps me," she tells me, looking over at me from across the bench, "I will survive and get off the streets. I will study and work."

My daydream evaporates. "You what?"

She cringes in embarrassment. "I want to be a beautician."

I don't quite understand the Spanish. "A what?"

"A beautician!" she shouts. Vicki dreams of making people look pretty, lifting others higher. Her life and her self-image are so ugly that this dream seems both sad and beautiful.

"A beautician, huh?" I ask. "Maybe you could make me beautiful. That's impossible, huh?"

Vicki laughs. "I like to paint nails," she says. "I was in a project once, and they took me to study painting on fabric, serigraphy, pottery. But after the courses ended, I could not keep studying."

"I think you would be a good beautician." Indeed, she has done an excellent job on herself tonight, as usual. "Did you hear me? I said you would be a good beautician."

She neither agrees nor disagrees. She leans over the concrete bench and aims a kiss at my mouth. I turn my face and let her kiss my cheek. Bolivian women give kisses on the cheek each time they part company, but Vicki does not leave. She stays, keeping us in an awkward state. I must say something, and yet how would it help? She's been rejected by her parents, and then by her world. To be rejected, or to *feel like* she has been rejected, by me too—does she really need that?

Little sister, I want to say, your depth of feeling and empathy may be greater than my own. And yet you founder in these very depths, drowning in your own self-hatred.

We pretend nothing has happened, and we continue to talk about making people beautiful.

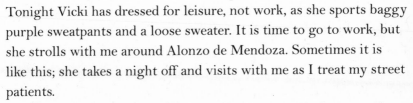

Tonight Vicki has dressed for leisure, not work, as she sports baggy purple sweatpants and a loose sweater. It is time to go to work, but she strolls with me around Alonzo de Mendoza. Sometimes it is like this; she takes a night off and visits with me as I treat my street patients.

Tonight my little sister is quite touchy-feely with the boys. She sits close to them, puts her arms around them. I can't stand to see this, so I try to concentrate on my work, treating children and mothers. At 1:35 a.m., I pack my things and prepare to go home. Vicki strolls over. "We should go and party sometime, Chi," she tells me, trying to make eye contact. "You can take me clubbing."

"I don't think that would be a good idea." I try to take control with a serious stare.

"Come on, Chi." She maneuvers about, shaking off my stare. "What is a little dancing and a few drinks? It won't hurt anyone." For street girls, "dancing" means that the man pays for the girl's drinks and the girl lets the man have sex with her.

"Vicki," I say, "you know I don't dance. You see these two left feet. Plus, I have the rhythm of a chicken."

She giggles. "I can teach the chicken how to dance." She grabs hold of my arm and scoots her hip against mine.

"No." I parry her hand away and back off. "Vicki." I look her square in the eyes. "No."

Vicki sits down on a bench. She pouts. I sit down too, on the other side. Cold silence. She looks out into the distance and sniffs, then sniffles. *He doesn't want to dance with me.* I can hear the words in her head. *He doesn't want to dance with me.* She believes me this time. *He will not dance with me!* She looks at me. Looks me square in the eyes. She narrows her eyes at me—out of hate or out of curiosity. "I wish," says Vicki, "I wish there were more good men like you out there."

Me too, I say to myself. Me too.

"You will be back tomorrow," she asks, "won't you?"

"Of course."

She walks over to the street boys. As she approaches them, her steps stutter. Vicki turns around and looks at me. I see on her face a look of pain—if not pain, then some sad question about her fate. When? Where? How?

Me too, Vicki. Me too.

26

Rain

February 14, 1998;
Calle de las Americas (a Street along Alonzo de Mendoza)

Alonzo de Mendoza needs this shower. The park has, appropriately, stripped naked for the occasion; all the prostitutes and drunks have run for cover—away, somewhere—leaving Alonzo de Mendoza bare of its human accoutrements, to be cleansed by the acidic rain of angry Andean clouds. Alonzo is now simply the stage for the smashing of water spirits into its face like flies into a screen window.

I am the only witness to this monotonous play.

Why am I out here? I told young Tina I would meet her tonight to check up on her gynecological ailment. She's not here. I am. But if, against the one-in-a-million odds, she had come out here and if she had then found herself alone, I would have lost her trust and a load of street credibility, so to speak. I spin around and around in my Gore-Tex jacket, searching the soulless streets. No one. Time to go back home.

Wait. I laugh on the inside. There's one other person as crazy as I am, running around in this freezing, sneezing weather. She is a girl, dressed purplishly from head to toe, running toward me, head hooded and arms holding her sides for warmth.

"Vicki!" I holler. "Is that you?"

She waits until she is before me to speak. "Chi!" Strobe-lightning takes flash photos of our faces as we look at each other. Vicki looks out of sorts, as if she left her favorite painting out in this rain.

"Terrible night, isn't it?" I ask, wondering why she's out here.

"Sure is!" she shouts over the moaning sky.

"Let's find some cover!" I shout.

We walk up the sidewalk, stepping over a sprawled, soiled drunk oblivious to both the rain and the small puddle of vomit beside his face.

"Where are we going, Chi?"

"I don't know," I say. "Where are the children?"

"Follow me. I will bring you to some of them." She walks northward. Do I detect a slight limp in her gait? We walk for five minutes.

We approach three orange Cotel Teléfono booths, their glass walls fogged up and stained by graffiti. "Where are you going to sleep tonight?" I ask her.

"I'll sleep on the streets," she says. "Where else?"

"Can you find any cover?"

"That's what I am looking for," she says.

"Where is everybody?"

"Right here," she says. I look more closely inside the telephone booths and see faces peeking out at me, four children jammed into each cubicle. I open one of the booths. They shake uncontrollably. "Joven Chi! Joven Chi! Cold night, eh?" They jump up and down.

"It's kind of chilly," I say. I walk to the next booth and recognize more of the children.

"I have a sore throat," a boy pleads.

"Look at my lip." The girl's lips are swollen to the size of small plantains as a result of an allergic reaction to paint thinner. "My bottom lip is busted." I treat the boy and the girl. Other children line up in the rain. I use the booth as my examination room. When I am finished, Vicki tugs at my jacket. "I need to talk to you."

We walk to a booth occupied by a single ten-year-old boy, José. "I need to talk to Chi," Vicki tells José. "Get out."

"Are you crazy?" José shouts. "It's raining!"

"I need to talk to Chi. It's private."

"Whatever!" he replies.

"It will just be a couple of minutes, José," I tell him. José leaves with a long grumble.

"What's wrong?" I ask her.

"My stomach hurts," she says.

"Why does it hurt?"

"One of the boys punched me in the stomach." She holds her tummy.

"Why did he hit you?"

"Because I would not give it to him." The rain batters the window of the telephone booth, muffling all words.

"What did you say?" I ask.

"He wanted me. You know. He wanted to get some."

"Oh," I reply, "so what did you do?"

"I said no," she says, without pride or shame.

"And then?"

"And then he punched my stomach out of anger. Chi, it really hurt. I kneeled over and started to cry. And then he left."

Boiling blood rushes to my face. I am no longer cold or wet. I am angry at the boy. I want to take retribution. To give him a strong punch to the stomach. Vicki is a child; she is poor; she is homeless; and she is a girl. Four strikes and Vicki is out. I wish I were there when she was doubled up in pain, trembling on the concrete. I wish I could have comforted her. But I was not there. She had no one to cry to. No one to hear her pain.

"Why didn't you call me?" I ask her. "I gave you money and my phone number so that you can contact me at any time."

"I know, but I forgot," Vicki whines. "I was too scared."

"Where is the boy now?"

"I don't know"—Vicki crosses her arms—"and I don't care."

"Yes, you care, or else you would not have found me. Am I wrong?"

"No," she whispers, the word curling out of her mouth as a wisp of steam. "I don't care. I don't care about anything. Don't you know yet, Chi? I don't care what happens to me. I'm garbage. Leave me alone."

"No. I won't leave you alone." You expect to be treated like garbage so you're never disappointed. You cauterize your heart. No one can hurt a dead girl. And yet who am I to tell you that you are alive? What good will it do if you believe you're a human being and no one else does? Can you survive on these streets if you insist on being treated with dignity? Can a street child afford self-worth? All God's children are created equal. But who really lives as if they believe this? One first world baby stuck at the bottom of a well generates more heartfelt anxiety than the 100 million children trapped on the streets of the developing world ever will. Should I foster hope in Vicki? "Vicki," I ask, "where is this boy? If you didn't want me to talk to him, you wouldn't have searched me out in the rain to tell me what happened."

Lightning cracks the sky like an egg and sparks her eyes, even in this telephone booth. She says, "I guess you're right."

"Let's go find him," I say.

"But it's raining." She holds her hand open, as if it were raining in the booth too.

"What's a little rain?" I ask her. "What is his name?"

"Eric," she says. I open the booth, and we look outside. Do we really want to go out there? On the streets, the strong abuse the weak, and justice is almost always of a poetic, accidental nature rather than purposeful. Can we rewrite this rule of the streets? José steps back into the phone booth. Our three minutes are up, and we walk back into the rain, unsure which way to walk, but we walk anyway, down Calle de las Americas, each of our heads huddled beneath a hood, mine Gore-Tex and hers cotton. We walk all the way down las Americas, make a turn and walk that way, and turn and turn again, checking the usual well-covered spots around down-town. For forty minutes we walk. For forty minutes the rain does not relent and neither does Vicki. She walks briskly down street after street as I wait for her to give up. I sincerely doubt we'll find Eric. But Vicki knows every nook and cranny downtown. And so we continue.

Finally, she slows her pace. She stands before a storefront awning. I stand next to her waiting for her to say she's given up, but instead she rears back her foot and kicks a human being huddled under-neath the awning. I had not even seen him through the gray sheets falling about me. The boy screams and holds his left leg tightly. "F— you!" the boy barks.

"You a—!" Vicki shrieks at him. The boy looks at me, wondering what I am doing here. He's big for a teen; his body has filled out early. A punch from his fist would probably double me over. I can't imagine what it felt like for Vicki.

"Calm down and step back," I tell Vicki. I pull her away from Eric, and then I stand before him. My heart races faster, faster. "Stand up!" I bark. Thunder punctuates my words.

Lightning strikes a mountaintop, and I can see the lines of fear on the boy's face as his head creeps upward along the door of the clothing shop. His brown eyes grow bigger and his top lip begins to quiver. Eric has seen me horsing around on the street, playing fútbol. He knows me as a doctor. Where is my compassion for this young brute?

"What do you want?" he asks in a trembling voice.

"Did you hit Vicki today?"

"No," he replies.

"You —ing liar!" Vicki barks.

"Shut up, Vicki," I say. "Did you hit her?"

Eric looks at me and looks at Vicki. He weighs the two elements that make up the world: lies and truth. He wants the best of both. "Maybe," he says.

"Maybe?" I yell over the thunder. Lightning splits the sky into two. Which side are you on? "What do you mean 'maybe'? It is either yes or no!"

"Yes." He creeps sideways along the wall. "Yes. Yes."

Eric probably ran away from a desperately poor family living in a mud-brick shanty in El Alto. Violence is a language to him, and he is well versed in many dialects. Club to the head. Knife in the side. Punches, kicks, scratches, whips. When he speaks, he wants people to listen; the streets twist every facet of human existence into a brutal farce. And so it is with me, too. I pick up the boy by his shirt and pin him against the glass door. Over his shoulder hangs the Closed sign. "Listen to me closely," I mutter gutturally. "You will never lay a hand on Vicki again. Do I make myself clear to you?" I look into the darting eyes of Eric. He could take a knife out of his pocket and stab me as I leave. He could tell the boys in his group; they could gang up on me. I don't care. "Do you hear me?"

"Yes, Don Chi," says Eric, remembering the serious look in my eyes. Yes, these streets are wild, but there are some people who care—who care, yes, but who will assert some control. "I will never touch her or hit her ever again!" he declares.

I let him go and he runs away down the street. I stand facing the Closed sign. Lightning flashes again, and I see my face in the reflection of the glass door. They are selling old leisure suits or something inside this store. What did I just do?

It isn't right, threatening children. Or is it? I don't care. She's my sister. I couldn't call her my sister if I didn't mean it. The first rule of the streets is "protect your own." From your birth until you meet God, that is all you have, and on the street your sister's life and your life are one and the same.

I turn around and look at Vicki, who smiles humbly at me. She's not really your sister, Chi. What if I had simply given Eric a stern lecture? Would he have changed? Would his friends? I won't take that risk. I'll do whatever it takes to make sure my sister is never again beaten or raped. We walk silently back toward the phone booths uptown. "I am glad that you told me about this boy," I tell Vicki.

"Me too," says Vicki, wiping her hair from her face. She rarely dresses up in the more fashionable outfits she wore when I first met her. What is going on? Was my initial instinct correct? Can a girl simply not keep up such an "extravagant" lifestyle on the street? Is Vicki on her way down? We reach Alonzo de Mendoza. It is clean. The excrement has been washed away, and the humans begin to return. We keep walking. The roads glisten.

I hail a taxi. Vicki gives me a salutatory kiss on the cheek. "Ciao," she says.

"Ciao," I echo. "Hey, by the way. Cut out the profanity, okay? You're better than that."

"Okay." She watches me sit down in the taxi. I will be dry and warm tonight. She will be wet and cold. Lightning zigs across the sky, and a sudden sheet of rain blasts Vicki. Her face is defined now by the falling water as it smashes and splashes against her cheek-bones, against the cartilage of her nose, against the enamel of her teeth. She smiles again. Little sister, find some cover.

27

Potato Chips

11:45 p.m., March 2, 1998;
Plaza San Francisco, Downtown La Paz

If it happens every day, can it still be a tragedy?

The selling of prepubescent female bodies is now the norm to me. The pimping and prostitution have become mundane and, yes, at times boring. Every night it is the same thirteen- and fourteen-year-old girls and the same drunks and the same fee and the same one-hour hotels. Nothing really changes.

I treat self-inflicted cuts to see those arms slashed up the next evening. I prescribe penicillin for syphilis so that the girl can be newly infected with her next trick. I administer oral rehydration therapy to tiny, malnourished street babies so that they may grow up to die early deaths, or worse, grow up to be prostitutes, ready to be beaten or raped. Is this God's intention for me? Is it His intention for these girls? Is this God's joke? Or His test of faith, even for those who cannot conceive of faith? Or has God simply forgotten about us?

Do I care? Sure I care. Just not right now.

Alonzo de Mendoza. Piggybacking their children in their colorful ahuayos, the girls sit and chatter together like American teenyboppers at a mall on a Saturday afternoon. And then, from among them, she stands up. Vicki. The boulder of my Sisyphean existence. Every day, I buttress her self-worth with apparently worthless words. Every day, I implore her to stop sniffing thinner. Every day, I tell her how she could earn money by selling soda pop or gum instead of her body—and yes, the juxtaposition of those three "items" now seems normal to me. Every day, she walks up to me, as she does today, and with a smile and a nod, ignores everything I say. Today she is dressed in red jeans and a purple cotton jacket, and she stands next to me as I stubbornly brood over the activities that transpire nightly at Alonzo de Mendoza.

"Hello," she says.

"Hello," I reply, tightening my crossed arms.

"Let's play soccer, Chi."

"Maybe later."

Vicki takes a deep sniff.

"Why are you still sniffing?" I ask out of habit.

"Because I like it."

"Well, I don't," I snap, surprised at my tone of voice.

"I know." She takes another sniff.

Silence.

"How was your day?" I ask. "Did you make money today?"

"I made five bolivianos."

"I thought your rate was six bolivianos."

"It was," she says with a smile and waits for me to say something. First, she quits dressing nicely; not that I really want her to attract more men. Now she lowers her fee. Maybe I was wrong. Maybe she has little potential, no true desire to get off the streets. Maybe I'm just easing her way into permanent homelessness. "Which street are you going to sleep on tonight?" I ask her.

"No street."

"Which hotel?"

"None."

"Where are you going to sleep?"

"In a beautiful home."

Silence. In a beautiful home? Is she dreaming? Or has she found a sugar daddy?

"An orphanage home," she clarifies.

"Really?" I jerk my head to look at her. Yes, it really is Vicki speaking to me. "When did you leave the streets?"

"Last week." She beams.

"Why didn't you tell me?"

"You didn't ask."

"Hmm." I am scared to believe her. I've pushed the boulder to the top of the hill. It sits there precariously. I'm betting it'll roll down the other side and then, just like Sisyphus, I will have to push it back up the hill. I look at her face, her glowing cheeks. Yes, this is for real! I say nothing, and she says nothing. We don't want this moment to end. Finally I ask her, "What made you decide to leave the streets?"

"Do you want to live on the streets, Chi?" She points her chin at me.

"N-n-no," I stutter. "Of course not."

Silence.

"How's the home?" I ask.

"It's good." She shrugs. "Beautiful, even."

"How can a dilapidated home with mattresses smelling like mildew be beautiful? Nice, maybe. But beautiful? How is it beautiful?"

"It's my home."

"Oh," I reply, made dumb by this simple, tautological answer that could be no closer to truth. "What do you do during the day?"

"We make arts and crafts. We wash our clothes. We play games. We talk. You know. Girl stuff. We talk about boys. Sometimes we even talk about you."

"I'm not a boy," I say seriously. "You know that."

"I know."

Silence. Vicki is not sitting too close to me. She's not flirting with me with her eyes. Has she learned how to be a sister to me, to her brother on the streets?

"So," I ask, still putting the pieces together, "why are you on the streets tonight?"

"Our curfew is midnight," she explains.

"Oh," I say. I wonder if she knows what time it is.

"What time is it?" she asks.

"11:30 p.m.," I tell her.

"I should be leaving now," she says. "Walk with me?"

We walk down Calle de las Americas in silence. I am so happy and she is so happy right now, I don't want to ask what I must ask. But I must. "How can you prostitute yourself while you are living at the home?"

"I don't."

"You said you made five bolivianos."

"I am selling potato chips now."

"Really. Since when?"

"I started last week."

It hits me. She doesn't dress in fancy clothes anymore because she has phased herself out of the business of prostitution. Her efforts, my efforts, our efforts—they have not been in vain. No, the exact opposite is true. By telling her story to a sympathetic ear, by internalizing my encouragement, by realizing that her worth is not housed in her sexuality, by going after Eric and punishing him for violating her body, by doing all these things and mostly by sheer power of will, Vicki has learned to value herself, her life, and her body. A miracle, a slow and steady one, has been playing itself out beneath my nose, and I just recognized it. "How's business?" I ask, the words now meaning something altogether more beautiful.

"It's difficult. I have to sell potato chips all day just to feed myself and stay alive. Sometimes I can buy a little treat for myself. I can't rely on men anymore to take me out and buy me things."

The cars and buses are honking ferociously at each other in Plaza San Francisco. A couple of street girls pass us and wave hello. We wave back, and suddenly Vicki stops in her tracks. "This is my street," she declares. "Thanks for talking."

"My pleasure." My voice goes soft. I want to tell her how proud I am of her. How happy I am. "You know," I say, "if you ever have trouble selling potato chips . . . I love potato chips. My mother tells me that I am too skinny and need to be fattened up like a little pig."

We smile at each other, and I give her a wink. She knows by now what I mean by this wink. A wink means "no" to prostitution. A wink is our mutual understanding that we are moving forward together toward a better life, hopefully, never to "walk" the streets again. A wink means she can count on me. Even after I return to Boston? I try not to think about it right now.

"Thanks, Chi," she says. "I love potato chips too." She has not smiled this much in months.

Slices of simple potato with a touch of salt, deep-fried in a kettle of oil. One greasy bag sells for one boliviano. Selling six bags takes eight hours. To earn one American dollar, the sturdy greenback. One trick earns a dollar too. In a fraction of the time. But those fractions of time have fractured her heart. By taking the longer, slower road, Vicki takes a needle and thread to her heart, attempting to sew the vital organ back together. To retransform meat into flesh and blood. She has committed herself to her own humanity, her own unique humanity.

I decide to walk home instead of taking a taxi. It takes forty-five minutes. It is not boring. The background is not drab. It is alive. Every life journey takes a million little steps. Each one of those steps must be walked with gusto and with care. Vicki has stepped forward on her journey. She takes a little step. Maybe two or a dozen or a hundred. I take a step too. I understand a little better now that I am here to walk with the children. To take each little step with the children, regardless of their directions, regardless of whether we seem to walk toward success or failure. Success or failure are not life. The walk is life. Yes, I must be present in the moment. If I walk every step with them, I may be surprised every once in a while by where we have walked, where we are going, and where we are. Tonight we stand within the halo of a minor miracle.

A minor miracle? Vicki has found love in her heart for herself. It is not a little step. It is a big step. A big step, and I must continue to walk with the children, however boring it might seem when we don't seem to be going anywhere. Walk with the children. Wherever they are going. It sounds simple, overly metaphorical, but nothing comes closer to truth.

28

Headbutt

11 p.m., March 10, 1998;
Alonzo de Mendoza

Only on the street are teenage prostitutes and working mothers the closest of friends. Mirta, a prostitute, brags about how she threatened to find the wife of one of her johns if he didn't pay. The other prostitutes and working mothers tell her that she did well and that they hope he still comes around to solicit her. Fernanda, a street-child mother, talks about how her lover made a fortune the other day—twelve bolivianos—and they went and got sodas as treats. Fernanda complains about a man who works on the street who stole five bolivianos from her. She was going to buy her baby a second diaper with the money. Most of the child mothers have only one diaper, which they constantly wash in the river.

"Chi, give me the soccer ball," says Christopher, whose eyes seem to have recovered fully, although I have not rolled out the sight chart for him. I hand him the soccer ball, and he runs off to kick it around with his brother Daniel. They play for a few minutes before acciden- tally kicking the ball into a man's chest. The man and his girlfriend scowl at the two street children and then walk on. Christopher and Daniel barely even notice and initiate a big soccer match.

I cut open the leg abscess of a street girl named Noemi in order to clean out her wound. Of course, I've applied lidocaine (a local anesthetic), and she doesn't feel too much pain. I am now completely accustomed to lancing out abscesses on these germ-infested streets and telling the kids to avoid infecting their wounds as they sleep on filth and excrement. I sew Noemi up, and she walks away without saying a word to me about anything, not even a complaint about how painful it was. I walk among the invisible children of La Paz, and ironically I myself sometimes feel invisible to them.

"Joven Chi, come here," Fernanda lilts.

"How are you, Fernanda?"

Fernanda shrugs. She raises her son on the streets; how is she supposed to reply?

"What did you do today?" I ask her.

"I took care of my baby." Fernanda typically takes pride in how she cares for her son, although, like all street children, she some- times doesn't seem to act rationally, from my overeducated point of view. Fernanda's son and the other toddlers of his playgroup chase each other and talk gibberish, just like the children at any suburban day care center in the United States.

"Don Chi," laments Fernanda, "my baby has diarrhea again."

I pick the infant boy up into my arms. He is small for his age. Street babies, born in blind alleys or in cheap clinics, are all runts. They start a few months behind and fall further and further behind. As I look at Fernanda's son, I can't help but think, *Maybe you should have stayed in the womb. At least it's warm and you get a constant supply of food from the placenta. Well, it's too late now. You came out, and you can't go back in.*

"Fernanda, how long has the baby had diarrhea?"

"One week."

"Why didn't you tell me a week ago?"

"I don't know. . . . I couldn't find you."

"I was right here in the plaza, and you know that. Do you want to let your baby die?"

"No." She hangs her head.

"Okay, Fernanda. You know the routine. Give your baby this special water every hour. If he doesn't take it, then I will need to take him to the hospital."

"I understand," says Fernanda. "That is why I am going to give this a chance. I am going to come back tomorrow morning at 7 a.m. Where will you be at that time?"

"Right here on this bench," I say.

"Okay." Fernanda carries her baby away and stands a few feet away. There is now a line of a dozen mothers with their babies.

"Okay, who is next?"

"I am, Joven Chi." A mother steps up, with her baby on her back. "My daughter has bad diarrhea."

"Really. How long has it been going on?" I quickly discover that most of the babies here tonight have diarrhea.

In the distance, several men watch me with seeming fascination. Some are dressed in suits, others in simple button-down shirts. They seem to be talking about me, or is it just my imagination? It is Friday night, also known as singles night on the street, and these men could be talking about the street prostitutes around me. Or maybe they want me arrested. Last week a man reported me to the police, complaining that I was pimping underage girls. A police officer came by and started interrogating me about pimping. Me. A pimp. I don't know the first thing about pimping. All the street-child mothers started to shout at the officer to leave me alone.

Three men, arm in arm, approach me. My voice quivers as I explain the diarrhea medicine to the mothers. I ignore the three men as they glare at me; I haven't gotten beaten up in six months of working on the street, and I hope I never will. The three men push their way past the mothers and stand before me.

"Who are you?" asks the man in the middle.

"Hey, I was here first," shouts a street mother. "Wait your turn!"

The man rears his head back and *BOOM!* Lights out. A deep, sharp, stabbing feeling from my forehead into the center of my brain robs me of sight.

"Aghhhh!" screams Fernanda. I recognize her voice.

I feel like I'm falling, and I grab whatever I can. Cloth. Skin, flesh, and bone. The man and I tumble down to the ground. My jaw suddenly throbs hard, and I can taste blood in my mouth. Did I get hit again?

The world is pitch-black. Where am I, and why am I here? Will they call a doctor? The police? They'll invite me to a soccer game, but I'll never join the team. I hope I survive. Feet shuffling. Scraping concrete. Grunts of pain. Cursing. The deep thuds of a torso being punched and kicked. "Stop!" I hear a voice shouting. "Stop!" Are the mothers being beaten? Are their babies falling to the concrete? Are the girl prostitutes being stabbed? I attracted danger to the girls, and they are being pummeled. Why am I here?

Boom! Boom! Boom! The lights come back on as if a switch had been thrown. What is this in my hands? The man's jacket. I must have grabbed it and pulled us both down. The street mothers, the street boys, the other street girls, and even the street babies have formed a large circle around me and this two-hundred-pound thug. We lie on the ground. The girls are kicking him and the children are pulling his hair with all their might. The other two men are trying to extricate their friend from the melee. They succeed and drag him away about forty feet. Having gotten some distance from the street children, they pick him up, and all three of them look at us for a moment. They concede defeat, but they still need to look at us for a few seconds. They run away.

"Are you okay, Don Chi?" asks Fernanda. Fernanda and the other street girls kicked my assailant into the middle of next week; he was the one shouting, "Stop!" They defended me and punished a man who hurt me.

"Are you all right?" asks Christopher.

My head is pounding with pain, and the world is still spinning. I taste salty blood in my mouth. "Yes," I say, "I am fine."

"Those men were terrible," says Fernanda.

"Do you know them?" I ask.

"No," she says. "We've never seen them."

"What did they want?" I ask.

"I don't know," she tells me. "Maybe your money. Maybe they don't like you because you are Chinese. Maybe they don't like it that you are talking to us."

"Umm," I say, assessing which sounds are least painful to make. "Well, I hope they don't come back."

A small child, no older than seven, exclaims, "Well, if they do come back, we will take care of them!" He flexes his biceps for us.

I am sitting on the bench now, holding my forehead and jaw. "Okay, who is next?" I ask. I want to finish my work as quickly as possible so I can find some ice and reduce my swelling face.

"Joven Chi, my baby has diarrhea," says a street mother.

"Oh, really?" I ask. I look at her foot. She kicked the man for me. They have brought me into the family now, with a flurry of kicks and hair pulling, saving my face from being embedded into the street. "How long has your child had diarrhea?" I ask.

"One week."

"Okay, you need to give your baby this special liquid for his diarrhea."

Baby

10 p.m., March 20, 1998;
Awning next to Casa de la Cultura
(Museum of Culture), Downtown La Paz

It is cold tonight, but not colder than any other night. That doesn't make it warm.

I just visited the two sites where the greatest numbers of street children congregate at night, Alonzo de Mendoza and Plaza San Francisco, where I played a hard game of fútbol with the kids. My body is sweaty and shivering. I now stand at the top of the steps leading down to El Cóndor, Casa de la Cultura. Along the rear doors of this museum of Bolivian art and cultural treasures, homeless bodies lie together like mismatched jigsaw pieces. I can't make out which legs belong to which heads. A blue tarp blankets this amorphous tangle of human flesh, which is asleep at the hour of 11 p.m. It must be drink night.

I silently pull back the tarp and see the face of César. I gently tap him on his good leg. César's body snarls, disengages from the mass; he blinks away his substance-induced coma. César squints his eyes to focus on me and then turns to another boy.

"Juan Carlos," he whispers into an ear, "Chi is here."

Juan Carlos shakes his head laterally as if to jiggle his brain into place. Once he recognizes me, he stands up and shakes my hand.

"Hi, Chi," he says. "How are you?"

"Good," I say, giving him my trademark firm handshake.

"Can you give us something to eat?" Juan Carlos asks, not a shred of whining in his voice.

"No," I tell him. "Maybe you should have used the money you spent on drinking for food."

He nods humbly. Juan Carlos and César are as close as any two brothers. César voluntarily joined Juan Carlos in prison so that the violence Juan Carlos would suffer might be divided between the two of them. Both Juan Carlos and César were beaten by men in prison, and César suffered a leg wound. César uses his good leg to gently kick awake the rest of his friends, who open their eyes in the fashion of a line of dominoes. On the end of the row are the homeless men, in their twenties and thirties, who drink both night and day. Equal opportunity drinkers, I call them. It is sad, really. These men are like fathers to the younger ones, and each father has taught each son to drink his blues away. Grandfather Time stands up to salute me in his drunken stupor. He is the oldest among them. How do I know? The white whiskers jutting out of his chin and upper lip give him away.

"Hello, Dr. Chi!" He opens his arms as if to hug me. "So nice that you could come and visit us."

"You're welcome," I say, unable to resist smiling. "You are drinking again, aren't you?"

"Drinking is good for the soul."

"Whose soul?"

"My soul! Ernesto's soul."

"And don't forget your liver," I say. "You shouldn't encourage these younger boys to drink."

"Ohh! I tell them that it is terrible for them. To stay away from that poison! I teach these children many things."

"Like?"

Ernesto opens up his arms and looks up at heaven. "'For God so loved the world that He gave his only begotten Son, that whoever believes in Him should not perish but have everlasting life.' John 3:16. That is just some of what I teach. There is an entire Bible these children must learn."

"Is that what you used to recite on the buses?" I ask Ernesto.

"No," Ernesto says. "I am the son of a pastor. I know the word of God inside and out."

I treat the various wounds and sore throats of each boy and each man, and after treatment each one quickly falls back asleep. In the middle of the string of bodies are two women. One woman looks as if she is about forty or fifty, and the other looks to be about seventy. Between them is tucked a little lump of blankets. From the end of the lump peek two little eyes and a smile. They are the eyes of a girl not more than four years old. The toddler hops out of her blankets and jumps toward me.

"What are you doing?" she asks me as I examine a boy's leg.

"I am treating these boys for their wounds," I tell her.

The cherubic child wears a soft fleece jacket with a hood. Her red corduroy pants complement her white plastic dress shoes. "Why?" she asks.

"Because they have cuts and bruises, and some of them are sick," I say.

"Why?" she asks.

"Why? Let me ask you a question first."

"What?" she asks.

"Where is your home?"

"Home?" she wonders. "Hahh! My home is right here." The girl cackles sharply.

"Where?"

"Right here. You are standing on my bed." She giggles.

"Where's your mother?"

"Right there. The woman sleeping over there." She points at the fortyish woman. "And right next to her is my grandmother." She points at the seventyish woman. "I sleep between them to stay warm. You know, it is cold at night." She looks at my jacket. "You should wear a little more."

Gee, this girl is a little smart aleck. She walks over to my medicine box and starts digging through it. She proceeds to pick up bottles of antibiotics and shake them vigorously. She opens a bottle and examines each individual pill as if it were a newfound toy.

"Hey, Doctor!" she yells. "What's this?" She takes a roll of bandages and sends it bowling ball–style down the corridor of Casa de la Cultura. "Bahahaha!" she screams in self-delight. "That's fun."

Wait. Wait. It finally hits me. This little girl is a third-generation street child. Her mother and grandmother live on the street with her. There are no runaways here. No parent here has abandoned a child. No child has run away from physical or sexual abuse.

I need to stop thinking about this and get back to work. César's leg wound needs cleaning. "Hey, little girl," I ask her, "what's your name?"

"My name is Rosa and I am three," she replies.

"Rosa, do you want to be my little helper?" I ask her.

"Sure."

"Please take the flashlight and shine it on César's leg."

"Okay," she says, taking the flashlight and turning it around in her little hands. "How do you make it shine?"

"You push this button."

Click. Clack. Click. Clack. Click. Clack. The flashlight switches on and off like a disco strobe. *Click. Clack. Click. Clack.* Rosa shines the light in her own eyes. "Ba! Ha! Ha! Ha!" she laughs. "I'm getting dizzy now. Ba! Ha! Ha! Ha!"

"Rosa, if you are going to be my helper, then you must shine the light properly on this man's leg."

"Okay, Chi."

I inject 2 percent lidocaine without epinephrine into César's leg. He yelps at the initial sting. The light wanders astray again.

"Rosa, I need you to keep the light on the leg."

"Oops. So sorry," she apologizes. I open the wound to clean it out, and then I sew four stitches into the boy's leg.

"Can you take a look at Rosa's ear?" asks Rosa's mother. "I am Catia." An old scar runs shallowly from Catia's nose to her left ear. Bags hang from her eyes, and her cheeks are like bulldog jowls.

"How long have you lived on the streets?"

"Twenty-five years," she says. "My whole life."

"Your whole life?" An entire life on the streets. A person who has never known the inside of a home, her only roof being the dark gray, raining skies of La Paz.

"Rosa was born here, and so was I," she explains.

"Where? Here?" I ask.

"On the streets here," she replies quietly. "We have both lived on the streets our whole lives. You have already met my father, Ernesto. You know, the soul-man preacher. My apologies, he is always drunk." But by the slur of Catia's words, I can tell that she, too, is more than a social drinker. Catia points down at the old woman lying next to her, looking at me as if I were a freak of nature. "Sleeping next to me is Monica. She is my mother."

Monica sits up. She seems to be the only sober one of the whole group—sobered by a deep sadness—with both her mouth and shoulders slumping. "I am Rosa's grandmother. I was not born on the street. Misfortune brought my husband and me onto the street, and we have raised our family here."

Three generations on the street. How can this happen? What

happened? I want to scream at the top of my lungs, "This is wrong!" But nothing comes out of my state of shock, just a faraway, glassy look.

"Could you check Rosa's ears for me?" asks Catia. "I think that she may have an infection."

"Hey, Rosa." I snap out of my stupor. "Hey, Señorita Flashlight! Get over here."

A drunken man at the end of the row glares at me, and I avoid looking directly at him. I believe he is Rosa's father.

"What do you want? I am busy." She is shining the light into the eyes of all her drunk role models trying to sleep.

"Rosa," I say, "leave them alone."

"What's that?" she points.

"An otoscope." I hold it before her face for her examination.

"A what?" She wrinkles her forehead and shrugs her shoulders.

"It is an otoscope. It is a little machine for looking into people's ears."

"Ohh." She exhales. "Test me."

I examine her ears. "Looks fine to me." She is lucky, in the perverted calculus of the streets, that her mother and her grandparents are all homeless. They live with her on the streets, and so do the family friends—an entire social network. She is twistedly lucky that this group of people drink too much. Their bodies with their dilated arteries provide alcohol-induced warmth in the cold of the Andean nights. She is lucky she has developed a spunky attitude, that she is not docile. She's smart. She's curious. And she does not shrink from the world. She has a chance of making it off the streets alive.

Rosa hops back into the bundle of blankets and pulls out her favorite toy. A duck. All the stuffing has fallen out of it; the duck is completely flat. There are no more quacks left in the poor little mallard.

An image pops into my mind: Rosa at twelve years of age is being picked up by a drunk businessman for a "Friday night special." Is she going to cut herself every day, like Mercedes? Will she survive like Vicki, selling her body for a dollar a trick? Will she give birth to a fourth generation of street children, not even distinguished by being the first? Will the cycle spin on?

My heart hurts at the thought. No. No! This must stop! The cycle stops here. I hope.

Dangerous hope. If I allow my hopes to fixate on one child, I will only be depressed for weeks or months or forever, until that child is off the streets like Vicki or until that child has simply disappeared like Gabriel and Mercedes. Where is my patience? What about simply walking with the children, wherever they are going? Patience cannot be an excuse for complacency. I may walk with the children, but I am also steering them in certain directions.

But how can one man reverse the injustices inherited by Rosa from three generations of street life? Where is God in this morass of human suffering? I don't know. Where are the billions of dollars the U.S. government spends on global humanitarian aid? It's really humanitarian aid with geopolitical/national security interests. Rosa, poor soul, is only worth helping if she has oil beneath her feet or a nuclear warhead pointed at the United States. She has neither. Rosa is only a child. But I will not rest until Rosa lives in a true home.

Rosa settles down into her mother's arms. Catia cradles her lovingly and kisses the top of her head. Catia wraps Rosa in the strata of blankets and tucks Rosa between herself and Rosa's grandmother. They slumber atop a cardboard mattress in the shadow of a blue tarp canopy.

Whoooohh! The cold wind blows. A cackle cuts through it: "Bahahaha!" Not knowing the joke, I laugh with Rosa.

Child One

March 30, 1998;
Casa de la Cultura

Sometimes you hear them crying from ahuayos on their mothers' backs. Sometimes you see them learning to walk, tripping among bottles of thinner and the feet of child prostitutes. Sometimes you hear them laughing as hard as any little baby in the world.

And sometimes they are so quiet you know they are on the verge of leaving the hard pavement forever. Born on the street, in a dark corner, in an alleyway perhaps, some little ones never leave their graves—like the cemetery kids.

Street babies and street toddlers are everywhere. There are so many, from corner to corner, I don't know where to start. I watch Rosa play. She has captured the hearts and the imaginations of me and everyone I work with. She is hope. As she learns to run across the concrete squares behind the museum, I think about this: Where *do* I start? With Child One. Concentrate my efforts on one child and bring her off the street. Make sure that her life is stable and directed. Then move on to Child Two and then Child Three and so on until all the children have a home.

I have to admit that this methodology probably will not produce a mass exodus of children from the street. But this is the way that makes sense to me. A public health specialist I am not; I don't care about cost-benefit analysis. I have been trained as a doctor. When I see a patient, I take care of that patient as best as I can. I go all out for that patient. I don't simply make sure that the patient is not dying and then push him out of my office. It's my responsibility to make sure that patient is securely on the path of healthy living for the foreseeable future. Rosa is my first patient.

"Hello, Rosa."

"Cheee!" She runs up the rear corridor of Casa de la Cultura and gives me a big kiss on the cheek. She knows her Bolivian manners.

"How are you, Rosa?"

"Good!" she screams cheerfully.

"Rosa," I whisper to her, "I am right here. You don't have to holler."

"Oops!" She covers her mouth with both hands.

"What did you do today?"

"Nothing." She shrugs her shoulders.

"Did you eat today?"

"Yes."

"What did you eat today?"

"Some bread."

Some bread to fill the stomach and trick it into believing that it is not malnourished. Bread is wonderful. Wonderful when it is with meat or vegetables. "Did you have anything else?" I ask.

"Ummm . . ." She places her hand against her cheek pensively. "Grandpa gave me some fruit juice."

"Well, that's good," I respond. "How's Grandpa?"

"Drunk." She imitates a drunk stumbling from side to side and then suddenly falling to the ground.

"Rosa," I suggest, "why don't you take the flashlight and announce my arrival while I talk to your mother?"

"Bueno!" She nods emphatically. "Chi is here!"

"Hello, Catia. Sit down on the steps with me, and let's talk."

Catia eases herself down onto the step as people ascend and descend around us. "How are you, Don Chi?"

"I am fine, Catia. How's business?" I ask, easing the conversation in the desired direction.

Catia looks down at her tray of glasses filled with fruit juice and floating chunks of odd-looking fruit. "Business is bad," she says. "People aren't thirsty and the economy is bad. I sell about six bolivianos in drinks every day. I give two to the person I rent the stand from, and I have to buy fruit too. Competition is fierce." Indeed, Catia echoes Daniela, who is likely competing against Catia for business tonight. They battle each other for that extra boliviano so that their daughters might diversify their diets. Adam Smith would smile if he could see them. Hurray for unadulterated capitalism.

"Catia," I ask her, "what do you want for Rosa?"

"What do you mean?" She clasps her hands together.

"What do you want her future to be?" I ask.

Catia looks far out into the distance at that ever-unreachable land beyond the horizon. "I don't want her to be *me*," she pushes out of her mouth.

I turn my head slowly to look at her. "What did you say?" I ask.

"I don't want her to be me," she repeats.

I want to object to her statement, to build her self-esteem, to tell her, "There's nothing wrong with you, Catia." But that would be patronizing and untrue. She lets Rosa go unattended at times; luckily Monica is always there. But the money for meat and vegetables often ends up in the bottom of a bottle. And the alcohol makes Catia vicious. She beats Rosa, pounding her head against the cement wall relentlessly. Where's the Department of Social Services? Where's Child Protective Services? Where's foster care? They're in the United States. Instead, Rosa has me. My job is to empathize, sympathize, and hopefully not eulogize.

"I don't want her to have my life," says Catia. She looks into my eyes, as I take my turn at looking far away.

"And what life is that?" I ask Catia.

"To live day by day on these three square blocks, selling fruit juice and earning six bolivianos a day. Not enough to eat a good meal each day. Too much to die."

Indeed, Catia actually falls backward each day, owing more and more to the man who rents her the fruit stand. She is like a slave, except that slaves are kept in houses.

"So, what do you want me to do for Rosa?" I ask, hoping Catia will allow Rosa to sleep at Yassela at night and pick her up in the day.

Catia places her hand on my hand. "I want you to adopt Rosa. Make her your own."

"Me?" I stall.

"Yes, you."

"Why me?"

"Because you can, and I can't."

"Won't she miss you, Catia?"

"Yes." Tears roll down through the crevices of her aged face. Rosa is the primary reason Catia continues living. "What is best for her is to stay away from me, or else she will grow up to be like me."

"Oh," I say, still stunned. "I don't think I can adopt Rosa."

"Why not?" she asks, half desperate, half relieved.

"Because," I say, "my life is crazy. When I am in Bolivia, I am always on the streets taking care of the children. When I return to Boston, I will be a medical resident, working all the time. Besides, what do I know about being a father?"

"I know you, Chi. I have been watching you for a long time." Catia shifts her body to face me. "You know how to take care of children and be a good father to them."

"Why can't she go to Yassela?" I deflect.

"Yassela orphanage?" Catia shakes her head and stands to leave. "No. I want Rosa to be with you, not at an orphanage."

I stand up quickly. "I thought you wanted Rosa to live in a home. If Rosa stays at Yassela, she can appreciate life on the other side. She'll learn skills for living and working. And if she learns to appreciate life in a home, she'll struggle hard to get off the streets when she gets old enough."

Catia closes her eyes, and a hundred wrinkles wash away. "You ask her if she wants to go. If she does, then you can take her to Yassela orphanage."

Catia and I walk to Rosa, who is playing under the statue of the big head. "Hola, Rosa," I greet her. "Would you like to sleep at the Yassela orphanage tonight?"

"No," says Rosa.

"How about we just visit the orphanage for an hour?"

"No," she says. "I want to stay here with my mommy."

Of course she wants to stay with her mommy. Any child would. She doesn't realize that the rest of her life is at stake, that if she stays on the street, she will live, die, and reproduce there. "There are dolls at Yassela," I say.

"What types of dolls?" she asks.

"All types of dolls," I lilt.

"Hmmm." She considers. "Can I take my duck?" She waves the lifeless piece of cloth in the air as I nod yes.

"Okay," she says. "My duck needs friends. But only an hour." Rosa does not know what an hour is; she just knows it's not too long. "Only an hour," I promise. Rosa looks to her mother, who gives an almost imperceptible nod.

"Okay, let's go!" she says. "Quack!"

As I carry Rosa away, I feel the eyes of Catia watching her baby, hoping that the invisible string between mother and daughter is not broken, at least not tonight.

The little hand of Rosa grips my own as my other hand knocks on the red wooden door of Yassela orphanage. *Boom, boom, boom.* A groggy social worker—Shana—opens the door. "Thank God you are here, Dr. Chi," she says. "Belinda has a painful ear and has been crying all night." Shana looks down at Rosa. "Who's this?"

"This is Rosa." I tug on Rosa's hand. "Rosa, meet Señora Shana." Rosa's lively spirit disappears into the night.

Señora Shana leans her head against the door. "Where did you find her?"

"At Casa de la Cultura."

Sara, peeking from behind Señora Shana's nightgown, points her finger at Rosa and yells, "Who's that?" The entire population of little girls and teens dressed in pajamas has gathered behind Señora Shana.

"This is Rosa," I say.

"Why isn't she at home?" asks Sara. "Why isn't she sleeping?"

"She doesn't have a home."

"You mean she lives out there with you?" Sara asks in disbelief.

"Sara, I don't live on the streets."

"It sure seems that way." Sara walks up to Rosa. "Hey, Rosa! How old are you?"

Frightened, Rosa manages to put up three fingers.

"Three? Three! You are a little baby." The crowd echoes her sentiment. "Come on, Rosa." Sara grabs Rosa's hand. "Do you want to play with my dolls?"

Rosa looks at me for approval and then lets herself down from my arms. Sara leads Rosa down three flights of stairs, step by step, and with each step Sara describes one of the dolls in the world of Sara.

Señora Shana and I walk down to Belinda's room, and I treat Belinda's ear infection with anesthetic ear drops and antibiotics. We tuck Belinda into bed and walk to Sara's room, where Sara sleeps as Rosa speaks to one of Sara's dolls. "And then my mother said, 'Get out of the street!' and I ran back to her. And then a mean man came over to Mommy and asked her for money."

"Hola," I sing to Rosa.

She looks up at me and says, "Chi, I want this doll."

I bite my lip. "I'm sorry, Rosa, but this doll belongs to the girls here."

Rosa looks at her long-lost friend with an out-turned bottom lip. Señora Shana leaves the room. "Come on, Rosa," I say to her. "It's time to go. It's three in the morning already."

Señora Shana returns with a different doll in her hand. "Here, Rosa," she announces. "You can have this doll." She is a sickly looking doll. The eyes are gone. Five strands of blonde hair hang precariously from her skull. She owns no clothes. Now *this* is the ugliest doll I have ever seen, worse than Mr. Quack. Rosa cradles the doll in her arms. She grabs a small brush off the bed and combs the doll's hairs. I want to tell Rosa to be careful; there's no Rogaine for dolls. I restrain myself.

"Thank you! Thank you!" Rosa shouts in glee, inadvertently waking Sara. "Rosa," asks sleepy-eyed Sara, "do you want to stay or do you want to leave?" Before Rosa can answer, Sara whines, "You should stay. You should stay."

The other girls, now awake, chime in with desperate pleas, all their motherly instincts awakened as well. "It's dangerous out there." Sara grabs Rosa's hand. "Stay here, and you can take hot baths, sleep in bunk beds, and play with us all day!" Rosa doesn't register the goodness of these amenities.

A semicircle forms around Rosa. She is trapped, forced to make a decision. Rosa brings Mr. Quack and her new doll closer to her chest; she looks at me with eyes that cry for me to pick her up and take her away, and I am about to pick her up when she peeps to me in her baby Spanish, "I want to go back."

I will not tempt Rosa with dolls or good meals. She trusts her mother and no one else. Perhaps in a few weeks or months, she will sleep under a roof, but tonight neither Rosa nor Catia are prepared to give up their rainy, blue-tarp nights together. I carry Rosa out of Yassela, and we return to mother, and Mother Street.

Rosa Must Stay

Casa de la Cultura

I have this fantasy. An upper-middle-class family living in suburban
Boston adopts Rosa. The adoptive mother plays with Rosa every
day and teaches her both English and Spanish. The father is gentle
and kind. Rosa attends a good school, she's a model student, and she
lives happily ever after.

I have this reality. I know of no suburban family ready to shell
out big bucks and loads of time to adopt a toddler off the streets of
Bolivia. Besides, Catia didn't want anyone besides myself to adopt
Rosa. I can't imagine trying to care for Rosa as I work thirty-six-
hour shifts for four years as a medical resident. And the whole idea
of "saving Rosa" by taking her away from her mother so she can
live far away in the United States—where she will undo her mestizo
culture in a proper first world setting—smacks of the worst kind of

colonialism. But is political correctness more important than the
health and well-being of a child?

As I watch Rosa play, Rosa's father watches me. He doesn't speak
to me, but he is generally respectful to me. He knows that I can help
Rosa, but he wants me out of his territory, away from his family.

Catia sits with me at the top of the stairs leading down to Casa
de la Cultura, well out of earshot of this man. We watch Rosa reach
for a bottle of alcohol Grandpa Ernesto is drinking from. Ernesto
shoos her away, and Monica swoops her up and drops her off among
a circle of children. Every day Rosa learns a little more of the culture
of the streets. She learns about drinking alcohol, how to stand up to
people, how to watch for "bad guys." She will eventually learn how
to fight, sniff thinner, cut herself and others, run, steal, sell her body,
and fend off male perpetrators. It is both bad and good.

Catia tells me of her day's events, as she often does. She tells me
of her difficulties, and we often talk about Rosa. It's like therapy.
Interestingly, no matter how hard times get, Catia never asks me
for money.

"Catia," I say, "I have taken Rosa to Yassela several times now, and
in weeks I will return to Boston. You must decide now. Do you wish
for Rosa to live at Yassela?"

"I don't know."

"What's the issue?" I ask. "You told me that you don't want Rosa
to be a street person."

"It's not that easy."

Catia and I both want what's best for Rosa, but what's best for Rosa
may not be what's best for Catia. She is a woman with almost nothing
to live for except her one and only beautiful daughter. And yet she is
willing to let her daughter go, under the right circumstances.

"I get into trouble every time you take Rosa to Yassela," she
tells me.

"What do you mean?" I ask.

"I mean I get beat up."

My heart drops. The lungs make a futile attempt to take a deep breath. "Who beats you?"

"My marido," she tells me.

"What does he do?"

"He hits me with his fists, especially when he is drunk. Sometimes he hits me with bricks."

The first time I took Rosa to Yassela, her father and I exchanged some meaningless greetings before I shuttled her away. It was the only time her father and I ever spoke, and it was apparently a prelude to a beating. Tonight Catia tells me of the time her marido tried to drown her in a river. And not long ago he tried to throw her off a mountain while Rosa pleaded for him to stop.

"Why didn't you tell me earlier?" I ask Catia.

"I don't know," she says.

"Does he beat Rosa, too?" I ask.

"Yes," she says. "He traumatizes her psychologically. When he is drunk, his mind is dulled. He doesn't want Rosa to play or laugh. She is required to sit quietly. When the child talks to other men, his jealousy comes out. He tells her, 'He should be your father!' And then he beats her."

By playing with other men, Rosa is reaching out for a father who can provide love, warmth, and food. A real father. Biology alone does not legitimize one's place in a family. Anyone can procreate. Even dogs.

"You see," explains Catia, "Rosa is a baby, and she does not understand. I scold her when she talks to men to keep her from getting beat and getting beat myself. He often accuses me of having affairs with these men."

"Why don't you leave your marido?" I ask Catia.

"It is not that easy," she says.

"Why not?"

"Because I love him," she says.

How can you love a person who beats you and your child? Yeah, yeah. I know about the cycle of violence in domestic abuse, but Catia is still a living, thinking human being; she can rise above "cycles." Can't she?

"He beats you," I say. "And he protects you. I know the system. Maybe you should ask him to protect you from himself." My words circle around the air like useless flies. "He doesn't take your money, does he?" I ask her.

She says nothing. My words embarrass her.

"He takes your money too?"

"Some of it. He drinks most of it away," she says drily, and then laughs at how silly her life is. "Chi, don't get angry."

"Angry!" I mutter. "I am past angry."

Rosa burrows her way under a mountain of blankets. Catia and I both look at her and wish and pray for the best for her. What's best for Rosa means a terrible beating for Catia.

"So, Catia," I dare to ask, "what do you want to do?"

She takes a shaky breath. "I want Rosa to stay on the streets with me. Rosa must stay."

What can I do? I can't confront Rosa's father. It will only make things worse for mother and child. And I can't approach child protection services because there are none. I can't do anything except go back to my room and pray. I look over to Catia's husband. He sneaks a glance at me and continues conversing with another man. "How can you love this man?" I ask Catia.

"Love." She exhales, closes her eyes. "Love is a curse."

Time is running short. In several days I will fly back to the United States to interview for medical residency programs. I need another minor miracle in order to help Rosa experience life off the street.

I find Catia in Plaza San Francisco behind her stand of fruit drinks. She stirs up the juice in five freshly poured glasses, and the fruit pulp floats up like fish eager to be fed. The plaza is quiet; the lunchtime customers have gone back to work, but Catia keeps stirring the fruit. "You know, he left," she says.

"Who left?" I ask. I spot Rosa with her wings out, flying toward the street. Monica, the ubiquitous grandmother, catches her. Rosa slams on the brakes and zips about in tight circles. She becomes dizzy and falls to the ground, landing on her rear end. "Ba! Ha! Ha! Ha!"

"My marido," finishes Catia.

"What?" I ask, shocked, happy, and already thinking of what to do next.

"He left yesterday," she says.

"Just like that," I say. "He left."

"Yes," she responds.

"Why?"

"For another woman," says Catia. Her jowls sag deeper than usual. The scar on her face seems to spring tributaries. She pronounces carefully, "He left me for a younger, prettier woman." Again, she stirs her fruit. "He took my blankets and my shoe-shine box and my money too."

Gee, this is like an American soap opera. Older man beats his wife and children, takes her money, and then leaves for a younger woman. Yet Rosa's father's abandoning the family makes my heart light. "How do you feel?" I ask Catia.

"Good and bad," she says, thinking, trying to place each component of this misfortune on the proper side of the fuzzy line between blessing and curse. "I feel good because I can use the money to feed Rosa, and I won't get beat anymore. I feel bad because I care for him. He was a part of me." Tears add salt to the fruit drink, and she quickly wipes her face.

Good riddance! Don't let the door pop you in the rear on the way out. I guess there really isn't a door. "How can I help you, Catia?"

"Help me protect and feed Rosa. And just listen," she says, "and talk to me."

"Okay," I say, "I will."

"Catia, I'm leaving Bolivia in a few days. Do you want Rosa to live at Yassela? She can try it out, and if either of you don't like it, you can bring her back home."

"Yes, I would like Rosa to live at Yassela. So if she wants to live at Yassela, you can take her there."

"Rosa, would you like to live at Yassela?"

"I don't like Yassela. One of the girls there hits me. They're mean to me."

"How about staying there just one night?"

"No. I want to stay here with my mommy."

I will leave for Boston tomorrow. Rosa and I sit in a posh restaurant in downtown La Paz. Her legs dangle, swing, and then dangle from the chair. Her mouth is full of rice, chomping with delight. We are surrounded by rich businessmen. How many days would Catia have to work to buy Rosa this meal?

"This is good," Rosa tells me, chewing on lean Bolivian beef. She rubs circles on her stomach.

"I am glad you like your meal," I tell her. "I want you to eat well every day so you can grow up strong and smart." I carefully place my fork on my napkin. "Did your mother tell you that I am leaving?"

"No."

"I'm going back to Boston soon, and I'm coming back in a month."

"Will you still come play with me when you're in Boston?"

"Rosa, Boston is in a faraway country called the United States. That's where I come from. When I'm in Boston, I can't visit any of you."

Rosa's fork falls to her plate. Tears threaten to break their dams.

"I'll be back, Rosa. It won't be very long until I'm back here. You won't even notice I'm gone."

Rice and beef grow cold as my napkin wipes away the tears, hers and mine.

I Want to Go Home

June 1998;
La Paz, Bolivia

I don't want to go home. I have been back from Boston for two weeks, and I will return to Boston in another few months. It is a beautiful day in La Paz. The sun cascades fat rays, fresh and yellow, down and further down through the thinnest of air, onto the tops of our heads, as the earth swings La Paz through cool eddies of mountain mist. The streets stretch before me like crisscrossing snakes baking themselves in their own sand tracks. I walk up and down the sidewalks looking for my children. Here they are. And there they are. I ask them how they did overnight, if there were clubs and knives in their lives and bodies. I wish, against the momentum of my own life, to live that cliché of clichés: to be there for them. I want to stay here in La Paz to protect and provide for my children. I don't want to go home.

In Plaza San Francisco I talk to half a dozen shoe-shine children. They wear ski masks all the time, even when they play fútbol. They claim the masks block out pollution and shoe polish fumes; some say they wear masks because they are ashamed to show their faces to their own customers. They greet me with a strong handshake and a warm "Cheeee," and they set their wooden shoe-shine boxes down on the concrete. They have to work hard for these boxes, saving fifteen American dollars to buy a comfortable spot for their customers to rest their feet while their shoes are being shined.

I say hello to "Mentisan," a twenty-six-year-old street woman who has lived on the street the last ten years. We affectionately nicknamed her Mentisan because I always give her the trademark lip balm for her constantly engorged lip, an allergic reaction to thinner. I do not know her real name. The children ask me which night I will return. I tell them, "Tomorrow night, and I'll visit all of you."

Beyond a heated street fútbol match, I see Catia holding in her arms her daughter, Rosa.

"Hola, Catia." I give her a Bolivian kiss.

"Hola, Chi. Rosa, say hello."

"Hola," Rosa responds shyly.

"How are you doing today?" I ask Catia.

"Good," says Catia. "It was a quiet night."

"What do you have planned for today?" I ask.

"You know: the same routine. Sell juice and soft drinks to earn some money."

Rosa removes a cooked chicken head from her mouth and pipes up, "I want to go to your new house."

Over the past two weeks, I've discussed with Catia the possibility of letting Rosa stay with me at a middle-class house owned by an American woman living in La Paz. Her name is Teresa. She allows La Iglesia de Dios to use a room in her house for whatever they need, as she lives in the rest of the house. I would like Rosa to stay in this room until I return to Boston and after that to stay in the home of a member of La Iglesia de Dios. She will visit Catia often, but she will learn to live in a home. And she will go to school.

"It's fine with me," Catia says, squinting against the sun. "Rosa can stay with you and the landlady, like we talked about. It will give me more time to earn money. You can bring her back tomorrow. It will be good for her to be off of the street for a little while. These streets are not good for little children."

"I want to go to your house," Rosa pleads.

I look into Rosa's eyes and begin to melt. "Are you sure that it is all right with you, Catia?"

"Yes. It will be good for her," she responds, and I take her response at face value. Catia puts Rosa in my arms.

Rosa immediately pounds on my chest with all her strength. "Shoulders! Shoulders! Shoulders! Shoulders!"

I place her on my shoulders, and she begins hitting my head with glee. "Say good-bye to your mom," I tell her.

"Bye!" she screams.

Rosa rides on my shoulders across Plaza San Francisco, and we jump into a *truffi* (a taxi-bus). Sitting in the center of the backseat, she stretches her neck upward and peers out the window. The farther south we go, the bigger her eyes grow.

She chews on the chicken head, probably a treat from her grandparents. The head has lost most of its meat, and I tell her, "You can throw away the chicken head now."

"You're so wasteful!" she scolds me. "*Malo chico!*"

Bad boy, she calls me. To Rosa, meat is meat, even if it is peeled off the crown of a sickly, featherless fowl. And we in the United States squawk at being served dark meat instead of white. We ride silently for five minutes, and then she tugs on my shirt. "Where are we going, Chi?"

"To my house in Calacoto."

"Where's Calacoto?" asks Rosa.

"It's a neighborhood about twenty minutes to the south."

"That's very far. Far, far away. Far away from Plaza San Francisco."
She nods, agreeing with herself.

The door opens before her. Rosa steps gingerly into the house.

"Hello, Doña Teresa. This is Rosa."

"Rosa, you are a cute little one," says Doña Teresa. "My home is
your home."

Rosa looks around as if she has walked into haunted catacombs.
As she takes a tour through the house, she carefully touches the
chairs, the carpet, the windows, and even the walls. I show her the
bed she is to sleep on, in her own room. She walks up to the bed
carefully and runs her hands across the comforter. She has seen beds
before, but she has never slept in one.

She stops in the living room to consider its enormity. She walks
into the kitchen. She cautiously turns her head to the left and then
to the right. Her eyes balloon as she notices, standing against the
wall, five twenty-gallon boxes of children's clothes donated by Park
Street Church. Rosa looks up at me, opens her arms, and jumps up
and down. "Baby clothes! Baby clothes! I am a baby!" she exclaims.

"You can pick out the clothes you like."

Before I can finish my sentence, Rosa has literally dived into
a box of clothes. Only her legs are visible as she wriggles her way
down toward the bottom. Her muffled voice is incomprehensible;
all I can hear is her happiness, and I smile. She rights herself and
sits atop the clothes.

I pick up a sweater from another box, and I hold it up before her.
"Do you need a sweater?" I ask.

She nods fervently, takes the sweater, and drops it on the floor.

"Do you need some overalls?" She again nods, takes the overalls,
and drops them on top of the sweater.

"Do you need a jacket?" The jacket falls on top of the overalls. Rosa digs clothes from the box she sits in and throws them on the pile. Within minutes, she stands beside a pile of clothes taller than herself. "Bag!" she demands. "I need a bag."

I open a plastic grocery bag. As Rosa carries the big pile of clothes, only her two little legs can be seen sticking out from beneath. A voice from within the clothes pile says, "Chi, I need to go poo-poo."

I help her drop the clothes into the bag, and I lead her into the bathroom. I make sure she understands how to use the toilet. Assured that she won't fall in, I leave her alone in the bathroom. From the kitchen, I can hear her dangling feet kicking the porcelain bowl.

"All done!" she announces. I walk back into the restroom to find her all dressed again.

"Did you wipe yourself?" I ask her.

"What do you mean?"

"Did you use toilet paper?"

"Why would I use toilet paper, Chi?" she asks.

I tear a handful of toilet paper and hand it to her. "To wipe your butt."

"To wipe my butt? Mommy and I only use that to blow our noses," she tells me cheerfully, but I insist that she use the toilet tissue for its original purpose.

"Doña Teresa, would you help me give Rosa a bath?"

"I think that is a great idea," Teresa says.

I turn the metal knob ever so slowly to make the water warmer a little bit at a time until it is nicely lukewarm. The clear water inches up the side of the cream-colored bathtub. Rosa comes in and watches me curiously. Her big brown eyes peer upward at my hands as the stench of human excrement wafts up from her shoes.

"What are you doing?"

"Getting a bath ready for you."

Rosa watches me intently as I stir the water with my hands and distribute the heat evenly.

"I can't take a bath," she tells me.

She needs a warm bath with real soap. Her skin should be free of human excrement from this day forth. "And why don't you need a bath?" I ask.

"Because it is cloudy and cold today," she says. "I will be cold if I take a bath."

I look at her lovely, round face. Her mother bathes her in the cold dirty river or in a restroom sink. Her survival instincts tell her to bathe only when it is sunny so that the water is warm and the wind does not make her shiver.

"I have a special machine that makes the water warm. Touch the water, Rosa."

Rosa carefully sticks her chubby little fingertips into the bath water. They reach in deeper and deeper. She lets out her cackling giggle as she realizes that this special machine actually works. The water heater, I explain to her, makes the water warm, even when the sun is gone.

Rosa jumps into the tub. Old dirt steadily gives way to the attrition of a good scrubber and warm water. She splashes water onto herself and giggles. She is happy for warm water! She is so happy that she jumps out of the tub and runs naked into the living room, screaming; she prances around in circles, cackling and leaving a trail of suds in her wake. Doña Teresa laughs hysterically. Little Rosa's cackle is infectious, and the giggles bubble out of me as I chase her around, trying to wrap a towel around her. She swings the white lace curtains to one side and peeks out.

"*Columpiar! Columpiar!*"

She jumps up and down in a frenzy as I throw a towel on her. What does *columpiar* mean?

"Columpiar!" she exclaims. "Columpiar!"

She presses her face against the window and points her finger at a wooden swing set in the yard below.

"Put on your new clothes and your shoes."

She runs into the bedroom and pulls on her new used OshKosh B'Gosh shirt and overalls.

"Rosa, you need underwear."

"No, I don't."

I give her a disapproving look. "Yes, you do."

She bounces like a rubber ball to the big cardboard boxes and digs out a pair of underwear.

Rosa laughs at the sky as she swings up in the air, telling me, "Higher! Higher, Chi!" I grunt and pretend to push her even harder.

We run inside and I blow up all the balloons bought just for her arrival. She starts hitting them, and hitting new high notes with her giggles.

And now it is 4 p.m., and I am hungry. She is too, she just doesn't know it. I make peanut butter and jelly sandwiches in the kitchen as Rosa makes a racket in the living room. She opens up every board game in the house and throws them together into one big game.

I set two plates of sandwiches and two cups of milk on the table and call her into the kitchen. She slams open the swinging kitchen door, and I catch it before it slams back into her face.

"Let's eat, Rosa."

"Okay. What's that for?" she asks, pointing at the dinner table.

"It's the dinner table."

"What is it used for? Why did you put the food way up there?"

"People eat at the table."

"Really?" she wonders aloud. "Why?"

"Well, it's where everyone eats: at a table."

"How do they eat at a table? No one eats at one of these, not even my mother."

"Oh," I reply.

Rosa climbs into a chair, reaches up on the table, grabs the sandwich, takes it back into the living room, sits down on the floor, and eats.

Four Days Later

For four nights in a row, Rosa has slept on a bed in the bedroom. I sleep in the living room. In the morning she sees her mother, sometimes to stay with her the entire day. The initial novelty of clean water, a warm bed, and plentiful food has worn off, and I am happy that she is getting used to these luxuries.

It is nine o'clock, and I tuck Rosa into bed. I close the door to her room. As I lie in my own bed, I let my mind go blank. And then a wave of pathos rolls through my chest. I want to adopt Rosa. I have wanted to take care of her as my own daughter for months now. It is inhumane to do anything less. I spend my last waking minutes walking through this fantasy world where I am Rosa's adoptive father and I am still working with the other street children of Bolivia.

I am awakened in the middle of the night by a wail. Rosa. I've never heard her cry like this before. I run into her room and let the light from the hall come in. Her face is streaked with tears. She sniffles and keeps her eyes closed to the light.

"I want to go home now," she cries.

"Why? What's wrong?" I ask.

"I wanna go home!" she hollers, and stomps her heels on the mattress. I pick her up and hold her in my arms, rubbing her back. Her tears soak into the skin of my neck.

"Rosa," I tell her, "you can't go home right now. I'll take you back in the morning. Remember our routine? You stay here at night and you see your mother in the morning." I rock her gently for a few minutes; she breathes slower and her eyelids grow heavy. Has she cried it all out? I lay her down on her bed, and I return to my own.

An interesting aspect of our biology: We can close our eyes, but we cannot close our ears. I can't keep from hearing Rosa crying for her mother and for home. "I wanna go home!" she screams. "I wanna go home!" I close my eyes even tighter. Children always scream when they receive their immunization shots; they are in extreme pain, but those shots must be given. This is no different. Tearing her away from her home is the most painful thing she could endure right now, more painful than living on the street with rain, wind, and disease, all of which she is used to. She'll get over it. She'll fall asleep eventually.

"I wanna go home! I wanna go home!"

I get out of bed and walk to Rosa's room. I pick her up in my arms, and she hits me in the face. "I want to go home. I want to go home. Chi, I want to go home."

She wants the arms of her mother. Of her grandmother. I carry her to her shoes and fit them on her feet. We walk toward the front door.

"Wait, Chi. Wait." She jumps down from my arms and runs into her bedroom. I follow her. Has she changed her mind?

"You forgot my new clothes," she tells me. She wants to leave this home permanently, never to return, and she wants to keep her new used clothes for life on the street. I pick up all the designer clothes and stuff them into a plastic bag. T-shirts. Pants. Overalls. Her face glows with happiness to have received so many presents.

"Chi, you are not folding them right!"

She takes the metallic blue overalls and painstakingly folds them to her desires. She then gently inserts them into the plastic bag. I watch her, and my heart weighs heavy with sadness. Why must Rosa return to the streets? Because her grandmother has been the only stable person in her life. Who am I? Just a transitory friend with a lot of cool toys. Of course Rosa is going to prefer the street.

"And where is my duck?" she screams.

I dig out her yellow duck from beneath the large white comforter.

"There's my duck. I have been looking for you, Mr. Ducky." She looks up at my solemn face. "Okay, I am ready to go."

I scrounge through the desk drawer for taxi fare.

"Shoulders. Shoulders, Chi!"

I lift her up onto my shoulders, and she gives me her signature laugh. It's a high-pitched giggle that emanates from the bottom of her lungs and gurgles up through her mouth and sprays out uncontrollably, like water blowing out of a pent-up hose. I smile sadly and giggle with her.

So with her clothes in one arm and Rosa on my shoulders, we leave the house. Only a few taxis are working tonight in the quiet neighborhood.

"How much to Casa de la Cultura?"

"Fifteen bolivianos."

"It's usually twelve."

"Twelve it is."

The low hum of the engine and the crisp, cool air blowing past our faces slowly hypnotize us. The brown, barren mountainside is studded with green, white, and red night lights. Far beyond Mount Illimani, the black sky opens up a million brilliant eyes—its stars— glowing, twinkling, free. Rosa's duck falls from her left hand onto the taxi floor. Her eyes are shut tightly. What does a street baby dream of? Certainly not Beanie Babies, Barbie dolls, or new Sunday dresses. Is she dreaming about a lollipop she gets once in a while? Is she dreaming about a warm Bolivian day when she can take a bath in the river? Is it a night when her father hugs her?

How could I fail like this? I was so close. A few more nights, and she would have gotten used to sleeping in a home. Yet she needs her mother. I am angry at her, at Catia, and at myself. Will Rosa become

a street prostitute, a shoe-shine girl with engorged lips who goes by
the name of her medication? My teeth are clenched in anger. What
hubris I possess, to take her away from her mother, if only to keep her
in the safety of a home during the dark nights. Her umbilical cord is
buried under hard concrete, and it is nearly impossible to unearth it.

"Is she your child?" the taxi driver asks.

"Huh?" The question jars me.

"Is she your baby?"

"No. I'm taking her back to her mother." I look at the taxi driver's
eyes through the rearview mirror. He awaits an explanation. "She
lives on the streets," I say. The taxi driver has not reached thirty
years of age. His complexion is rich cocoa brown, and his eyes are
jet-black.

"What do you mean?" he asks me.

"She's a street baby."

"What?" His face contorts uncomfortably.

"She's a street baby," I repeat.

I am confused at his inability to grasp this fact, considering he
sees street children every day.

"So where are her parents?" asks the taxi driver.

"She lives with them. Her mother is a street woman, and her
grandparents also live on the street. This child's name is Rosa, and
she is four years old now."

He grows quiet, and the car's low hum grows loud. Rosa breathes
deeply in sleep. The streets are empty. The sidewalks see no feet.
My mind wanders.

A throat clears, softly; it is clogged with tears. I hear sniffles. Part
of me does not want to turn to look at the taxi driver, but I do, just
to see if he is okay. His cheeks glisten with thin, slow tears. He does
not bother to wipe them. They begin to fall from his cheeks faster
and faster. His white shirt darkens with translucent spots.

"My daughter is her age," he peeps out. "She's four years old too.

I love her very much. Very much." He continues to cry. "Where does she sleep?"

I tell him through the rearview mirror, "Casa de la Cultura."

"You mean on the sidewalk in front of all the stores?" he asks.

"Yes."

"How does her mother survive?"

"She sells fruit drinks at the plaza."

"Does Rosa have a father?"

"Sort of. He is there sometimes. When he is there, he is drunk and beats Rosa and her mother. Thankfully he left them."

"So why are they still on the streets?"

"Rosa's mother is an alcoholic, and that makes it difficult for Rosa. Most of the time her grandmother takes care of her."

I look down and see Rosa's head against my chest. I look at her eyes. She has awakened and now stares out the window. My heart sinks. How much of our conversation has she heard? I feel that I've just betrayed her. Did I just destroy her idolized and rose-colored view of her mother, one of the two people in the world whom she trusts? Did I compromise that bond?

"How are you doing, Rosa?"

"Fine," she whispers in a sleepy voice. She does not look up to acknowledge me. Her eyes are staring out into deep space.

The taxi driver takes a furtive glance at Rosa and darts his face back to the road, as if it is too painful to see her. What is his daughter like? Does she laugh like Rosa? What if one room was made available for every tear cried for these street children? Pity is useless and unwanted. Give me rooms. Give me clean water. Give me loving arms. Pity never built a home.

"Where are we going, Rosa?" I ask.

"Home," Rosa says. "To see Grandma."

"Why?" I ask.

"Because she does not drink," says Rosa.

I adjust myself in my seat and look deep into the sky, contemplating the bond between words and life. "Alcoholic." The word rings in my head and echoes through the stars. We arrive at Casa de la Cultura. Rosa has fallen asleep again in my arms. I carefully position her to one side and dig in my pocket for the taxi money.

"You take good care of her," says the taxi driver. "It's cold tonight. You should give her your jacket."

"She has a jacket in the bag," I respond.

I place a little red-hooded jacket on her tiny body. The manipulation wakes her up, and she opens up a lion's yawn.

"You make sure you take good care of her. Good care of her. You are responsible for her," he pleads as he takes the twelve bolivianos.

"I will," I tell him. "Don't worry."

I walk across one of the main streets and find Monica, who stands next to Ernesto and four other disheveled men. Her face breaks out into wrinkles as she sees Rosa. Her smile knows no teeth.

"Hello, Chi," she says. "Rosa, did you have fun today?"

"Yes."

"What did you do?"

"I took a bath in a bathtub. I washed my hair. I washed my clothes. I ate lots of food. I played with toys." She reaches out for her grandmother.

"Give Chi a kiss good night."

Rosa kisses me on the cheek and yells out, "Good night, Chi. I will see you tomorrow. We can play again."

I ride home in a different taxi, watching the sky at first and then closing my eyes. I want to go home. The words echo from the stars, and from every cardboard bed, from every empty bottle of thinner, from every fresh razor slash. I hear it as a scream, as a wail, as a cry, as a demand, as a shout, as a prayer, and I cannot close my ears. I want to go home. The tears burn down my face.

EPILOGUE
2006

Since 1998, the paths of these children have radiated in all
directions.

Not long after Rosa's father left her and Catia, the Bolivian Street
Children Project began helping Catia, Rosa, and grandmother
Monica by paying their rent on a tiny apartment. Catia and Monica
continued selling fruit drinks and school supplies on the streets, but
they no longer slept on the streets. Rosa, for the first time in her
life, had a real home.

The Bolivian Street Children Project was founded in an attempt
to bring attention to the plight of street children around the world.
Our goal is to return to the abandoned street children in La Paz,
Bolivia, their childhood, their rights, their dignity. We also strive
to equip our children with the ability to become role models and
agents of constructive change. In the early years, we simply walked
the streets, as I had before, talking to the kids and treating their
various ailments. With a growing group of staff and volunteers,
we have made approximately six thousand street visits.

In 2001 the Bolivian Street Children Project started its first
home, Hogar Bernabé, in La Paz, Bolivia. Our homes specifically
serve abandoned street children, who, by definition, have no adult
supervision or caretakers. In my eyes, these are precisely the children to whom we are called to respond in our charity of love and
kindness. Abandoned street children in La Paz have an average age
of 14.4 years, and more than 50 percent are boys. Nearly 90 percent
of these children have been physically abused, and more than 90 percent of these children use paint thinner. Of the abandoned street

girls, more than half of the girls are pregnant or have children, and 38 percent have reported being sexually abused.

With the building of Hogar Bernabé, I have satisfied, in a rather humble manner, one of the three requests of Daniela, Vicki, Gabriel, and others: to build a home for them. Hogar Bernabé is home for ten abandoned street children. We provide our children with holistic care. It is not enough to give them food and clothing. We must give our children the opportunity to feel safe. To know love. Besides physical problems such as dental cavities and wrongly healed bones from past beatings on the streets, the children suffer from suicidal desires, depression, posttraumatic stress disorder, drug addiction, and the entire book of psychological disorders. Some have difficulty attaching themselves to others; others attach too easily. Most believe they will eventually be abandoned; in the first days off the street, some street children follow me and staff members around the home, making sure we don't leave them.

Children at our homes live in a safe environment, with a high staff-to-child ratio. We do not utilize corporal punishment. An in-house tutor catches the children up on missed education. Our staff and our psychologist help the children recover from physical, emotional, and sexual trauma so they can take their first steps toward a future free of murder, rape, and homelessness—a future, perhaps, with peace of mind and spirit. Through both academic and technical education, the children learn to sustain themselves within the mainstream economy. Some of the children at Hogar Bernabé aspire to become lawyers or businesspeople. Through tenacious studying, one child is now the top student of his grade level at school.

Sometimes people ask me why we have only ten children in Hogar Bernabé. First, one cannot bring too many children off the street and into the same home simultaneously; the instability causes mass exoduses of children back to the street. Second, with our high staff-to-child ratio, more than 60 percent of our children stay in our home until they are prepared to sustain themselves in the outside world. Others who work with street children in other homes privately admit that their retention rates are in the single digits. Thus, our home for ten children rehabilitates more children than two or three homes housing fifty children each.

Our second home, Hogar Renacer, opened in 2005 as a transitional home for children who have recently left the streets. It is used as a bridge for children not yet ready to live with stricter rules and responsibilities. In 2006 we hope to open a third home, and if we can secure the funding, we would like to open four more homes for abandoned street children and street babies. We also hope to build a small school, a library, a soccer field, and microenterprises where children learn trades in realistic settings.

I cannot take credit for the successes of the Bolivian Street Children Project. Over the last decade, donations have appeared in my mailbox just in time to cover my bank account that was overdrawn by hundreds of dollars. I have survived several close calls on the streets. Some call it fate. I call it God.

In addition, 95 percent of the real work is done by the wonderful team I have been blessed to work with, along with two dedicated boards in Bolivia and in Boston: Francisca Martínez Alave, Ben Branham, Kristy Branham, Juan Carlos Arteaga Flores, Luis Javier Yrusta Campos, Luis Carlos Ruiz Carreño, Carola Contreras Céspedes, Luly Quispe Condori, David Copa, Moisés Hurtado Céspedes, Rosario Quiroga de Castellón, Hernán Oliveira Durán, John Eggen, Michelle Eggen, Luis Gonzalo Fernández Pereira, Mary Frances Giles, Kristin Huang, Kep James, Noemí Karageorge de Rivero, Kurt Leafstrand, Laura Leafstrand, Luis Fernando Morales Medina, Vernonica Mendoza, Nils Cajareico Nauro, Gigi Ohnes, Karla Eliana Saavedra de Fernández, Deb Veth, George Veth, Antón Villatoro, and Thania Villatoro.

I have crossed paths with many of the street children I met in my first year in La Paz. Some of those children, sadly, I have never seen again.

A street girl spotted Mercedes on a bus going to the red-light district in 1999. I have not heard news of her since then. If she is alive, she is an adult by now. Maybe she is a prostitute. Maybe she sells ten-cent soft drinks on the corners in La Paz. Maybe she is married. Maybe she is a mother. Maybe she made one final razor slash.

Alejandro cooks at a local restaurant in El Alto, providing for himself, his wife, and their child. He was the catalyst for our project in 1997. He has done more for the children than he knows. I am excited for him and proud of his accomplishments.

Jorge continued to live at Bururu orphanage until he was promoted to a nicer orphanage with more opportunities.

Fernando moved from Bururu orphanage to another orphanage a couple of years after I first met him.

Gabriel reportedly traveled to Cochabamba, and I have not seen him since I washed lice out of his hair in 1998.

Tómas left Bururu shortly after the accident and was spotted on the streets a couple of times during the first year thereafter. Some people at the orphanage knew he was never going to stay. I disagree. A child will fail if you expect him or her to fail.

Anna committed suicide in 2001 in El Alto. She hung herself from a metal bar that held up a shower curtain. A street boy who was passing by told the authorities that Anna was one of the street children, and he walked on. No one else claimed or identified her.

Javier is a homeless man, spending most of his waking hours drinking and committing petty crimes. When I told him that Anna had killed herself, Javier was silenced, shocked, and saddened. Having lost his lover and his unborn child, he almost shed a tear. But he did not. He walked on. I have not seen him for nearly two years.

Maria's burial structure was destroyed because the cemetery permit was not renewed. Although Daniela and her mother continue to have a frigid relationship, both Daniela and Natalia now live with Daniela's mother. Daniela sells fruit drinks on a downtown corner.

Daniel Chávez remains a street boy, eight years later. He is currently one of the older boys who abuse younger children, physically and probably sexually. Christopher Chávez lives in a home for street children. I have not seen them in two years.

Juan Carlos and César continue to sleep on the street, often inebriated and sometimes committing small crimes.

Vicki is doing remarkably well in a home for teenage street girls. I bumped into her in 2005 on one of the main streets of La Paz as she was running off to a class for beauticians. She has a small baby girl, and they are doing well together. It has been a long journey since the days of child prostitution and selling overgreased potato chips.

Ernesto, Rosa's grandfather, died on the streets in 2000, from alcoholism. Rosa spotted her biological father once over the last eight years. He did not acknowledge Rosa during their brief encounter. Rosa's grandmother, Monica, continues to sell trinkets and other small goods every morning beginning at 8 a.m. in Plaza San Francisco. Over the years, multiple attempts were made to assist Catia in taking responsibility for her daughter, but she continued to lose her ongoing battle with alcoholism, regularly putting Rosa's life in danger. Rosa was eventually adopted by a loving family. She is doing well in school and aspires to go to college.

In April 2005, Catia disappeared from the streets.

I completed my Harvard residency program in internal medicine and pediatrics in 2002. I now split my time between Boston and La Paz. I work several months each year at the Boston Medical Center at Boston University School of Medicine, where I am a hospitalist in pediatrics and internal medicine. My dual roles as a Boston hospital doctor and a Bolivian street children advocate are made possible by Boston University's Dr. Barry Zuckerman, Dr. Bob Vinci, Dr. Jeff Samet, and Dr. Jeff Greenwald, all of whom value the work we provide for the marginalized in both Boston and Bolivia.

Do you see our invisible children? Economics and technology

widen the moats and heighten the walls between us in the developed world and the poor of the developing world. Political parties distort our vision. Many on the left wish us to believe that our street children are innocent and helpless victims. In contrast, those on the right often define these children as violent, lazy vermin deserving of their torture. Street children are not good or bad, but rather complex human beings with good and bad qualities—just like us all.

Do you see our invisible children? Have you focused your vision on them so that you may judge them? Tell me what is black and white in their world of gray; I myself am so often confused. Is it wrong for a street child to steal a piece of bread to survive one more day? Is it right to give a street child money, knowing he may use it to buy drugs? Is it better to leave him penniless, knowing he might starve? Forced to choose, do you help the street baby or the street boy or the street girl?

Do you see our invisible children? I take issue with the current tilt of American Christianity. The "wealth and prosperity gospel" says that Christians, because of their belief in God, receive gifts from heaven. Does this mean that the street children need only believe in God to find themselves living in loving homes with food and medicine? Does the popular understanding that God helps those who help themselves mean that the street children do not help themselves and that they deserve to be starved, murdered, and raped?

Sometimes my anger gets the best of me. I yell and snap at those I shouldn't, as well as those I should. What is anger in the cause of the street children? Perhaps it is passion. My passion is still youthful and strong. My body, however, has aged. Where once there was a healthy tuft of hair, there is now a smooth patch of scalp. As my workouts become more difficult, my waist widens. My spiritual blind spots remain, but I am more aware of them and am searching for others yet unknown. My hypocrisy weighs the same as it used to. My family, children, friends, and colleagues will readily attest that I am far from a saint. Sometimes I do not treat the children as well as I would like. Working with street children is mundane and often hopeless. For street children, it is always about "me"— not unreasonable since no else cares about them. Through all the troubles, I try to remain present in their lives, but sometimes at a cost. The heartbreak, stress, rage, and hopelessness have contributed to the many valleys of my life.

To know the street children is to have one's life transformed. So many of the peaks in my life have come from being present with the street children. I truly enjoy seeing the children play and smile after being cured of various diseases. To play soccer with a street child and see him or her happy for a millisecond is one of the most treasured gifts I can ever receive. My other peaks are my marriage to my caring wife, spending time with our daughter, Grace, and looking forward with great anticipation to our new daughter, Lily, from China, and another infant due in June 2006.

I still struggle with my lifelong conundrum: Why did God take my sister Mingfang and not me? Why must our children suffer on the street? Why is such evil allowed to be inflicted upon our children? Intellectually, I have come to accept that God has created us with free wills. He also allows us our evil, our neglect, and our blindness.

Will you decide to see my invisible children? My children ask for your money. But more important, they ask to be seen, to be known as human beings and as children. Tell our stories, they told me. To Daniela, a hundred dollars made me rich. The street children flounder in absolute squalor. They ask for your understanding and empathy and not necessarily for your sympathy or forgiveness. They ask to live with dignity.

Our lives are short and fleeting. What is the legacy we leave behind? Maybe my legacy is a few square blocks of La Paz, Bolivia, where all the children have homes.

Our children die not from disease or malnutrition. Our children die because they are poor. In reality, most of us do not even watch the children as they die, for we dare not let ourselves see the children. See my children.

No, you needn't help them all, because we simply can't. In fact, I prefer that you help just one. That is, help one child at a time. There are 70 million street children in the world. With your help, there will be one former street child. One child in a home. And then two. Three. Four. Five, six, seven. . . . A girl named Rosa, a baby named Elisa, a boy named Jesús. . . .

You can donate to our efforts at Kaya Children International, P.O. Box 337, Lincoln, MA 01773 or online through PayPal at www.kayachildren.org. The Bolivian Street Children Project is a nonprofit organization.

Chi-Cheng Huang, MD
La Paz, Bolivia, April 2006

Acknowledgments / Chi Huang

Kristin Huang, my wife and my best friend, for her support and encouragement during difficult times.

My daughter, Grace, for making me laugh every day and for showing me what is truly important in life.

My father, mother, and sister, for their continued support.

George Veth, Deb Veth, Ben Branham, Kristy Branham, Anton Villatoro, Thania Villatoro, Kurt Leafstrand, and Laura Leafstrand (Bolivian Street Children Project board), for believing in our work.

Daniel Harrell at Park Street Church, for providing me the initial opportunity to go to Bolivia.

Park Street Church, Bethany Church, Christ Church of Houston, and churches in La Paz, Bolivia, for helping us build homes for our children.

John Chung, for allowing us to run our homes in Bolivia.

Dickler Foundation, for believing that we can make a difference in the lives of children in Bolivia.

Kep and Debbie James, for their guidance and wisdom.

Tobi Nagel, Arthur Kim, Michael Balboni, Mark Valle, Reuben Gobezie, Richard Rhee, Steve Swanson, and Manish Shah, for their prayers, support, and friendship.

Tom Petter, for his teaching.

Irwin Tang and Josh Busby, for their lifelong friendship.

Barry Zuckerman, Bob Vinci, Jeffrey Greenwald, and Jeff Samet at Boston Medical Center, for the support in allowing me to care for people in Boston and abroad.

Joel Katz, Marshall Wolf, Jane Sillman, Bruce Levy, and Howard Hiatt at Brigham and Women's Hospital, for the mentorship and guidance in my development as a physician during residency.

Paul Farmer and Jim Kim at Partners in Health, for preventing me from becoming disillusioned and for allowing me to focus on the poor.

Laurence Ronan at Massachusetts General Hospital, for providing me the opportunity to be an internist and a pediatrician.

Sherry Penny and Pat Neilson at Center for Collaborative Leadership at the University of Massachusetts, for teaching me about leadership.

Susanna Finnell and the honors program at Texas A&M University, for providing a college student so many opportunities to grow intellectually and socially.

Bobby Slovak at A&M Consolidated High School, for teaching me to think critically as a high school student and for opening my eyes to politics.

Elaine Smith at A&M Consolidated High School, for encouraging me to enter into science.

Chrissy Hester at A&M Consolidated High School, for her support and encouragement.

Residents in the Boston Combined Residency Program in Pediatrics and the Harvard Internal Medicine and Pediatrics Program, for keeping me on my toes clinically.

Acknowledgments / Irwin Tang

I thank my family for supporting me in the writing of *When Invisible Children Sing*. I thank Chi for our lifelong friendship and the opportunity to help him write this book. I thank Sabine Zenker, Nancy Truong, Lucia Bardone, and Gay Talese for their help on this book. I thank the editors at Tyndale House—Janis Harris and Lisa Jackson—for recognizing the importance of this work. I thank Wes Yoder for finding a publisher for the book. And I thank every person I met in Bolivia.

Online Discussion *guide*

TAKE *your* TYNDALE READING
EXPERIENCE *to the* NEXT LEVEL

A FREE discussion guide for this book
is available at bookclubhub.net, perfect
for sparking conversations in your book
group or for digging deeper into the text
on your own.

www.bookclubhub.net

*You'll also find free discussion guides for
other Tyndale books, e-newsletters, e-mail
devotionals, virtual book tours, and more!*